SHOPPING
CENTRE DESIGN

to
Dorothy

SHOPPING
CENTRE DESIGN

N Keith Scott

VNR

International

VAN NOSTRAND REINHOLD (INTERNATIONAL)

First published in 1989 by
Van Nostrand Reinhold (International) Co. Ltd.
11 New Fetter Lane, London EC4P 4EE
©1989 N Keith Scott
ISBN 0 7476 0045 7

Designed by BDP Design, Preston

Typeset in 9/10pt Palatino by P's & Q's, Liverpool

Printed and bound in Hong Kong

British Library Cataloguing in Publication Data

Scott, N. Keith
Shopping centre design
1. Shopping centres. Design
I. Title
711'.5522
ISBN 0 7476 0045 7

CONTENTS

CREDITS

ACKNOWLEDGEMENTS

Because this book is more derived from personal experience of shopping centre design than a theoretical, historical or technical work there has been little need to draw on the knowledge of others in the course of its preparation. Hence the slender list of acknowledgements.

On the other hand the tuition I received over the last 35 years from people and companies across the entire spectrum of retail development activity has comprised the longest and most diverse education course known to man. Estate Agents, Solicitors, Development Companies, Property Funds, Property Managers, Local Authority technical officers, local development orientated politicians and retailers of every description have all been tutors to my widening fund of knowledge.

Above all, I am grateful to my firm, Building Design Partnership, for the opportunity it has given me to develop skills on an astonishing range and size of retail project. I have been engaged in schemes as small as £1m and as large as several £Bn and throughout I have had the support of the immense design resources of BDP in all professions.

On the specific matter of professions fees for development work I would like to thank David Ives and Harold Couch (partners in the Estate Consultants Donaldsons and Hillier Parker respectively) for their contribution to the accuracy of my text. Eric Whittle, Vice-Master, Queen Elizabeth's Grammar School, Blackburn, for checking and acting as critic to the evolving manuscript; Professor Sir George Grenfell Baines for acting as second critic and for continuing a 35 year crusade to reduce my proclivity to purple prose to a pale mauve.

My colleagues Janet Jack, Stuart Boott and Roy Taylor contributed their great expertise to the sections on Landscape, Fire and Cost Control: indeed they wrote the basic text.

BDP Graphics are responsible for the design, page layout and the whole 'feel' of the book. John Green heads the section but special thanks are due to Carole Houston and Theresa Gale for all the detailed work, sifting through a mountain of illustrative material, and ensuring that the book appears in its present form.

Except where noted I took the photographs and did all the freehand drawings. My son, Quentin, drew the plans throughout: his young eyes enabled him to produce a standard far more accurate than anything I could have achieved.

For sheer time, dedication and patience nobody could rival, let alone better, the contribution of my secretary, Anne Reynolds. Her tireless devotion to the task of typing, editing, retyping and keeping my spirits high when I might easily have succumbed can only be dimly grasped by those who have actually tried to put a book to bed.

Lastly, public recognition that my myopic dedication to the task of creating urban centres of distinction has only been made possible by the support and tolerance of my wife, Dorothy. An artist herself, she has followed the conception and creation of every shopping centre I have worked on. (I draw exclusively on the dining room table: never in the office). She has followed me round and aided my understanding of literally hundreds of shopping centres in all five Continents and has long ago ceased to question the dichotomy between my obvious addiction to designing better shopping centres on the one hand and my chronic aversion to shopping on the other.

FOREWORD

Over the last 40 years, many of Britain's town and city centres have been substantially rebuilt as we have tried to provide them with retail and commercial cores capable of serving the community into the 21st century. New retailing methods, pedestrianisation of main shopping streets and planning for carborne shoppers have been adopted as the essential elements of modern town centre development.

In retrospect, however, we now realise that the results of most of this rebuilding, much needed as it was at the time, have not been entirely satisfactory. Schemes which were entered into with a spirit of genuine commitment to improving and enhancing the attractions of towns have not worn well, despite the skills and resources which were available.

It is generally acknowledged that town centre redevelopment can only be achieved through partnerships between the local authority and the private sector. While finance necessarily comes in most cases from the developer, backed up by a pension fund or insurance company, the concept is usually the contribution of the hard- working professional team.

In this collaboration, nobody plays a more vital role in creating a successful development than the architect. It is after all he or she who provides the designs for the buildings and layouts which are seen by the general public and by which the entire scheme will be judged.

Keith Scott refers to the remarkably few 'well-known' names in the architectural profession who have entered the field of town centre design – one which probably has more impact upon the lives of the ordinary person than any other type of development. But what explains this reluctance?

The answer is perhaps that the 'well-known' names are often unable or unwilling to work in a multi-disciplinary team. They are rather more used, it appears, to exploiting their individual brilliance unfettered by such mundane concerns as controlling building costs or considering financial returns.

To produce good architecture, to have this all-important ability to work as part of the team, as well as being able to communicate with the outside world, are qualities bestowed on very few people, and Keith Scott is undoubtedly one of this small but talented band. His book examines in considerable detail the complexities facing the developer on any town centre scheme and explains how such highly successful developments as Carlisle and Ealing were pieced together and are now acclaimed by general populace as well as property professionals.

We all realise that mistakes have been made in the past; but these have, perhaps, helped us to understand more clearly that towns are for people and that people like to identify with a place of their own. The worst mistake of all lay in trying to produce a perfect selling machine which had no sense of identity with its location. The author has clearly travelled extensively in order to study at first hand developments in the United States and Canada which have had a major influence on shopping centre design in the UK. It is reassuring to have him confirm that North American practice is not being slavishly copied over here but is being properly and sensitively adapted to a style of architecture which is essentially British.

The problems of competitions, particularly the complexities of setting up a major competition and the unprofitable use of much professional time, are of major concern. Nobody has found the perfect solution, but Keith Scott has examined the matter and leaves me, at least, convinced that if only we could find a simple answer, then the development world would be a far happier place!

It was a great pleasure to be asked to write this short foreword. I conclude by expressing my conviction that much of the content of this book will be of interest to the 'ordinary person' as well as to those who have been involved in the professional side of development over past decades.

RONALD A GAMMIE, Senior Partner, Donaldsons (Chartered Surveyors) London

20.10.88

INTRODUCTION

The number of top class architects designing shopping centres is astonishingly small, yet the potential is vast. On the face of it the retail world offers limitless opportunity of self expression, so why the reluctance to get involved? Why is it that virtually none of the luminaries of the architectural world is credited with the design of the 28,000 shopping centres built in North America or of the 650 built in Britain since the 50's?

Clients from either the public or the private sector would not, in the main, dream of commissioning any of the half dozen firms whose names might appear in a list of top architects. In December 1986 the American magazine 'Progressive Architecture' polled 325 architects from 25 North American cities and asked them to name their best architects. They were, in order, I.M. Pei, Richard Mier, James Stirling, Robert Venturi, Kevin Roche, Arthur Erikson, Aldo Guirgolo, Arata Isozaki, Cesar Pelli, Philip Johnson,. Mario Botta, Norman Foster, Helmut Jahn, Kohn Pederson Fox. Only one has built a shopping centre (as distinct from specialist shops supporting a larger development) and one other to my knowledge has designed a specific shopping plaza – but it was deemed impractical and never built.

The list, one of several polls in the issue, provided entertaining and controversial Christmas reading. Every architect would want to shuffle the rankings and introduce other names, but, in the context of this book, a serious question is highlighted. If only half a dozen of these 14 names could be agreed as common ground, is it not extraordinary that they have contributed virtually nothing to the billions of pounds worth of retail investment in the built environment? The situation is especially calamitous since by definition this investment is placed either at the heart of our urban settlements or at a confluence of trade routes and so occupies a position of maximum exposure.

The old developer's adage of 'location, location, location' as the three criteria for a successful shopping centre tells us all we need to know about the importance of the environmental impact of the built form which results. Trade is a prime function of human activity and its physical manifestation ranks second only in quantum to shelter. The Greek agora, the Roman forum, the souks of the East and the galleries and market places of the West have been the worthy subjects of endless research and numberless scholarly papers and books. Yet the thousands of shopping complexes, the scores of thousands of small 'strip centres' and the hundreds of thousands of individual shops built since the end of the Second World War have engaged the attention of none of the supreme design talents of our century.

The result in Great Britain can be judged by examining the list of Civic Trust and RIBA Awards and Commendations in search of retail schemes. Of the 3500 Civic Trust accolades only 6 have been awarded to shopping centres and in the highest eschelon of prizes, the RIBA Regional Awards of 350, only 3 have been given to central area retail developments – in order, The Brunel Centre, Swindon; Milton Keynes and The Lanes in Carlisle. In short, the scene is very depressing: and if one were a truly modest person one would omit the fact that BDP were involved in three of the former and two of the latter.

There must be a reason for the lack of awards for retail schemes, and there is. Rather there are a multitude of reasons and they have to do firstly with the attitude of the architects themselves and then of developers, funding agencies, estates consultants and local authorities. Indeed, the issues polarize round the architects on the one hand and the rest of the team on the other. When they have been asked, architects, never notable for their proclivity to accept advice, have often taken an egocentric view of their contribution. They frequently tried to impose a divine right to rule; then, when denied, adopted the petulant stance that if they could not have the ball they would not play.

Hence the rest of the development team have a view of architects which was summed up for me 25 years ago when one of the most famous developers in the country told me on my first central area job, 'Young man, there are about six firms of architects in this country to whom I would happily go with a shopping centre problem. There are about 10 other firms I could use but I know I will have to wet-nurse them through most of the difficulties. The rest I wouldn't pay with washers.'

Whilst writing this book I have told that story to several of today's leading clients, they tell me the names vary slightly but the numbers remain the same.

Twenty five years of continuous application to a subject should bring some measure of experience which might be of interest to others. I therefore offer this personal anthology of what it has been like to work in a firm of designers which can by common consent be numbered among the six most experienced in the UK.

A glance at the Contents page and a flip through the illustrations will show the extent to which I have drawn on the work of my firm. Those who know me best will recognise the degree to which my opinions have been formed by the jobs on which I have worked personally.

The book is light on history and academic theorising – primarily because as a still practicing architect I have time only for using the lessons that history teaches. It leaves no space for assimilating history in the depth required to present and catalogue it for others. That task is left either for academics or my retirement.

What follows, then, is aimed first at young architects who, at the start of their career, have already some grasp of the enormous opportunities and responsibilities that confront the designers of a central area or an out-of-town retail complex. My purpose is to alert them to the attributes they must display if they are to win the confidence of the vast and varied client body that awaits them. It is also a guide to the minefield of conflicting attitudes they will discover as they meet the full spectrum of society from developers, through funding agencies, local authorities and letting agents to the environmental lobbyists.

Secondly, the developer world may find it instructive (if not amusing and/or irritating) to know what at least one architect thinks of them and their attitudes as I have observed their evolution since 1962. It may come as news to them that, save for the fact that they are the clients and we are the employed (so prompting discretion as the better part of valour) we think the numbers of top class developers are just about the same as they give for architects.

Thirdly I hope the book will be read by people whom I regard as the ultimate client. That is by interested members of the public who have a special role in monitoring the quality – and quantity – of commercial redevelopment.

These people include publicly elected members of local councils who take prime responsibility for approving what gets built. It also includes technical officers of local authorities who have the task of advising elected members of the relative merits of the many proposals which confront them.

Finally some chapters will be of special interest to what these days is called the Environment Lobby. This now comprises a vast complex of bodies, some with statutory status, some with great credibility stemming from their size and composition, some self-appointed pressure groups and some simple busy-bodies who are guaranteed to pop out of the woodwork to expound on any environmental matter.

This last group is, however, unlikely to be influenced by what I have to say because, in my unvaried experience of them when their minds are made up they are incapable of being swayed by argument or fact.

I doubt too whether my efforts will be of much interest to the great majority of architects who have never worked in the developer world and prefer not to sully their hands with this kind of commission. They have got it into their heads that there is something inimical to quality in the tensions that inevitably arise if an essential result of the solution is profit. After nearly 30 years I suppose I must assume that I am well tainted with the developer disease: indeed one of my colleagues suggested an alternative title to this book 'Working for the Developer: or, I did it Their Way'.

1

THE EARLY YEARS – HOW IT ALL STARTED

1960 – 1970

After the Second World War

Signs of a change

Dealing with the motor car

The servicing problem

The policy to demolish decayed town centres

The American solution

The resultant deal of American towns

Britain's town centres under threat

Blackburn: an early example of central area clearance and redevelopment

The value of political vision

Starting afresh in the town centre

And in the inner housing areas

A modest defence of architects in the 60's

Lessons from Blackburn

Working with politicians

1

THE EARLY YEARS

The 60's were the Cavalier years of the shopping centre industry – some would say the Cowboy years. When we survey the concrete tank traps, the wind swept terraces and the empty cul-de-sac arcades in dozens of innocent towns like Portsmouth, Gateshead, Ipswich, Burnley or Derby we are tempted to conclude that the whole commercial world had taken leave of its senses. How could everybody have been so naive? Surely a child could have told us that they would be a disaster? Why could not the planners see that the vast windowless hulks of building juxtaposed with layers of glassless, blackeyed multi-storey car parks would destroy the character of our towns? How could developers be so stupid as to think that just anything would let as long as a group of shops was strung along a mall?

All very sensible questions and easy to put with the crystal clarity of hindsight. It is hard even for those now approaching retirement to remember the atmosphere of euphoria which pervaded the shopping world in those days. It is worth stepping back to see how it happened.

After the Second World War
In 1945 the country was economically bankrupt and though we had won a war it seemed an eternity before any benefits accrued. Rationing for food, clothing and building materials continued: so did military conscription. Young architects were nurtured in the belief that good architecture was 'responsible' architecture, and that meant designing everything – buildings, structure and all components – to a minimum. Everything was minimal. We spent hours

designing houses that had tiny rooms and little or no storage space. We cut circulation to a degree that forbade anything as big as a wardrobe to go upstairs so it had to be built in. We had a competition in the office to see if we could design the first floor of a three-bedroomed house so compactly that when you arrived at the top of the stair all vertical surfaces were occupied by doors and doorframes. The inevitable 4 inch surface between doors, where a partition defined the rooms, was the place for a light switch. Skirtings were cut down to 2 inches high and timber windows had such narrow frames that they remained fragile and 'whippy' until the 24oz glass was in and the putty set. Double glazing was something they did in Sweden.

Our architectural imaginations were crippled, so that intellectually a whole generation was affected. It took us – the whole nation – most of the 50's to nurse ourselves back to life. The 1951 South Bank Exhibition was crucial to this process. It was as if the first snowdrop had illumined a bleak midwinter landscape. Then, as the tide turned, waves of architects took trips to Sweden and Switzerland where there had been no war and the architectural magazines told tales of splendour that excited our parched minds.

In the beginning the new 'Swedish Modern' style was a fad or fashionable game played by the cognoscenti. Our parents, rooted firmly in the 20's and earlier, could never see the sense in it but the tide was now running strongly and there was an irresistible urge to strike out in new directions.

Marketway shopping centre, Llanelli
Many pedestrian centres were built through-out the 1960's. Some were covered but nearly all had appalling shop front designs.

Merseyway shopping centre, Stockport
A precinct left open to the sky devoid of retail ambience or 'theatre'. Concrete galleries, dull paving, endless ramps and flat roofs predominate.

Signs of a change

The signs were favourable: thousands of acres in city centres still lay derelict, the rubble merely swept from the roads into vast heaps, either back onto the site whence it had come or into craters and old quarries. Where there was no war damage, especially in the northern industrial towns, the Victorian fabric looked tired, dirty and in desperate need of repair. Streets were becoming clogged with cars as petrol rationing ended and a new affluence brought the dream of individual family mobility into reality. But the universally attainable mobile capsule was rapidly becoming immobile and its passengers were taking longer to get across town than were people on foot.

The shops lining the streets were almost all serviced from the street itself, and ever bigger pantechnicons serving many shops in a chain added to the accretion of noise, smoke and physical congestion.

Dealing with the motor car

In 1963 came the seminal work from the Buchanan team 'Traffic in Towns'. The basic thesis was that urban forms were dense agglomerations of human activity and facilities, and the demand for universal access to these nodes by individually operated vehicles was just an impossible dream. No matter how spacious the roads themselves, no matter how sophisticated the management of those roads, the sheer logistics were such that one had a straight choice: either ample capacity roads and no town centres or pedestrianised town centres and no cars. It is difficult to overestimate the impact of the Buchanan Report. Our thinking about the planning of town centres was revolutionised and overnight, it seemed, we were all talking about how to pedestrianise our streets and where to build multi-storey car parks.

But there was a snag. It was easy to find sites for multi-storey car parks and to propose pedestrianisation, but violent opposition from traders met every traffic free proposal. Retailers could not rid themselves of their fixation with the idea that every customer should be able to drive up to the shop door and park. It took years of persuasion and many trips to the newly pedestrianised hearts of Cologne, Stockholm, Munich

and Rotterdam for them to realise that cars bring only one family at best to each small trader. The parking turnover is barely 5 or 6 a day and the shoppers also shop elsewhere. While it is stopped and empty, the vehicle is blocking a view of the shop display from across the street and when it moves off and another car manoeuvres in its place the street becomes a dangerous river which shoppers cross at their peril. Now, nearly 30 years on, a careful study of 400 towns by Erdmans, the letting agents, has established that rents are 45% higher in pedestrianised streets than for shops in similar vehicular streets.

The servicing problem

Nevertheless the car problem could be solved within the existing city fabric. What could not be solved so readily was the servicing. So dense was the fabric of cities that there was no possibility of lorry access to the rear of the shops. All were serviced down narrow alleys from the main street at the front. The answer came with inexorable logic. Were not the great majority of these shops Dickensian relics anyway and at the end of their useful life? The small businessman who used to occupy the upper floors had long gone. Their office windows were clouded with cobwebs and the rooms were ankle-deep in pigeon droppings because nobody had repaired the gap in the roof.

The doctors had evacuated to smart group practices in the suburbs. The solicitors were a bit slow to move but the architects, chartered accountants, engineers, insurance societies, building societies and the tatty little upstairs hairdressers had all disappeared either to purpose made buildings beyond the shopping centre where they would merge and expand (long before the Big Bang) or to ground floor premises among the shops where they could catch the impulse buyer as well as the long term customer.

So had not the time come for a major restructuring of our city centres? The arteries of our historic towns were designed for people on foot or on horse. The more recent of them had been made wide enough to take a horse and carriage but such transport was for the well to do. Universal car ownership and centralised warehousing for chain store distribution was the straw

Rotterdam, Linjbahn
After total wartime devastation Rotterdam was cleared of all vehicles and pedestrians filled the shopping plazas. People do not insist on driving to the door of every shop.

Market Street, Manchester
Empty offices above shops in central Manchester.

that broke the camel's back. Shops were amalgamating, selling greater ranges of goods and requiring much more floor space and storage per unit. There were just not enough sizeable units to be had in any town centre in Britain. The age of the big shop unit and the supermarket was at hand.

The policy to demolish decayed town centres

The answer seemed obvious. The town centres or whatever was left of them after Hitler's bombers must be demolished and the whole area comprehensively redeveloped. The nation was breathless with admiration for the clarity of the notion, and politicians could see votes in countless numbers as reward for leading the electorate to this new Jerusalem in their own town. Developers' eyes gleamed in contemplation of the profits to be made from simple forms of tailor-made shopping emporia, and contractors could see work stretching into the next millennium. Architects, ever alert for an ego trip, caught a breath of its heady scent and magazines like the 'Architectural Review' explored the theoretical possibilities without sullying itself with the economic consequences. We dashed out and bought 'Civilia: The End of Sub-urban Man,' but could not understand the impenetrable text so we looked at the mesmeric montage pictures and gave it away as a Christmas present. Sir Frederick Osborn of the National Garden Cities Committee called the idea 'an odious damned lie' but Sir Hugh Casson said 'isn't it time we tried it?' and since he had made such a jolly good shot at the 1951 Exhibition we decided he was right.

Academics will complain that this is to sight read the music and some of the notes are wrong but surely the theme is right. Only those who were involved in the first comprehensive central area developments can fully recapture the excitement. We really did think we were embarking upon the first major overall review of the urban fabric since the days of Haussmann and L'Enfant.

The American solution

American developers had pioneered the shopping centre as a building type in the early 50's but they never seriously considered putting these vast complexes in town centres. Firstly they had no ready means of land assembly through compulsory purchase powers. Secondly people did not want to live in the characterless urban wilderness of false fronts and wirescapes so vividly described in Sinclair Lewis' 'Main Street', so they had already fled to the suburbs. Thirdly land was cheap and apparently infinite as the town gave way to the prairie – developers just followed a freeway out of town until they came to a satellite community or, even better, to a confluence of freeways from which several communities could be served. The plan of the centre was simple and the formula in essence never varied. Two major anchor traders were placed dumb-bell fashion at either end of a pedestrian mall which was lined on both sides with small unit shops. To get from one anchor to another shoppers were obliged to pass by all the small shops. In the North the mall was covered; in the South the climate was judged to be perfect so it was simply let in. The mall roof was omitted and shade was given by canopies and trees.

A Montage from 'Civilia: The End of Sub-urban Man'
Much of the imagery here is taken from the Blackburn central area development.

American mall systems
Two typical out of town malls in the USA. University Towne Centre shows the more flexible layout ideas of the late seventies with the Ice Capades rink. Parkway Plaza is older (opened in 1972) and is planning a mid-mall attraction. Both are single level, about 1m sq ft, three miles apart yet together record about $250,000,000 per annum in sales. Each uses 80 acres of land – much of which is devoted to parking 4500 cars.

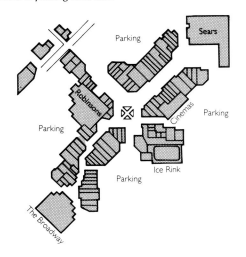

University Towne Centre, San Diego

Parkway Plaza, San Diego

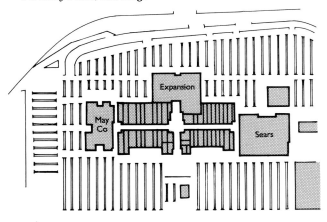

London's green belt boundary

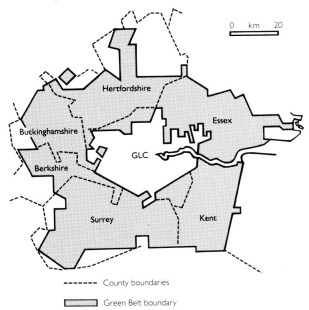

- - - - - County boundaries

☐ Green Belt boundary

The resultant death of American towns

Great department stores like Filenes and Jordon Marsh built outlets in the new malls on the edge of cities and either closed or severely curtailed their in town operation. Boston was particularly sad because it is one of the handful of cities in the USA which has real character. Most American towns are products of the 20th Century. They are built on flat land for ease and economy, and the streets are laid out in a monotonous grid iron. The whole place has the flaccid character of a day-old waffle: the sky is laced with a tangle of telephone wires and electric cables. But Boston is built on hills, and it has lovely in-town parks, elegant Georgian houses, churches and meeting rooms and the streets meander with the same elusive mystery that we find in Bath in England.[1]

Britain's town centres under threat

Here in Britain land was precious and open space irreplaceable. We had been through the laissez-faire phase of ribbon development in the 30's and had been shocked to see how towns could be linked by thoughtless expansion. Long before the war it was impossible to see countryside between Manchester and Bury and residential speed restrictions were continually in force between Bradford and Leeds.

In the mid 40's planners like Abercrombie had warned of the need to preserve the countryside that was our heritage and the concept of the green belt girdling the cities was established. Onslaught will forever be made on this priceless asset because its development is a cheap option and one cannot blame those whose business it is to maximise return on investment for trying constantly to nibble it away. They are especially encouraged when a laissez- faire or 'market force' government is in power and the Tory minister's firm commitment to blocking needless out of town development was a wonderful Christmas present in 1986 when environmentalists were becoming extremely concerned at the plethora of applications for megacentres near every big city in Britain. Many local authorities also prefer the easy solution of building new in a field to rebuilding the inner cities where the social as well as infrastructure complexities are formidable.

Central government too is not exempt from criticism in this respect. Certainly a good case could be made for overspill communities in most of the 32 New Towns that had to be built to solve the problems of the war-torn cities. In the northwest, however, one has to do an acrobatic feat of special pleading to convince anyone that the Central Lancashire New Town should have been allowed to destroy thousands of acres of fertile, pleasant landscape to develop a new community based on the Preston/Chorley axis. Only in the dying gasp of its 15-year mandate did the Development Corporation start major rehousing in the old industrial Plungington district to the north of the town centre, and very admirable it is. So admirable indeed that it makes even more shameful the wilderness of out of town housing to which few slum-cleared residents wanted to go. It is significant that to this day no name could be agreed for the New Town – and none ever will.

Blackburn: an early example of central area clearance and redevelopment

To return to the heady days of the 60's, of complete land clearance and a story of a town in the north of England. In 1960 Blackburn was a sorry sight: more accurately, it was a sorry site. The cotton weaving industry on which it was founded had virtually disappeared and was

9

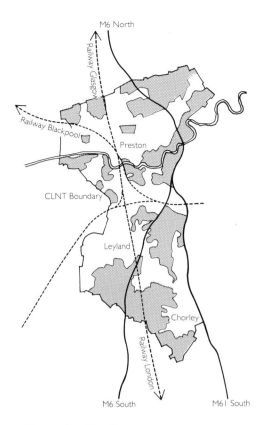

Central Lancashire New Town
Based on the three existing towns of Preston, Leyland and Chorley.
They contain hundreds of acres of derelict land or of low quality
buildings that are ripe for renewal. The shaded area shows land
within the designated area which was classified as being of medium,
high or very high visual quality in the rural landscape. Development
should have been concentrated in the existing communities.

certainly doomed. Man-made fibre and foreign
competition had wrung its neck. The town was tucked
away in the Rossendale valley and to get at it from the
west one had to take a branch road off the A6 or the
newly built M6 or change trains at Preston and take
a local line. There was no quick route from the south
and east and bleak Pennine moors guarded the north.

The town centre of Blackburn was an archetype of
the planning problems described earlier, but it had one
priceless asset which few communities are granted and
for lack of which many still founder. The Town Council
was led by a charismatic and visionary politician who
was of Scottish birth and to his deathbed at the age of 87
sounded as if he had just arrived from Aberdeen. He was
of Labour persuasion and had been grounded in the art
of the possible, having been Parliamentary Secretary to
Labour's equally charismatic Cabinet Minister, Barbara
Castle, Blackburn's MP until she retired in 1979. His
name was George Eddie and it was to him that the
Laing Development Company made a presentation in
1961. They said, in essence, that they knew the Council
was a major landowner in the town centre and a few
peripheral acquisitions could deliver practically 15
acres at the very heart of the town for redevelopment.

Blackburn lay in the heartland of the Co-operative
movement and a large CWS store sat rather off-pitch
to the northwest of the town centre. Laings had an
agreement in principle with the financial arm of the
business, the Co-operative Insurance Society, to fund
a scheme on condition that the CWS would be offered
first pick in the new development.

The value of political vision

Eddie saw the potential for a new Blackburn and
proposed that council deliberation of town centre
matters should be removed from the political arena.
This was done by the simple device of making an
executive committee of the leaders of the three main
political parties and calling them The Town Centre
Redevelopment Committee. For over 10 years they
each had mandated powers from their own party
caucus to take the widest planning decisions. No doubt
great battles were fought behind the party caucus
doors but when the three came together as a committee,
decisions were made with astonishing speed.

Their first act was to invite the Laing team to make
an official visual presentation of their ideas and their
in-house design team was given three months to show
what it could do. The presentation was made in the
Blackburn Art Gallery in March 1962 and the Press
were invited.[2]

A fortnight later Maurice Laing rang BDP's founder
partner, George Baines (every person mentioned in
this story has since been knighted) and said that Laings
had a job in Blackburn and the council wanted it to be
designed by a northern firm; would the newly created
Building Design Partnership take it on. We were
appointed and for the next 15 years until Phase 3
was completed, BDP laboured to give Blackburn
a new image.

Starting afresh in the town centre

In these days of care and conservation it is difficult
to recapture the spirit of excitement and the demand
for complete renewal that pervaded the 60's. It is
therefore worth quoting from a letter from the Leader
of Blackburn Council that was printed in the brochure
of the Laing proposals:

'Like most industrial towns in Lancashire, Blackburn
is a product of the industrial revolution. It grew up
without any apparent sense of planning, with few
buildings that can lay claim to real architectural beauty,
and with a crowded shopping centre totally inadequate
to meet the needs of modern traffic. Drastic change in
the way of re-planning and re-building is inevitable.

'This brochure tells just how the town shopping centre
is going to be rebuilt. It is a plan that has vision and
courage. This is not a case of knocking down a street
and rebuilding. Blackburn is going to have the sense
and courage to knock down its whole town centre,
replan it, and build in accordance with modern needs
and ideas. We propose to do that with 150 acres of our
town centre in addition to clearance areas all over the
town.

'The pages that follow tell the story of an up to date
shopping centre segregating shoppers from traffic,
of roof top car parking, of underground servicing,
of open spaces and the provision of all amenities
essential in a modern town centre. The Town Council
is unanimous in its support for this plan. We have
great faith in the industrial future of this town and
we believe it will become the shopping centre for a
very wide area. We are certainly prepared to invest in
its future prosperity. On behalf of the Town Council
I congratulate all the staff of the Laing Development
Company Limited, who, in co-operation with the staff
of the Blackburn Corporation, have produced this
magnificent town centre plan. May it soon become
a reality.'

Victorian Blackburn, Lancashire
*Photo circa 1960
The city was decayed
and unsuited to
modern trading
requirements.*

Blackburn, Lancashire
*The 'New Blackburn'
envisaged in 1962.
The same view point
illustrates the intent
to renew 150 acres.*

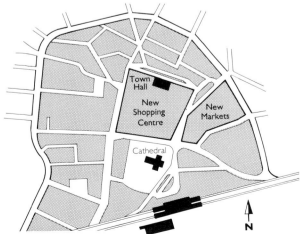

Blackburn town centre
*In May 1962 Blackburn Council approved this visionary plan for
its town. In 1988 it would be deemed megalomania for it meant
sweeping away 150 acres of primarily Victorian fabric and starting
again.*

Blackburn old clock tower
Blackburn markethall clock tower immediately before demolition in 1962. Its destruction would be unthinkable in the mood of the 80's.

Booth's corner
The old E H Booth corner in King William Street, Blackburn. Most buildings in the street were decrepit and beyond viable repair. Even the Booth shop had exceeded its useful life though in the climate of the 80's many would argue for its retention. Surely contemporary architects of quality could be trusted to design buildings tailored to 20th century use which would be at least as distinguished as this?

Blackburn Phase 1, 1964
Taken from the same position as the photo of Booth's corner in King William Street.

It is beyond dispute that the public at large was convinced that total demolition and renewal was the answer. A river flowing through the edge of the centre was culverted and a new 3 and 5 day market built over it on a raft (this was a separate contract not designed by BDP). The old market was vacated, the building demolished, the clock tower felled and away we went on a cleared site using the 20ft (6m) crossfall to create basement service below a traffic free pedestrian precinct of single-storey shopping. We demolished some worthy buildings like Booth's corner and Thwaites Arcade, though much was so decrepit that at the sight of the bulldozer it fell down of its own accord. Three separate phases were completed and they incorporated many subphases. The only factors that stopped Sir George Eddie and his Committee driving on to phases 4 and 5 as proposed in the Laing submission were a combination of the ever more insistent cries of the conservation movement, advice from the letting agents that the centre was becoming overshopped and his own wearying progress into advanced years.

The achievement, however, stands. Blackburn remains the most comprehensively redeveloped non-bomb-damaged town in Britain and it is much loved and respected by residents. It is one of the 5 new town centres to have been given a Civic Trust Award and one of only two covered by the illustrious Architectural Review. It has been featured in magazines, seminars and lectures all over the world.

And in the inner housing areas

Just as exciting, and equally noteworthy, Blackburn's housing problems were solved almost completely within the town boundaries. At the peak of the rehabilitation programme 800 council houses a year were being gutted and modernised and, even more pioneering, rows of solid privately owned Victorian terraces in areas like Queen Street were refurbished, the streets landscaped, children's play areas laid out and car laybys discreetly defined. So notable was the achievement that photographs of the finished work were displayed at the UN Conference on Human Settlements in Vancouver in 1976. At that time most other Lancashire towns were building beyond the suburbs, filling ponds, felling trees, scooping top soil away and putting in drains and sewers for new housing estates in the countryside.

Of course, if we were doing it again we would be less violent with the town's fabric. We would not dream of demolishing the old clock tower and Thwaites Arcade would be refurbished. The basement servicing would still work below 15 acres (6 hectares) of pedestrian walkways and shoppers would still be able to park right over the shop they wish to visit.[3]

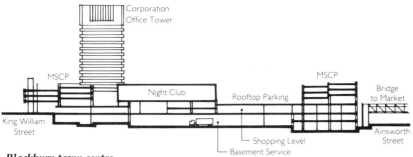

Blackburn town centre
Elevation and section of the first and second phases. The concern to sweep away the Victorian 'rubbish' and start anew is apparent.

Blackburn town centre
The 20ft cross fall from King William Street down to Ainsworth Street allows pedestrian access from the west and bridge level access to the New Markets to the east without changing levels. Basement service underneath with excavation only at the western side. Roof top parking prevented daylight in the malls and when they opened into squares they were left open. Draught problems resulted. The malls are open 24 hours; to close them would seal off the town centre.

Queen Street, Blackburn
Houses before redevelopment.

Queen Street, Blackburn
Houses after redevelopment. People were temporarily decanted from their homes and returned after the houses had been renovated; an exercise in management as much as design.

A modest defence of architects in the 60's

Whilst architects are expected to wear sackcloth for their misdemeanours in this period we can cheat a little and wear a cotton vest next to the skin. It is not the business of architecture to prophesy: that is the job of the fine arts – music, literature, painting. Architecture relies for its being on patronage and it is the architect's function to mirror to the highest possible level the civilisation he or she serves. The corporate will of a society must be interpreted and the skill with which this is done separates the men from the boys. This is no defence for some of the architectural nightmares which have been visited on some of our towns (true design talent will always be as rare as snowflakes in June) but if the architecture of the 60's and 70's is in bad odour, and in the context of shopping centre design in particular it leaves a lot to be desired, then the failure is a corporate fault. The concept of Comprehensive Central Area Redevelopment was almost universally applauded. Parents loved the safety of the pedestrian malls; relieved never to have to snatch the toddler from under a lorry's wheels; delighted that the rain no longer swept into the baby's pram and their teenager had somewhere safe to meet friends on the seats near the Kentucky Fry. It may well be fashionable to deride the Arndale Mall as a generic type (any architect trying to defend it at a RIBA branch meeting let alone at Portland Place would be either lynched or carted off to the funny farm) but from the safety of these pages the view is proffered that the only things wrong with them were: that in the process they sometimes knocked down some jolly good buildings; that in the desire to get roof-top car parking or servicing, developers and their architects forgot the human need for daylight (much more of that later); and that the vast majority suffered very low quality aesthetic design as a result of poor developer patronage and low quality design talent. All three are capable of remedy and we shall see how.

Lessons from Blackburn

Blackburn provides many lessons that have been invaluable. First and most important, a community like any business organisation is only as vibrant as its leaders. Sir George Eddie had a vision for his town and he was quite disinterested in the enabling detail. If you see a town that is going nowhere you can be sure it is being run by nobodies.

Secondly, it is best if the vision comes from the political side rather than the technical, because politicians are best placed to dominate their party caucus and persuade the public into supporting their ideas and renewing their mandate.

Thirdly, a visionary must be in power to be effective. In the rare periods when Blackburn had an abberation and voted Tory the whole Town Centre Development team ground to a halt though it was composed of exactly the same people. Sir George was simply not Chairman of the Committee.

Fourthly, quality attracts quality: the reverse is also true. When excellent technical officers get wind of an exciting place to be they beat a path to it. Never have we worked with technical officers more skilled and decisive in getting things done in all departments than in Blackburn during the years 1962-1970. Once clear about the Town Centre Redevelopment Committee's intent they knew they had a mandate to implement.

That clarity repercussed directly onto the work and the morale of outside consultants.

Fifthly, since central area work is very long term owing to its extraordinary political, legal, estate and technical complexity, nothing can be done if the project is treated as a political football. If the political balance is marginal and if the game stops every three years and the teams change ends it is imperative that the policy towards the central area redevelopment remains intact.

A town centre is the beating heart of the community and few of the issues concerning its physical health have anything to do with politics. The drive towards redevelopment should come from a leadership that is united across the political spectrum. Councillors will undergo pressures enough without dissipating their energy sniping in opposition then spending the first 6 months of each new administration unscrambling everything that the previous incumbents put together. There is no significant issue in a central area redevelopment proposal which can be illuminated or assisted by the application of political dogma.

Working with politicians

One is sometimes asked whether town centre redevelopment work is easier with a Labour or a Tory administration. Here is a fertile field for losing friends and influencing nobody, but one or two thoughts have occurred over the years. The retail world is by and large singularly immune to central government policy. The litmus paper reacts strongly to the economic health of the nation and that has always been crucial. The most dramatic example was the energy crisis in the early 70's and the collapse of many secondary banks. The shake out of cowboys in every branch of the industry was profound, very beneficial, and had nothing to do with politics.

On the local scene, however, observation of political ideology does prompt a tentative view. Tories tend to cling to the belief that theirs is the party of private enterprise, pragmatism and business acumen, all very necessary attributes of a developer. One might assume therefore that a meeting of minds can be anticipated. In fact this does not follow. Tory councils are usually made up of self-made businessmen and they own drapers shops, small jewellers and confectionery stalls. They are generally freeholders and have a very acute sense of what is good for their own business, but it would not occur to them to spend time working out what is good for their competitors. In short, they are strong on detail, light on strategy and getting them to take the broad view on a project involving every trader in town can be very hard work indeed.

Labour councillors tend to have a quite different perception. They are frequently blue-collar workers, almost always in the PAYE tax bracket and they are often given great articulacy by support from academics from the local polytechnic. Together they know little about the arcane world of business – indeed tend to deride it – but this leaves them free to be visionaries and they are quick to grasp overall strategy. Implementation and practical matters make them short-tempered and they are prone to retreat into rhetoric. That cuts little ice with a developer who is seeking to get on with the job, or with a fund who has a simple requirement to find a safe home for 20 million pounds of the society's money.[4]

Arndale Mall, Manchester 1970's
Safe, free from traffic and out of the rain.

1. Washington Street was the shopping heart of Boston but already when I was a student there in 1953 it was dying and much worse was to follow. We will trace the revival later but for now just note that nearly all the thousands of shopping malls that were built in the USA were sited on the edge of town on greenfield sites – with disastrous results for the fragile fabric of the already characterless city centres.

2. At the time I reported for the now defunct 'Architect and Building News' and the editor asked me to go along and write an appraisal of the scheme. I was highly impressed with the overall planning of the huge development which completely swept away the decrepit Victorian fabric of Blackburn but was aghast at its visual impact with a choppy sea of cars covering the whole roof area at one level. I said so in the article.

3. It is certain however that I would be locked in conflict with conservationists over my advocacy of pulling down the old Market Hall and the rows of Victorian hovels. The preservationists would be arguing that they were part of our priceless heritage: I, to the contrary, would be maintaining that they were of little architectural value and if modern architects could not do better than that we should take up knitting.

4. Once I worked with a Liberal majority. That council did not survive the ensuing election. The Labour successor immediately unravelled everything the Liberals did so I could not possibly offer any view that would command credence as to that party's foibles in a development context. Labour sacked us within the first week of its mandate.

2

THE MIDDLE YEARS – REAPPRAISAL: COUNTING THE COST

1970-1980

The British example: Brent Cross

Some reasons for failure

The architect's contribution

The developer's attitude

The planner's role

Where were the preservationists?

The influence of the traffic engineer

2

THE MIDDLE YEARS

By the early 70's the shopping centre industry and the public at large had begun to take stock of what had been achieved. The energy crisis and its attendant financial difficulties meant that the whole construction industry was withdrawing within itself and consolidating. Inflation seemed set to grow worse and at its peak in 1975 the cost of living rose at an annual rate of 24% while the cost of building was escalating at an unnerving 1.5% per month.

Many of the straightforward easy sites had been developed and only the problem areas were left. Furthermore people were becoming restive about the architectural quality bequeathed to them under the banner of comprehensive redevelopment and the environmental movement was growing in stridency and power. All the ingredients of uncertainty were manifest, so many of the big names battened down the hatches, closed down their development activities and elected to become managers of their vast estates – many of which were highly profitable.

A British example: Brent Cross
The Brent Cross Centre, in London, is a good example and not just because it was the biggest in Britain when it was built. All the classic principles of American malls are on display. The big anchor stores are perfectly located and of a quality that attracts the motorborne shopper from miles away. John Lewis and Fenwicks give the necessary West End chic at either end of the dumb-bell, and along the mall's length W H Smith, Boots, C&A Modes and Marks & Spencer are inserted at regular intervals to keep the lateral pull of shoppers under full impetus. The scheme is not well enough toplit but the malls are furnished with seats, plants, fountains and small food outlets. Just as important, and overlooked by those who did not do their American homework properly, it is superbly managed. One could eat off the floor, as the saying goes, and that kind of cleanliness and attention to repairs is the biggest key to success after location and layout. Brent Cross was opened in 1976 and in a retail sense it represents the apogee of achievement of first generation malls in Great Britain.

Where it went wrong was in the quality of its external architecture. The inside was fine for its vintage. Great care was taken over every detail because the success of the venture from a commercial standpoint rested on the internal design and ambience. Full size mock -ups of sections of the mall were made to ensure that everything was considered. What escaped notice was that in transferring the American experience to Britain, the shopping centre was to be set right in the middle of suburbia. Indeed most new British developments were planted in the town centre. In the USA the shopping centres were out of town so the visiting developers parked their cars and charabancs as near to the

entrance as possible and dashed inside to study the interiors. The crass exteriors were never given a glance.

If one can argue for a moment (and it should not be attempted really) that indifferent quality architecture can be tolerated in an out of town centre, it matters greatly if a building block of even a quarter the size of Brent Cross is imposed on English towns like Gloucester, Salisbury or Winchester. Furthermore it matters just as much if the town is hardly a well-loved tourist centre. Wherever they live, people want to identify proudly with their town and the opportunity should be grasped to give a wholly new image to places like Bury, Rotheram and Oldham.

The failure of the development world to rise to this challenge will remain the greatest single criticism of those years between 1960 and 1975.

Some reasons for failure
There are several reasons for the failures and it is unfair to blame the developer for the whole dismal parade of town centre developments. After all, although the developer is a client and has a patron's responsibilities he is not an architect. It is not his business to design the exterior of buildings; so what were architects, planning officers and the environment lobby doing whilst city centres were being ravaged? Sadly, the answer is the same as when one asks what sociologists were doing whilst families with small children were being allocated flats in high rise apartments. Not a lot: the silence of the protest was deafening.

The architect's contribution
Take architects: they were quick to see the possibilities and in the beginning some well known names were commissioned. A number of things went wrong, however, and a crisis of confidence set in between the developer and the architectural profession which has never been resolved. The architectural world back in the 60's was still in its early modern movement phase and addicted to slogans like 'less is more', 'form follows function', 'decoration is a crime', and many more.

They added up to a desire to design simply and directly with new materials or at least with old materials in a new way (like glass, steel and concrete) faithfully following the dictates of pioneer thinkers like Le Corbusier, Walter Gropius and Mies Van der Rohe. The rectangular boxes which resulted looked cheap and were exactly what the developer wanted. If the architect could chat the planning officer into believing it was great architecture, who was he to argue?

Furthermore architects, in Britain at least, were still trying to decide how to create new buildings of many different kinds because a whole generation had

Brent Cross Centre,
London
South elevation.

Brent Cross Centre,
London
Main mall.

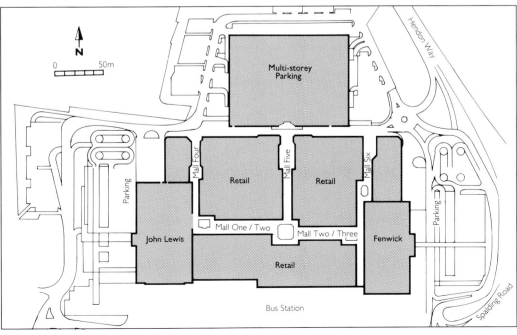

Brent Cross Centre,
London

**The Gallery,
Philadelphia**
*A stark exterior broods
over the city. Not a
window in sight.*

**Stamford Mall,
Stamford, Connecticut**
*A desolate exterior,
an insult to the
urban fabric.*

**The Piazza Navona,
Rome**
*One of Europe's
greatest outdoor rooms.
Lessons abound here
for every urban planner.*

designed nothing of quality or permanence since before the Second World War. The older practitioners who were commissioned to produce shopping centres found the criteria inimical to their traditional training which had rejected the modern movement. The younger generation, on the other hand, were in the thrall of the euphoria of the modern technology and they decided that it was exactly what our rehabilitated towns and cities needed. The philosophy fitted well with the idea of comprehensive redevelopment.

Developers' disenchantment with the architectural profession set in quite early. Although delighted with simple blank boxes the developer was not prepared to put up with someone who thought he was God's gift to the shopping public. Some of these 'simple' boxes turned out to be extremely costly. The architect wanted to detail them in boardmarked concrete with all the shutter bolts arranged carefully in patterns and the contractor said it was needlessly expensive. For perhaps the first time architects came up against a whole class of clients who were as autocratic as them. There would have been a rapport if these clients had been Medicis – men of taste and letters, but every word they uttered revealed them as Philistines and they boasted of it. They had not, specifically not, employed the architect to create a work of art for them, nor to build something that would elevate them as great patrons. The architect had not been retained to play prima-donna but to create a building in which money could be made.

The developer's attitude
Developer clients had seen what had happened in the USA and the profits accruing. To them investment was a straightforward business transaction: you could trade in shopping centres as you could trade in equities. They were not minded to bow to opposition from paid professionals who simply could not grasp that time was money. Aesthetic considerations were well down their list of priorities; frankly the subject bored them.

Some architects tried the resignation ploy and were amazed when the client snapped their hands off and waved goodbye. As recently as 1985 a well-known architect who had strayed inadvertently into the development world said in an argument over standards 'This, I am afraid, is a resignation issue'. The client just surveyed him bleakly and said 'It's a pity you feel that way: if you do decide to resign, do me a favour, do it very quickly.'

As the 60's wore on mutual suspicion intensified. Architects could make neither moss nor sand of a client who could not give him a settled brief, who had no motivation for building other than to make money and with whom he had the utmost difficulty in striking up an intellectual dialogue. Developers came increasingly to feel that architects epitomised the view that the letters ARIBA stood for Always Remember I'm the Bloody Architect and decided that there was room for only one decision-maker on the job. They also concluded that the architect as aesthete was a supernumerary and they would be far better off with a professional who knew his place like an engineer, a quantity surveyor, a lawyer or an agent. In fact the developer took the same view of architects as Frank Lloyd Wright, took of engineers: 'All I want an engineer for is to tell me how much and where'. By mutual consent highly sensitive design-orientated architects left the commercial shopping centre world and have so far not returned.

If the developer's view of architects is unflattering, the profession's view of the commercial field is fully reciprocated: to the degree that the Royal Institute of British Architects, the elite architectural press and the cult figures of the profession regard architects who meddle in the commercial world as pariahs who have sold their aesthetic soul for a mess of pottage. Tragically there is much evidence to support that view.

The planner's role
The planner? In the first decade of town centre renewal planners were rudderless in a fast moving tide. We will see later that only a minority had any architectural training and they too were subject to the same heady wine of the modern movement that inebriated private architects. The majority had, from an architectural and aesthetic point of view, no idea what was going on. Few had done any basic field work – and the situation is no better today. Greater affluence and mobility is fine but if travel abroad for a planning officer means lying on a beach at Lerici rather than spending a morning looking, learning and sipping coffee in the Piazza Navona, little of benefit to towns back in England can be expected.

Into this badly-informed and ill-prepared pool dropped applications for central area schemes by the score. They were submitted (hardly the right word to describe their cavalier authors) by a type of person who was prepared to go straight for the jugular if any opposition was mounted by technical officers. Councillors, on the other hand, relied for their position on public election and they were eager to be seen as men and women of vision who had attracted new trade and hence new affluence to the town. If, by approving a scheme, nagging traffic problems could be eased, parking could be solved and household names in new supermarkets and quality shops could be brought into the city that surely outweighed subjective arguments about the quality of the townscape. Aesthetics were always matters of opinion anyway and nobody could argue definitively between good and bad. There were no votes there. So the planning officer was thanked for his view and told that there were greater priorities than whether the walls of the new shopping centre should be brick or concrete or wiggly tin. The schemes were approved.

Where were the preservationists?
So what were the preservationists, the environment-alists and the protection societies doing? Not very much either. They were in fact a fairly new breed, and had a low profile.

Never before in planning and architectural history had any group of people, as distinct from individual patrons in the Renaissance, proposed to tear down whole areas of our towns and cities and rebuild them along completely new lines. Renewal was always taking place and there was an occasional outcry when some quality building was under threat. Groups like the Georgian Society and the Council for the Protection of Rural England were on the alert for individual acts of vandalism but the scale of this new phenomenon caught them unprepared.[1]

Preservationists had also to avoid the charge of being opposed to any kind of progress and let some of the proposals take place before they could be sure of their ground and point to the folly of what had been done. They had a particularly difficult time over the subject of new road proposals.

Demolish

New Ring Road

Preston inner ringway
The panorama of the rim of Avenham Park from the River Ribble. The Borough Engineer recommended that the southern ringway should break through the houses where shown, fell all the trees and put a four-lane highway on stilts in front of the houses. The photograph below shows the parkland that would have been destroyed.

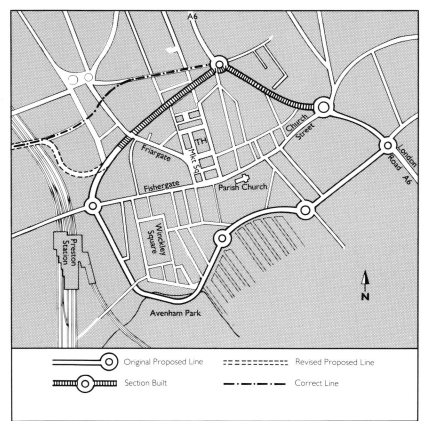

Original Proposed Line   Revised Proposed Line

Section Built   Correct Line

Preston inner ringway
Plan of Preston in 1958 with the Borough Engineer's ring road proposals round the centre. The southern section would have demolished hundreds of houses and severed the town centre from Avenham Park and the River Ribble. The Central Lancashire New Town Corporation demonstrated the folly of this plan and the line was abandoned. The northern section has been built as indicated and as predicted is too tightly drawn for the commercial sector to 'breathe' properly. The revised line for the completion is shown and its efficiency can be gauged from its contortion. The correct line has been studiously ignored. Engineer-led solutions of this kind plague many a town.

Demolish

The influence of the traffic engineer

Everyone could see that towns were grinding to a standstill and something had to be done. However, whilst new roads meant pulling things down, they rarely meant putting anything up; so there was never any horrible new building to criticise; only a lament for what had disappeared. Environmentalists were by nature drawn from among the ranks of the aesthetes and they were much more at home debating subjective, qualitive issues with architects than they were dealing with engineers. These very practical chaps smiled patiently when lectured about the grain of the city but said they had put the whole problem to the computer and the answer was irrefutable. If people wanted to move about the town on four wheels the buildings would have to go.

Examples are legion but Preston's inner ring road is a classic. Engineering 'logic' proved impervious to every environmental argument and so the monstrous road was allowed to swathe through the fabric of the town and it will remain forever a monument to the stupidity of allowing so called quantitative arguments to hold sway over qualitative considerations. 'So called' because even quantitative arguments can be fallacious.

In spite of the traffic counts, studies of model split, origin and destination figures and the rest of the jargon that was used in the 60's to justify the proposed line of the road, it is now a matter of daily observation that the road has been built on quite the wrong line.

Thus the country went through the Decade of the Engineer when that chief officer was frequently the most powerful man in the local authority and a very valuable ally of the comprehensive central area developer. Environmentalists took a while to get their act together and though the judgement of history will be critical of their speed of reaction it will applaud the notable contributions they made once organised.

Take for instance the London Ealing experience. Design issues are discussed later but in the context of environmental concern local people had spent several years in the mid-70's fighting a massive scheme whose content and road proposals would, in their opinion have destroyed the character of their town. They took expert advice, they learned from the experience of Public Inquiries nationwide, plotted their campaign carefully and succeeded in persuading the minister to reject the developer's scheme. When the local authority, who had supported the proposal, had licked its wounds, prepared a revised brief and issued it to competing developers, each was advised to consult the Ealing Action Group before putting pencil to paper. This our team did and at the close of a tense but very professional evening meeting in one of the committee's homes one of the ladies said 'I hope you have found the evening instructive. I can tell you that if we like your plans for our town centre you will find us very supportive. If we do not we will destroy it.' A group of environmentalists had come of age and could not be ignored.

---

1. *I was a member of the Lancashire Branch of the Council for the Protection of Rural England in those days and found it pleasant talking shop where some worthy solicitors, one or two titled gentry, an excellent portrait painter, a school master specialising in geography – and a very young architect met 3 or 4 times a year for tea and buns in a committee room at County Hall. We were confronted by these new steely-eyed people called developers. They were backed by clever QCs and had immense financial resources. They 'had us for dinner'.*

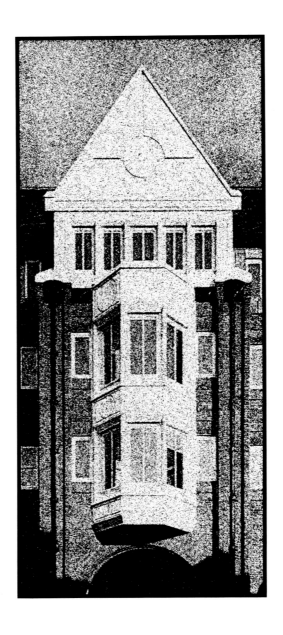

3

THE LAST DECADE : THE DEBATE ABOUT STYLE

A personal experience of six schemes

A poll to ascertain preferences

The public call for a new direction

Examples from experience

The tile vernacular

Sheer size and absence of windows

Tentative moves from functionalism

Different client motivations

Responding to changing taste: Blackpool

The Ealing Broadway Centre, London: full-blooded vernacular

Ealing High Street elevations: a pastiche?

The high-tech alternative

The later phases of Ealing

Ealing: the final phase

Carlisle: outright historicism

Consistency in the malls

To roof or not to roof the malls

The architectural character of The Lanes, Carlisle

Why a Fund prefers to demolish and rebuild

Maintaining the continuity of the street

Minimising the impact of big buildings

A big building in a small town: Bentalls at Kingston-upon-Thames

Kirkgate Market, Leeds

Waverley, Edinburgh: a different problem

Waverley: pedestrian flow as a planning determinant

Lessons from Waverley: living with others

3

THE LAST DECADE

School of Architecture, Houston University
A grotesque reduction of the canons of classical architecture to the level of nonsense.

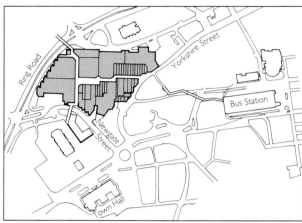

Rochdale
As at Blackburn, the footprint of this 11-acre scheme could destroy the scale of Rochdale. The home and birth of the Co-operative movements in 1846, the new Pioneer store is 25,000 sq ft – and that is the smallest large space.

Hillingdon Civic Centre
This exuberant melange of oddly shaped forms was immediately welcomed by a public that had wearied of seeing the results of demanding quick, cheap buildings. Jobs like this are neither easy to design or quick and cheap to build, yet the building heralded a massive swing in public expectancy.

Debenhams, Blackburn
The third phase of Blackburn. The Council wanted a good department store in the town: the store knew it and could dictate their terms. This is the view from the cathedral close with the greenery and mature trees. No windows were permitted by the retailer: the curtained glazing at the right are the management offices of another retailer.

Whilst there is an abundance of experience of shopping centre design and the public is broadly satisfied with what has been achieved in trading and convenience terms there are grave reservations about the way it has been done.

Powerful influences are at work on today's architecture, and architects, as a profession, have begun to resolve the inherent conflicts. Many problems remain and they are germane to central area design as well as to buildings generally: some of them can be defined.

The bewildering array of new building types from the second half of the 19th century onwards was promoted primarily as a consequence of the invention of the lift and the internal combustion engine. The challenge demanded a complete reassessment of architectural forms and standards. Lifts have meant that the height of a building is no longer constrained by the number of stairs people are prepared to climb, and though we could build high long before the 19th century (see any Gothic cathedral) the ability to stack floor upon floor released whole new design possibilities. Similarly the legion of places required to make, house, sell and repair motor cars, buses and aeroplanes and their derivatives and accessories has called for types of building previously unknown – quite apart from the profound environmental effect the machines themselves had on our towns and countryside.

Wherever one looks new structures abound and only a stylist of the most reactionary persuasion could believe it right to ignore the possibilities of new building forms to express new building briefs. It is surely a functional as well as an aesthetic nonsense to make a factory for making baked beans – or for making anything – look like the temple of Abu Simbel or to design a polytechnic in the style of a Greek temple.

A poll to ascertain preferences

In the wake of the reaction against some of the dogma of the early Modernists there is strong criticism of the products of those ideals. In 1984 Thames TV News conducted a poll in which some 4,500 viewers took part. They were asked to name their most and least favourite buildings completed in the post war years – a time span of 40 years which ought to iron out some of the more extreme swings of fashion. Top of the poll came Hillingdon Civic Centre, second the Aviary at London Zoo, third Waterloo Bridge, and fourth the Ealing Broadway Centre. At the bottom, starting from the least liked at no: 50 was the Ashton Estate at Roehampton, at 49 Robin Hood Gardens, Poplar, at 48 Trellick Tower, Paddington, at 47 Alexandra Road Housing, NW8. All four buildings were designed by ardent advocates of the Modern movement – epitomised in the public's mind by the epithet 'Brutalism' and all featured precast or in-situ concrete as their prime external finish.

The buildings that topped the list were even more intriguing. At number one, the Hillingdon Civic Centre was the first public building in Britain to explore thoroughly the possibilities of a high Romantic or Picturesque approach to contemporary architecture and was the subject of great controversy in architectural circles. The arguments centred on abstruse topics like formal complexity, fussy detailing and unclear relationships between plan, section and elevations. Clearly these matters have gone straight over the heads of the man in the street for whom it was built and the public have said quite simply that they like it.

The second and third choices are not buildings at all in the normal sense. The Aviary at London Zoo is a lace-like structural extravaganza to contain birds in the open air and Waterloo Bridge is an engineering triumph, sensuously undulating with long low arches as it crosses the river. It is notable that in each case the lead designer by the very nature of the structures was not an architect, but an engineer.

The fourth choice, second in normal architectural terms, is a shopping centre discussed later but when the poll was held the building was still wreathed in scaffolding and could scarcely be seen let alone appreciated. Here too, although the building was the subject of fierce arguments among architects, the public were not prepared to wait until the builders had gone before declaring their approval.

The public call for a new direction

It is relatively easy for the general public or architectural critics to say what they don't like. It is more difficult to be specific about the reasons for their dislike – and even tougher to be an architect and have

to do something about it. In 1985 the Prince of Wales put his finger as close as anyone to the pulse of the debate by telling an architectural gathering at the RIBA centenary celebrations that what people would like to see again in our buildings is a richness of tone, texture and form that many contemporary architects had ignored. Those in the audience that night at Hampton Court Palace could feel the ripple of guilt and ruffled dignity washing through the 600 or so professionals. At least two architects could not stand the criticism and stalked out in high dudgeon. The rest stood on the velvet green lawn, shuffling uneasily: the President's face stiffened into an icy mask. Most of us knew the Prince was right.

We are therefore presented with an interesting situation. The mid 80's are years of affluence, especially in the southeast, unprecedented in these islands. Admittedly there are 3 million people unemployed, but the 20 million who are employed are demanding quality in every sphere and are well able to pay for it. But alas Formalism and their machine-age derivitives have been exposed as a joyless cul-de-sac and we find ourselves in a period of footloose pluralism which is as worrying in its licentiousness as the fridgity from which we have just fled. One has lost count of the isms and fetishes with which academic commentators label each new experimental expression.

Many architects who have either consciously or unconsciously chafed for years under the strictures of hardline modernism have broken out into a rash of eclectic decoration which leads to charges of pastiche and clip-on architecture. Some take the view that their role is that of a 'stylist' like designers in the industrial field who take the basic functional form of the product and 'package' it for the consumer market.

Examples from experience

We are now on controversial ground and since completed work is, for good or ill, the most powerful advocate of a point of view there follows a description of a few central area buildings where BDP was appointed. We start at the beginning, not only for BDP but for the shopping centre industry, and take Blackburn Town Centre designed between 1962 and 1964. There were no precedents for so extensive a redevelopment in a small British town. Stylistically both the design team and the client agreed simple direct forms and the only hint of controversy arose over the cladding. The client had assumed that since he wanted simplicity and flexibility of construction that would rule out brickwork – which in any case was in short supply at the time – and we would specify precast concrete panels with perhaps an exposed aggregate.

However, having studied concrete as a facing material as a student and noting how it stained in our northern climate, one had made a vow never to use it as a finish material. We were then in search of an alternative finish and the thought occurred that if the faience of the Persians had lasted 2000 years the material should stand the ravages of northern Britain. Studies were done, practical matters researched and the tiles on all three phases of Blackburn and subsequently throughout the Rochdale centre came to be specified.

The tile vernacular

In the present discussion two points are relevant. First, both schemes were built in the context of wholesale demolition so there was by definition no existing urban fabric with which to merge. We were creating a new environment as irrelevant to the decrepit buildings on the edge of the town centre as were the new shopping centres to the surroundings in the New Towns. Cumbernauld, Runcorn and, later, Milton Keynes, are good examples; they were isolated from the residential areas and made no attempt to integrate as a seamless entity.

Secondly, the technology of tiling gave us the opportunity to develop a hierarchy of scales which helped to give meaning to the huge buildings we were called upon to design. The individual tiles, the wide soft joints for thermal movement and the large precast panels all gave scale, and the client was afforded flexibility for breaking through the walls or remodelling them at a later date to cope with differing sizes of shops.

Sheer size and the absence of windows
The size of individual shop units creates the most significant architectural problem for central area designers. Throughout the last three decades we have had to live with the fact that the big units want to grow ever bigger both in floor area and in height. Traders also insist that they make contact with the shopper only in the mall. If the architect proposes windows in the external wall the developer concludes that he has picked a chap who does not know the elementary rules. If the architect suggests a picture window and a balcony in the customer restaurant of Debenhams so that shoppers could eat looking southwards over the cathedral green he is told to forget it. The trader may want to re-position the departments and put, say, white goods where the restaurant was. What use the window then? Anyway, who wants to eat looking out over grubby old Grit-town? Far better a plastered wall with a mural of a sunny beach on the Costa del Sol, lit with recessed fluorescents behind lace drapes and a plastic palm tree: very flexible – a resignation issue perhaps?

In short the problem is to integrate a windowless rectangle about 120 ft long and 16 ft high (36m x 5m) into the delicate fabric of an English town and now that the comprehensive redevelopment phase is behind us we are required to weave such huge shapes without seams into the warp and weft of the city. Frankly it cannot be done without resort to artifice. Since fenestration is the straw with which architectural bricks are made an architect who is denied windows is looking for some other scale and texture-giving device to replace them. That leads to ideas like expressing the structure, arcading the wall surface, breaking the skyline, corbelling the cornice, delineating the floor levels with different coloured brick, putting in blind windows, making maximum capital out of each minor excuse for changing the materials, and charges of 'pastiche', 'pseudo', 'clip-on', 'whimsy' and 'historicism' fly with gay abandon.

These design issues faced architects as the reaction against the faceless developments of the 60's began to assume the force of a universal clamour. It is not easy to go deliberately against the training of a lifetime. Serious designers think long and hard about what they are doing and accept some starting point for their work. Those of us trained in the 1940's and 1950's had celestial visions of the 'ville radieuse' as our icons. Some now realize that whilst they had much to teach in terms of a new clarity of rational thinking to meet the challenges of the 20th Century, the actual solutions they proffered were flawed. Some designers from that prewar generation of students are still unable to face the possibility of error in their mentors and find themselves increasingly lonely in a hostile world.

Rochdale shopping centre
View from the main approach road. The staircase, lift towers and motor rooms are played for all they are worth.

Rochdale shopping centre
View of the pedestrianised Yorkshire Street – the main shopping street in Rochdale.

Rochdale shopping centre The forms enliven the back of Littlewood's and the new Market Hall. The modelling is imposed.

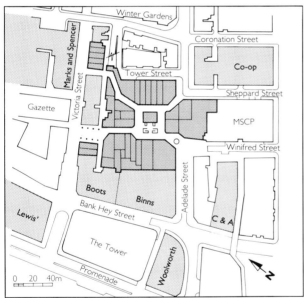

Hounds Hill Centre, Blackpool
Surrounded by major stores all that was needed was to draw an 'X' across the area to link the big units. Forty small shops converge on a central space and the existing multi-storey car park was extended to cover the new scheme and bring shoppers down into the middle of the development.

Tentative moves from functionalism
To demonstrate the change that occurred compare the design approach at Blackburn and Rochdale in the 60s with the Hounds Hill Centre at Blackpool in 1972.

Note that the first two take their name from the town itself because they were so comprehensive they precluded any other development in the town for many years. Once the total redevelopment decade was over and we moved into the 70's, centres were named after their district or given non-geographic names like Cascades, Quadrant, Olympia, Queensway, Bell, or any one of two dozen saints making them sound anonymous, characterless, and sometimes just plain silly.

Blackburn has been described and the only thing to add about Rochdale is that we wanted to make it like Blackburn – but more so. We were determined to pursue the strong form-giving qualities that the various functions suggested but we worked even harder to accentuate the angular, sharp profiles that could be obtained by modelling the lift shafts, stair towers and split-level car parks. We did not eschew surface relief and decoration; it simply never occurred to us.

With hindsight one sees that in the absence of texture and scale-giving surface decoration we instinctively reached out for richer forms to avoid the bland windowless walls at Blackburn. We struggled to impart richness to the walls of the huge anchor store at Rochdale and each lift tower and tank room was given a sloping roof to echo the choppy sea of Victorian roofs round about. In retrospect some of the form-giving was misapplied and an element of serenity was sacrificed.

It is important too that we had the rare advantage of working throughout these years for one client and our relationship carried on with the Laing Group not only through Blackburn and Rochdale, but Blackpool (Hounds Hill) and Ealing Broadway. We therefore grew together as a team and cut through the need to learn about each other's design philosophy with each new job.

Thus at Rochdale the only matters of real debate were not the architectural style or the use of tiles as a finish material but the colour of the tiles themselves. Even on that issue the debate was not between client and architect but between architect and town council. We had assumed that because Blackburn had been well received (it had just been given a Civic Trust Award) Rochdale would be happy with the same white tile. We were knocked off balance when the Leader told us that they liked Blackburn but they wanted something different for Rochdale. We said it was a good job people had not thought that way in the 18th century or there would only have been one Georgian square – but acceded to their view and proposed the variegated earth brown colour in which the centre is clad.

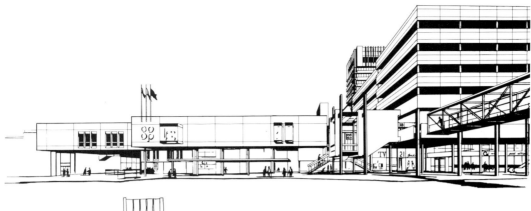

*Blackburn
shopping centre*
Ainsworth Street
elevation.

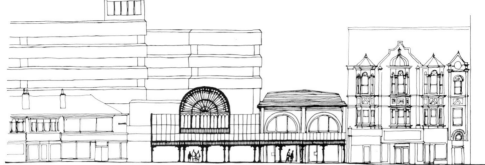

*Hounds Hill
Centre, Blackpool*
Victoria Street
elevation.

Different client motivations.

The most significant difference between working as an architect for a specific client on an individual building and working on a central area scheme is that for the latter the real client is the general public, or more narrowly the people in the local community.

The former circumstance is relatively straightforward. The architects' job is to analyse the brief and synthesize it into a creation with which both he or she and the client are happy. As long as the two get on well together and hit the same wavelength, they are home and dry. The only constraining factor is planning permission and in the great majority of cases this is forthcoming – though each may have to exert a good deal of pressure or guile in the process. Failing agreement with the local planners, client and designer are at liberty to press their convictions in a higher court. If they have a good case the appeal will grant their point of view.

The latter circumstance, the central area scheme, is far more confused. The architect has a client in the developer who pays him, but in so far as the client is in business primarily to make money and see growth on his investment, the real client is the shopper who, in a competitive world, must be persuaded to come to our client's centre rather than any other. Shopper rejection strikes terror into a developer's heart because as Isaac Stern said of concert audiences 'if nobody wants to come, nothing will stop them'.

The architect of a shopping centre must understand that when a developer says he does not like the design what is really meant is that he does not think the public will like it.

In fact most developers would approve a Chinese pagoda in the Rows at Chester if they thought it would put a couple of pounds on the Zone A rents. That is not meant in any way disparagingly, it is merely to point out the difference in motivation between the designer and the person who pays the fees.

A further point of difference between these two client worlds and their motivation is that for developers time is money. The last thing they want is for their architects to be locked in battle with the Royal Fine Arts Commission and a Public Inquiry over the design. The idea of public displeasure with his or her proposals is anathema. A Peter Palumbo London Mansion House affair is inconceivable in the shopping centre arena.

Responding to changing taste: Blackpool

Thus the reason for the marked difference between Rochdale and Blackpool is not that the architect suddenly changed his spots or that the client developed a sudden taste for whimsy. Rather that public opinion was on the move. Before Laings got involved in the Hounds Hill site, Blackpool had been combed over by most big developers in Britain. They had all proposed a huge comprehensive scheme and had come up against public and therefore Council hostility. They were too late – the day of the megalomaniac scheme had passed.

The message from council members and technical officers to us was that not only were the townsfolk unlikely to approve a proposal to knock the famous tower down, but that since the shopping centre was to be built immediately adjacent they would like something that fitted in with the tower buildings in both style and materials. Having been brought up just 17 miles away from Blackpool and observing at fairly close quarters its Coney Island mentality in the Golden Mile one had not previously suspected its citizens of being overly concerned with aesthetic matters; but here was a challenge indeed.

The prize therefore fell to those who saw opportunity in the smaller scale and we were presented with a tight site hidden behind shop fronts and linked by big department stores. Both the ground floor plans and the elevational treatment show the light years of difference between Blackburn and the Hounds Hill Centre.

Others will judge our success but we tried to give a responsible answer to the question asked. First we

Hounds Hill Centre, Blackpool

made a survey of the most appropriate materials, for in that location the abrasive action of wind-blown sand requires buildings near the promenade to withstand a constant sandblasting and salt is highly corrosive. We concluded that we could not improve on the Victorian's choice and the flint hard Accrington engineering brick was chosen for the walls, with cast iron for the structure – after all, Central Pier was still standing.

Architecturally we arcaded the brickwork, modelled the cornices, experimented with re-entrant angles to deepen shadows and went a long way towards the more extrovert ideas at Ealing. Yet it was all still rather hesitant and the multi-storey car park shows how far there was still to go to achieve a happy architectural resolution.

Having chosen cast iron for the structure we were on an easier wicket. The very nature of the material and its method of manufacture precludes long slender sections so we were thrust into problems of joints, connections, thicknesses and casting limitations. We knew there would be neither time nor sympathy for us to evolve a 20th Century cast iron design philosophy so we went to the manufacturers who had served the building trade so well in the 19th century. We winkled out a workshop in a little town in Derbyshire after a chance visit to Buxton had drawn our attention to an extension to a canopy on the main street.

We stretched the factory to and beyond its limits but what resulted was a large cast iron atrium, and the thrill of working with the foundry engineers was very satisfying.[1]

The public took to what the development team had achieved and throughout the deep retail recession of the mid-70's the centre stood up well to economic pressures and both the lettings and the rent levels stayed high. Interestingly, and to add piquancy to the architectural evolutionary story, 10 years after the astringency of Blackburn, Blackpool's Hounds Hill Centre was also given a Civic Trust Award....

Hounds Hill Centre, Blackpool

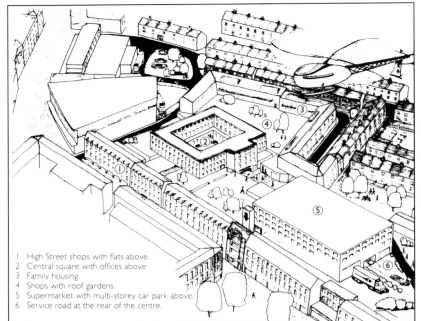

1 High Street shops with flats above.
2 Central square with offices above.
3 Family housing.
4 Shops with roof gardens.
5 Supermarket with multi-storey car park above.
6 Service road at the rear of the centre.

The Ealing Study Group Scheme, 1978
The perspective shows the gulf between the resident's idea of their town and the developer's. The former is cosy, sensitive and respectful of the town – but impractical and therefore unfundable. The latter maximises the economic potential; but is an environmental disaster.

The gulf is, however, more imaginary than real. The built scheme has almost as much retail area as the EMI scheme but the relief road is dropped and all access to the scheme is from the south-east and south-west corners. Through traffic on Broadway is still congested but pedestrian access from the housing to the south is maintained. Compared with the Ealing Study Group scheme the BDP scheme keeps the idea of an arcaded front to High Street, and an open town square in the heart of the development, roof gardens over the parking and overlooked by the offices. Nearly all the houses are saved and a new close, Carillon Court is built.

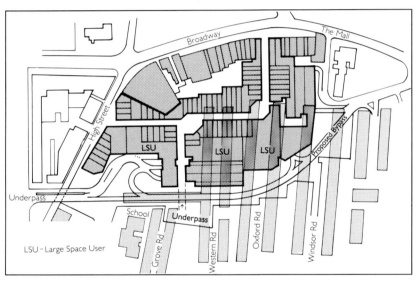

Ealing Broadway: The Grosvenor-EMI Scheme, 1974
The proposals laid over an Ordnance Map show the implications:

1 the roads destroy scores of houses;

2 the shopping centre is a commercial island with access by pedestrian tunnel or across primary roads;

3 daylight is excluded from the scheme.;

4 roof-top servicing compromises design and limits vertical expansion.

Council's revised brief resulted in two fundamental changes:

1 the housing remained largely untouched;

2 the southern relief road was eliminated.

Ealing Town Square, BDP Scheme, 1980
Note the proportion of the open Town Square relative to the project as a whole. The malls are not daylit due to the multi-layered, multi-use scheme. A library, a huge office block, a sports and leisure centre and 1000 cars all had to be stacked at the upper levels above the shopping. A vital difference between a new shopping centre and a new town centre is that the latter can regenerate a whole area. In Carillon Court the first units sold in 1984 for £36,000. In 1987 they were changing hands at over £120,000.

Oxford Road, Ealing, 1979
Planning blight is a terrible disease to inflict on a community. Whilst planners, conservationists and developers fought over the Grove people tried desperately to get out of the area. The vandals, the winos and the drug addicts were quick to move in.

The Mall, Ealing
The gabled elegance of Edwardian England. The brief was to reflect this in the new town centre.

Ealing Town Centre
The central square is open and a glazed arcade protects the shop fronts on three sides.

St Mary's Church, Ealing
St Mary's is a fine characterful Victorian parish church: an excellent work by the architect, Toulon. Its distinguished tower was an inspiration for the twin towers in the main court of the Ealing Broadway scheme.

The Ealing Broadway Centre, London: the full-blooded vernacular

Shortly after completing the Blackpool Hounds Hill Centre, Laings and BDP won the competition to redevelop the town centre at Ealing and found the wheel of conservation had been cranked another full turn. Local action groups had organised themselves to oppose what they saw as the destruction of their characterful London suburb and it was clear both from reading the competition brief and from meeting their representatives that when they talked about 'reflecting the spirit of Edwardian Ealing' they were really suggesting historical replica.

We had deep reservations about this approach but our entry made an attempt to recognise the scale and materials of the buildings we saw around the town. Architecturally we clearly impressed the Council and our scheme was judged to be the best on offer. Once we had won the job the fascinating stage began, because, having put our hand to the plough, we determined that the style should not be a surface veneer. For their part the local council were determined to achieve a quality of external design that matched anything else in Ealing.

The townspeople had also asked that there be open air in their town square. The local action group had

actually made a model of their ideas, showing such a space as a focal point. This indicated that they had gone full circle from traditional open squares, through the claustrophobic closed mall phase and back to the town meeting place. The idea of a glazed atrium as a focus for their shopping centre was not an option as far as the residents of Ealing were concerned. The development fraternity however has been critical of this aspect of Ealing, and the Fund made it a condition that we demonstrated how to glaze in the central space should they ever want to do it. The Council were quite happy for us to give that undertaking because they said a request to do so would never be given planning permission. We shall see: 125 years is a long time. The square is a delight on a warm June day but the central space is deserted in rain and the winter wind swirls through the adjoining malls.

A later chapter deals with the detailed design of centres like Ealing. This discussion focuses on the architectural approach and the visual impact that central area schemes make upon people in this period of stylistic uncertainty. Our competition entry showed elevations that were in dire peril of falling between two stools. In the offices above the shops, we offered window proportions and spacing which reflected the scale of High Street and, even more importantly, Bond Street

Ealing High Street
The elevation at the competition stage. The Edwardian character of Ealing had not been fully understood or reflected. Most of the competition time was optimizing the commercial potential of the plan making sure it met with the brief.

a few hundred feet away. Here was a clear model for the best qualities of traditional Ealing. What eluded us in the frantic rush to get a competitive bid together was a coherent stylistic wholeness.

Ealing High Street elevations: a pastiche?

In fact the layered hierarchy of shops, parking and offices did offer possibilities of a good design solution, so gradually a discipline was established which gave rise to the much publicised High Street elevations. We took from Edwardian Ealing its gables, bay windows, highly modelled brickwork and above all its proportional elegance, and through numerous design review meetings there emerged a satisfactory resolution of the problem given the concern, even suspicion, that local people had of our intent.

For others the result is a pastiche. Pastiche, however, is a French word meaning a jumble, a pot-pourri, made of bits of other works or imitations of another's style. The High Street elevations are none of these things. The design is not irrelevantly imposed or out of context.

The module of fenestration offers flexibility of partition layout and the bay windows are a joy to be in and look up and down the street. Of course there are wholly modern and 'clean' ways of detailing elevations which meet these functional requirements equally well, but the overt stylistic references had great value in establishing our credentials with a community that had seen itself as only just saved from desecration and was therefore hypersensitive. We were especially fortunate in having on our team a designer who was uniquely talented and committed to the value of a 'scenic' approach to architecture. Indeed given a completely free hand he would have moved the elevations even more in that direction.

But, diverting and challenging as this experience was, this line of thought is a cul-de-sac. That is not to denigrate culs-de-sac. We have all been in perfectly charming dead ends and enjoyed exploring them. They are not, however, going anywhere and to make progress we have to recognise their limitations, retrace our steps, and try another avenue.

Ealing High Street
The developed elevation of the office block with greater formal and detailed richness gets closer to the Edwardian spirit of Ealing. This fine pencil drawing by Francis Roberts, the senior associate on the team, shows the final design virtually as built.

Houston skyline

The high-tech alternative

Meanwhile Modernists with their withering dismissal
of anything that smacks of joy let alone whimsy in
the main street must make their own case before their
holier-than-thou stance can be accepted. The American
city of Houston has more notable high-tech office
blocks designed by more luminaries of the 20th century
architectural firmament than any other city in the world
– per square mile at least. Buildings by Philip Johnson,
IM Pei, Skidmore Owings & Merril, HOK, William
Pereira, CRS, Ulrich Franzen and some very fine
local designers like Lloyd Jones Webster all jostle
for attention and they are a unique guide to the
development of the North American office block
over the last two decades. In the last analysis however
and after many visits the city is simply boring. The
buildings are sleek, skin tight, highly efficient, hugely
expensive and a statistician's gold mine. But the only
space that repeatedly lifts one's spirit is the Piranese-
like atrium of the Republic Bank and the only building
to add delight to admiration is the exterior of the same
block – with all its Gothic overtones.

Republic Bank, Houston

Republic Bank, Houston

The later phases of Ealing

At Ealing the reward for the design team was that with the High Street elevations we had secured the confidence of local people, and they trusted us to explore different aesthetic solutions. The public discussions we had in a packed town hall were among the most rewarding, though challenging, memories of the job. If any confirmation were needed of the Royal view that what people are looking for is pleasing forms, materials, tones and textures, it was amply given by the people of Ealing at those meetings. If they expressed that demand by calling for a return to familiar forms from an Edwardian past it was only because that was the last time an architectural style had offered such delights.

Without exception no 'functionalist' architect in Britain has consistently displayed a felicitious touch (especially on major buildings) throughout the 40 years since the end of the Second World War. Indeed one has to go back to the buildings of Charles Rennie Macintosh and Charles Voisey to see characteristics of delight last taken right through a building with utter integrity and conviction.

On the world scene there are instances of 'modern' designers who were sensitive to the tactile qualities that people instinctively crave – but none worked in the retail field. The names stand out like beacons in a barren landscape; Frank Lloyd-Wright and Eero Saarinen in the USA. Alvar Aalto and a small group of people influenced by him in Finland and (to a lesser extent) humanist designers like Asplund, Bergman and Jacobsen in Scandinavia. Lesser mortals have to win their spurs in the way we did at Ealing before being allowed to proceed along more radical lines.

The design evolution over the time span of this enormous project (one of the most extensive of its type since Blackburn) was quite dramatic in its shift from historicism to functionalism. At the beginning of the scheme we would not have found it easy to 'sell' the east elevation with its tall, spare library windows and there is no doubt whatever that our mirror glass solution to the Broadway office block would have received summary rejection.

Take the east elevation first. Unlike the western High Street the ground floor presented the classic problem of windowless backs of the shop units and these faced gardens and houses. Above the shops was the single floor of the library, and three trays of car parking. Thus only the library gave opportunity for fenestration but at least there was some height to the room so allowing a major scale and dignity to that floor.

At the base, brick corbelling and lush planting soften the rear wall of the shops and above the library we took our first steps in trying to enliven the facade of a multi-storey car park with medallions of metal screening to break the monotony. The problem is that as soon as screening is added to relieve the black hole of the car deck the result can look like a prison. At Ealing the detailed handling of the three elements of shop, library and multistorey car park is rich but with no overt historical reference and, perhaps because the east side is not so prominent as the west, we got away with it.[2]

The Broadway facade is the most extraordinary of all in the context of the history of the centre. Designed as part of the overall plan but for a different client we came up against a view of office requirements which differed

Ealing Broadway: the multi-storey car park
Metal screens clad the apertures of the car decks and an element of decoration was added to break up the prison-like appearance of rows of metal bars. Note the decision to terminate the expression of structure below parapet level. An unbroken skyline results – restful to some; boring to others.

Ealing Broadway: the east elevation
The full length of the library sitting over the retail stores. The walkway leads from the housing areas into the scheme.

Ealing Broadway: office building
Mirror glass elevation.

*Kenzo Tange's
Hanna Maurie
newspaper
headquarters, Tokyo
Faceting relieves the
blandness of mirror
glass.*

*Olivetti Building,
Milan*

BHS in Wakefield

markedly from that in the main scheme. The Broadway
client had little knowledge of the tortured history of the
Ealing project: nor was he interested. Bay windows and
complex elevational modelling were anathema to him
('no good for letting; limits freedom of partition layout;
complicates servicing runs; jolly expensive'). Our new
client was quite happy with brick and stone trim but
there was to be no compromise over what he saw as
fundamental matters of speculative office planning.
(Although differing in their approach to the office
market both blocks have been satisfactorily let at
the asking rent.) On the other hand the planners
and populace loved what we had done on the
High Street side and demanded more of the same.

A resolution to the problem called for careful
negotiation and patience. Architecturally the last thing
we wanted was a flat chested stripped down version of
the High Street solution though for a time we seemed
to be heading that way.

Eventually we struck out in a new direction and looked
at stone cladding the whole block. The developer would
have approved, but stone (especially the polished
granite option that one of our ideas produced) was
rejected by the planners. It was while experimenting
with polished faceted stone (still giving a perfectly
flush interior) that the breakthrough came.

Ealing: the final phase
The idea of losing brickwork and stone trim as a
finish material was not looked upon favourably by
the planners so we retained brick in vertical columns
to express the structure and interposed stone corbels
and cappings as functional elements where brick was
not suitable for either weathering or technical reasons.
This left the panels between brick piers and it was
while studying the reflections from the faceted polished
stone that the thought arose that the drama would be
enhanced by mirror glass.

We had never designed a mirror glass elevation before
and had reservations about much that had been done.
Since the material was not condemned by either client
or planner we worked out an approach to using mirror
glass because its potential for banality is fairly evident.
We came to the conclusion that there are only three
conditions in which one should use the material. The
first is where the job is out in the countryside on a green
field site, where with minimal detailing the building
can be made to 'disappear' into the landscape of field,
trees and sky. A beautiful example of this effect can be
seen at Saarinen's Bell Telephone Corporation Research
Laboratories in Holmdel, New Jersey, USA, built as long
ago as 1957.

The second is in an urban situation where there is
something truly worth reflecting. The idea is used
effectively in Milan where an Olivetti office building
is tucked into characterful old back streets quite near
the cathedral. To keep the integrity of the flat reflecting
surfaces on a non-airconditioned building they had
gone to the lengths of opening the windows on scissor
stays so the windows pushed outwards absolutely
vertical.[3] Nearer home a mirrored refacing of British
Home Stores in the High Street at Wakefield gives
beautiful reflections of the cathedral opposite.

The third condition is where, although mirror glass is
both appropriate and agreed by the client, there is really
nothing worth reflecting. In those circumstances there
is no point in trying to reflect mediocrity. The solution

then is to facet the wall surface into a series of recessed and advancing planes (and these need to be quite pronounced to break up the continuity of the images) or to angle the various elevational components rather like the complex bevelling of mirrors in Louis XIV boudoires. A very successful example of the former is Kenzo Tange's Hanna Maurie newspaper office headquarters in Tokyo where the images are further fractured by heavy tree planting so making the kaleidoscope of building images appear to float above a sea of greenery.

Since at Ealing we were expressly forbidden by the client to indulge in recessed and advancing planes in the structure of the exterior wall (that was just another way of saying bay windows) the angled faceting of the wall surface itself was the only remaining option. Although a mirror glass elevation would have been unthinkable at the time of our initial appointment, the long process of negotiation and experience of the early phases of the development stood us in good stead. We might otherwise have forfeit the trust we had built up with the community and at the same time have lost credibility with one of our biggest developer clients.

Carlisle: outright historicism
In the context of concern for creating a central area scheme in today's shifting sand of pluralistic design two further examples are relevant. Both were produced at the same time as the Ealing Broadway Centre and both were set in the heart of historic towns.

The first at Carlisle had some similarities to the problem at Ealing; the second, a scheme in Edinburgh had none. Like Ealing, Carlisle had, over an even longer period, been threatened by what the townsfolk considered the destruction of their medieval city. Buildings of enormous size and dubious quality had been proposed to replace the tightly knit lanes which crossed the city from the old main street called Scotch Street (the high road to Scotland) to the line of the long-vanished Roman wall on Lowther Street. Twenty years of acrimony between the local citizenry and developers had soured relationships and by 1979 a decision had been taken by the City Council to develop the area themselves with directly employed consultants and to control the the form of the buildings. BDP were appointed with Donaldsons, the Estates Consultants, to advise the Council – the first time we had acted for a community without a developer client.

As at Ealing, the townspeople had an image of what they wanted but in the direct consultancy at Carlisle we had the responsibility for advising them what was commercially viable as well as civically desirable. Crucial to starting on site was our ability to persuade a financial institution to provide the millions of pounds needed to build the scheme; all the local authority could contribute was the land and the will to see the development happen. The mix of uses and the layout of the retail spaces was the subject of much debate both in committee and with local bodies, and central to all considerations was the physical image of the city.

The old main streets, Scotch Street and English Street, were the focus for one debate and the internal character of The Lanes the focus for another. At the junction of English Street and Scotch Street there was a group of three terraced buildings which, whilst not of great architectural merit, had late 18th century charm, were perfectly in scale with the old town square and were

listed Grade II for their group value. We were sure we could design something in a contemporary way which would be equally sympathetic to the local scale and materials and we spent hours sketching ideas. Similarly we carried these proposals northwards along Scotch Street and were keen to demonstrate that modern architecture had come of age and could be trusted.

Then one bleak winter's night we were telephoned with the news that the listed buildings had fallen down. There was no extreme weather condition: the poor things had simply grown tired of waiting to be saved. They had had no fabric maintenance for over twenty years so they gave up the ghost and died.

This dramatic event concentrated the Council's mind. An urgent decision on their replacement had to be taken and within hours the chairman reported that the ghastly hole in the terrace made them realise how much they loved their town square. Whilst they knew the lanes would have to be dramatically restructured, they wanted faithful replicas of what they had always known as Scotch Street: 'Give us our town square back again ' were the exact words of the instruction.

We did our best. Although an exact replica would have been easy from the photographic records, the needs of a major entrance into the heart of the shopping and the requirements of the major variety store at that point (with floor to floor heights that were inimical to the old elevations) made an exact copy impossible.

Further north along Scotch Street we then had the job of designing individual shop units and we proposed houses over them in such a way as to carry on the tradition of one-off buildings as they were added to the street. Housing is a fraught subject in the context of shopping centres and no institutional fund would readily agree to houses over shops if they had the choice. The subject of mix comes later so here it is enough to remark that whilst housing in town centres is a beloved topic among planners and architects, developer's eyes glaze over at the mention. Environmentally housing over shops is its own justification by day or by night. The sense of life and animation given by plants, curtains, people and lights is self- evident but the development world considers the legal, management and design problem to be a hassle they can do without. At Carlisle, without the veto of a developer, we were free to propose what we felt was the right solution. When we went to tender for a fund they were told the housing was a requirement and they could like it or lump it. It has been a great success, though the elevations themselves could be improved. (One never gets a second chance – it must be wonderful to be a painter or a composer.)

Consistency in the malls
Inside the scheme itself the architectural expression was a fascination to everyone on the development team – architect, agents, Council and the Fund. Having been obliged to seek a straight historicist expression for the exterior, some were in favour of a logical extension of that philosophy throughout the development. After all, the argument ran, the old lanes were the cross streets of Carlisle, the new lanes must have the same flavour. But whilst one might argue a case for an open town square in the heart of a southern town like Ealing, even southerners question the idea of open malls – although one or two do exist, like the King Edward Centre at Windsor and St Martins in Leicester.

Carlisle: the old town square
A sketch in the summer of 1977 after receiving the commission to redevelop seven acres of the city.

Carlisle: the old town square
Some months after BDP's appointment in 1979 the listed buildings to the right of the centre fell down. They grew tired of waiting to be saved and simply died, so the instruction to reconstruct facsimilies became imperative.

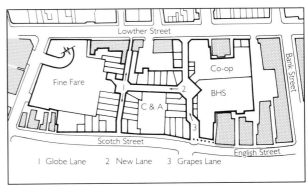

The Lanes, Carlisle
Two plans contrast the street and lane pattern of the old city with the new. 14 lanes threaded between Lowther and Scotch Street; they were too closely grouped to allow modern retailing. Comparison with the new plan shows that few of the old large shops are as big as the smallest new units.

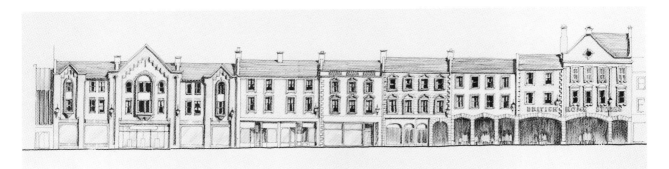

The Lanes, Carlisle
The new Scotch Street elevation at the south end.

The Old Lanes, Carlisle
Globe lane was the best preserved and probably the most nostalgic of the 14 lanes which linked Lowther Street to Scotch Street. The starting point for many townspeople was to preserve as many as possible intact.

Early studies for The Lanes, Carlisle
Local people were determined not to have claustrophobic covered malls and were only with difficulty persuaded to accept the roof glazing. The floor and wall finishes are all of external materials to enhance the feeling of being out of doors.

The Lanes, Carlisle
Model studies to explore the idea of rebuilding the lanes in the style of old Globe Lane. Several roof profiles were modelled to prove that light and air would still enter the lanes.

To roof or not to roof the malls

In Carlisle the thought of open lanes never occurred to us until it was brought up as an issue by local people. They said they abhorred closed, claustrophobic, roofed -in malls and wanted the fresh air and the sun in their streets. Their vehemence suggested some underlying trauma and it was not until we learnt that Carlisle people went regularly to Newcastle for variety and comparison shopping that it dawned on us that a roofed mall to them meant Eldon Square.[4]

We suggested that whilst they might think they like shopping with snow clogging the streets and rain soaking the baby's pram the Funds knew they did not. Indeed a quick round of enquiries confirmed that although the competition was hot to fund the scheme none of the front runners would come to Carlisle if the condition to be imposed on their investment was a scheme open to the sky. Their prime requirement of growth in value could not be guaranteed with such an archaic notion. At this point models came to our aid. We made a number of them to 1:50 scale with various designs of lightweight roofs all fully glazed with continuous glass louvres down both sides of the vertical faces of the rooflight. We assured the populace that the

ends of The Lanes would be left open and poured balm on the still vociferous lobby of doubters by assuring them that although they would be dry they would still be frozen stiff and the temperature in the windswept lanes would not be discernably less than that they had always experienced. The incidence of pneumonia in the city should drop only marginally.

The architectural character of The Lanes, Carlisle

Eventually glazed roofs were approved and we turned to designing the 'lanes' – for it was as much as our job was worth to call them 'malls'. We argued that in the novel form of a glass roofed street we should explore new elevations rather than slavishly follow what had been done before and that there should be a continuity of materials, because as Ealing took shape many of us felt that the spirit of the external architecture had not been sufficiently carried through into the internal malls. We had been seduced by the reasoning that historically interiors were never made of the same materials as the exterior so why should malls look like the external envelope? That may be true but the stylistic continuity of a Georgian or Palladian building from outside to inside is indisputable. We had also argued that shopping is fashion orientated and the interior must

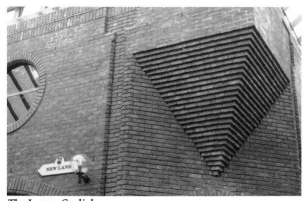

The Lanes, Carlisle
In response to the desire for an outdoor feeling in The Lanes the finishes were brick walls and stone floors. Care was taken to introduce rich modelling into the details because in the narrow lanes the quality of the design and the workmanship can be studied at close quarters. In fact it only takes a touch or two to create the right ambience.

The Old Market, Carlisle
A bold sandstone arch into the old Carlisle Market Hall was the inspiration behind the design for the new entrance to Globe Lane off Lowther Street.

Old Globe Lane Entrance, Carlisle
This charming brick building with bold, elegant windows became available for inclusion in The Lanes scheme when the main contract was nearly complete. The Fund opted for complete demolition rather than rehabilitating the old fabric.

respond to whim. True again, but changing fashion in the heart of a permanent entity like a city should happen within a context which has an inside-outside integrity. Therein lies the distinction between the shopping centre as a civic building and the ever changing shops themselves which may switch tenants and character as often as a picture in a frame.

We therefore set about designing The Lanes as if they were streets with a glazed roof. Brick was carried into the elevations from the surrounding streets and the floor was paved in sandstone and granite setts as a continuity with the floorscape of the medieval town square. We turned against the stylistic imagery of Scotch Street to pursue new means of solving the difficult problem of providing a lively first floor of windowless storage above continuous glazed ground floor windows. Sketches illustrate the problem and how we tackled it. The Lowther Street elevation lining the East side of the development presented different problems. Firstly the street is not so sensitive as Scotch Street with no important historic buildings. Architecturally it is in fact a non-descript thoroughfare and so there was no need to replicate former or existing buildings.

Globe Lane, the most cherished of all the Carlisle lanes had at its junction with Lowther Street an elegant three storey structure with huge first floor windows and flowing tracery which gave the facade a hint of Art Nouveau. It was not originally part of the Council's ownership and had therefore not been part of the site. A common problem with central area development is that the boundary moves with bewildering swiftness and frequency throughout the design and even the building period. Any desire to design with finite rectitude and build in a single contract without alteration is soon knocked on the head by experience. Thus it was that right up to an advanced building stage this elegant but structurally neglected building was not part of our considerations. Suddenly it became available, it was bought, and the debate as to whether we should renovate or demolish and rebuild was engaged.

Why a Fund prefers to demolish and rebuild
On this issue our preference for reinstatement was over-ruled by the Fund who had been in place since the start of work on site and whose influence increased. The Fund had tendered on specific conditions and every change or amplification of the project was subject to

New entrance to Globe Lane, Carlisle
In the rebuild of the entrance building off Lowther Street a stronger statement announcing the old lane was required. The design developed from the bold arch to the old Market Hall. A first floor restaurant gives interesting views down Globe Lane and out to Lowther Street.

Lowther Street, Carlisle
Arches like this frame the entrance to the two ground level service yards. They give continuity to the street elevations which would otherwise suffer a severe break to give access to pantechnicons.

Lowther Street, Carlisle
As a street of no distinction, the historical constraints were not so severe as Scotch Street. The canopy from Grapes Lane comes out over the pavement and comes as low as possible to give weather protection. The 'cut-out' was required by the fire officer for his engine. Note the new entrance to Globe Lane in the distance.

their approval – free from every risk that could be anticipated and eliminated. It makes a good deal of difference if you are a Fund investing people's life savings as pensions rather than an oldtime 60's developer who was an entrepreneur and who took risks that fell little short of gambling. Hence on a renovation versus demolition issue the Fund will almost always identify components which are part way through their life and cannot be cut out and replaced. The Fund is probably tied to a 125 year lease and wants the assurance that everything in the building fabric will stay the course. That usually argues for demolition and new materials – and so it did in this case.

We therefore looked for an expression that was appropriate to the importance of the entrance to Globe Lane and found our inspiration in a fine sandstone arch that gave into the old Market Hall from Scotch Street. From that came the arcuated design announcing Globe Lane off Lowther Street and the hierarchy of side arcades, window sizes and brick detailing led to an expression of Post-Modern architecture that is quite singular in Carlisle. In contrast, the entrance to Grapes Lane had no inhibitions; no buildings worth keeping. Here we let the roof of the glazed arcade generate its own bold geometry to come in a broad sweep out

over the pavement in Lowther Street. The uncompromising modernity of this gesture has been much commented upon in the Carlisle context and a final judgement will be made on the basis of how well its ample lines have responded to the small scale of historic Carlisle.

Maintaining the continuity of the street

The task of dealing with the diffuse and uninspiring architecture of Lowther Street produced another design solution worthy of comment because it relates to the problem of dealing with ground level servicing off a main street. If, as at Carlisle, ground level servicing is unavoidable then it is important to locate the service yard well inside the scheme so that buildings can line the street frontage. Otherwise the street is lined with a boundary wall – or, worse, no wall at all. Since Lowther Street was the only street from which lorries could gain access to the shopping centre we wanted to ensure that its limited quality would not be further dissipated by wide apertures for pantechnicons. Some form of architectural continuity seemed essential so we revived the idea of huge archways spanning the openings between brick piers. It works well and could be developed further: it costs money but the main street of a city is worth it.

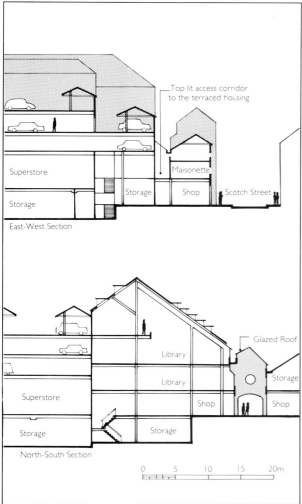

Carlisle, The Lanes
The large buildings were masked from Scotch Street in the east-west section. Housing over the ground floor shops hide the recessed trays of multi-storey car park and the bulk of the library. The Fine Fare superstore (all 55,000 sq ft of it) is buried within the site and makes no impression on this sensitive street.

Globe Lane, Carlisle
The final appearance of the lane where functional solutions triumphed over artifice. The mass of the library is brought down to the scale of the lane before achieving its full height deeper in the site. The bay windows are much in demand to look up and down The Lanes; they could have been much larger.

Minimising the impact of big buildings

The difficulty of grafting on to the intimate grain of a city some of today's very large commercial and parking structures would tax any designer. Whenever one builds in towns and cities in Britain the plea of the conservationists is always for a compatibility of scale. This is often confused with size. As a result, no matter what degree of care one takes over the articulation of the elevations, if the size is thought to be too big for the grain of the town, it will be rejected. BDP only just got the Halifax Building Society Headquarters in Halifax finished in time. It was opened in 1961, won an award in every competition for which it was entered and is probably the practice's best known building. If it were to be proposed now it would meet great opposition. A glance at the plan in its context would be enough to condemn it, let alone the realisation that its height throughout is at least twice that of any surrounding building – other than the Society's own computer block.

In Carlisle we felt the only way to overcome this problem was either to put large space users in the centre of the site and allow them only a single storey presence on the streets (BHS and C&A) or locate them right in the middle of the development and permit them no external expression at all (Fine Fare and the new County library). A variant of this last option was to allow a major space user who was located predominantly inboard to make an external impression only on to a street of lesser quality (the County Store on Lowther Street). Another street, East Tower Street, is simply a traffic sewer for vehicles along the northern boundary of the site and it seemed appropriate for it to be overlooked by the multi-storey car park. Not that this excuses an inept elevation, buildings should have no 'back' elevations, and a deliberate attempt was made here to take a stage further ideas for car park facades with complex grilles and rich brick details. In this way the environment lobby was mollified, but the Royal Fine Arts Commision thought the architecture quite dreadful

Before the architecture of our age can be said to have reached maturity it will have to demonstrate that it can adapt itself to a whole range of building size and sit comfortably in any type or style of urban fabric. When The Lanes was designed the pressure of public opinion made us opt for discretion as the better part of valour and so far as Scotch Street is concerned the challenge was frankly avoided. One cannot blame the people of Carlisle for their caution. They were terrified of 'modern' architecture and there were enough horrors in the city centre to justify their concern.

Palazzo Farnese, Rome
A huge building of much bigger scale than the mediaeval city surrounding it.

The Bentall Centre, Kingston-upon-Thames
Wood Street entrance.

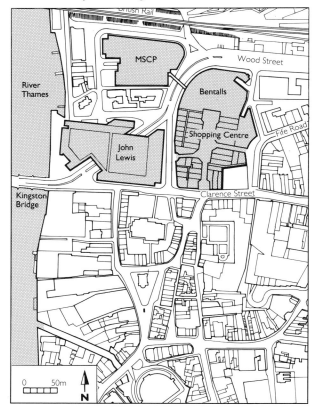

The Bentall Centre, Kingston-upon-Thames
Clarence Street entrance.

The Bentall Centre, Kingston-upon-Thames
Plan showing the impact of the new centre, a multi-storey car park for 1600 cars and a department store for John Lewis. John Lewis spans a new freeway to take vehicles north of the town centre and relieve congestion. The imposition of these enormous buildings may work because fortuitously they are all to the north of the old town centre and no retail activity takes place beyond the railway line. The scale of the existing town centre will not be disturbed.

Nevertheless, the Palazzo Farnese and a hundred more Renaissance palaces must have appeared like gargantua to the Lilliputian gothic cities upon which they were imposed and the Victorians too laid about them with cavalier abandon. They built a mass of buildings, many of which were wholly inimical to the size of the town. They are now almost without exception listed and any that are not will be fought for tooth and nail.

Few of us feel the need to check back on the preceding scale of the town before commenting on the appropriateness for location of many masterpieces. One wonders what chance Wren would have had with his designs for St Paul's Cathedral in the face of the Royal Society for the Protection of Tudorbethan England.

It is exciting and challenging to be part of the current debate surrounding the modern movement. A solution must be found which is recognised as valid, not by ivory towered critics who are irrelevant to the course of modern architecture, but by the populace for whom it is built.

A big building in a small town: The Bentall Centre, Kingston-upon-Thames

BDP is now wrestling with an archetype of the problem. In Kingston-upon-Thames just outside London a new shopping complex and a department store to be called the Bentall Centre is being built. The total area is 750,000 sq ft (70,000 sq metres) and its single block will be the largest building in the town centre. There is absolutely no way such a Goliath can be tucked behind some small

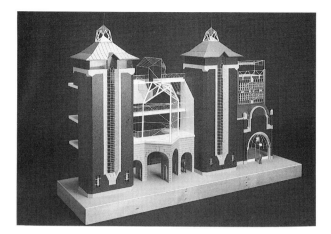

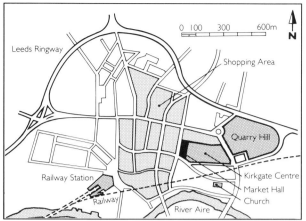

Kirkgate Market, Leeds
Lightly shaded area shows the main shopping district of Leeds. Dark shaded area indicates the 26 acres of pedestrianised shopping that will be added by the Kirkgate Centre and the Quarry Hill development. Parking for 3000 cars is accessed directly from the motorway system. The 1904 listed Market Hall is shown in solid colour.

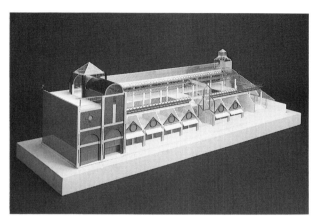

Kirkgate Market, Leeds
This sketch shows the need to break down the scale of the new buildings.

Kirkgate Market, Leeds
Study models showing proposed entrances to the Kirkgate Market.

terraces aping another age. There is a revivalist frontage by Aston Webb based on the Wren facades of Hampton Court Palace and this must be retained. It is the biggest single elevation in town but its size will pale into insignificance beside the new extended scheme. Across the road John Lewis is building a large department store and its designers face the same difficulties. The problem is to integrate buildings of such alien scale into the close woven fabric of a charming London suburb.

Kirkgate Market, Leeds
Similarly at Kirkgate Market in Leeds we are involved in an enormous scheme which when laid over an Ordnance Map of the City makes a profound impact on even this big city centre. The problem is eased because one complete elevation – the one nearest the city – is

provided by a magnificent Victorian market hall and one third the length of the southern side is occupied by another row of listed buildings. On the other hand, the lack of retail ground floor shop front facing the street is inhibiting and virtually the whole of the remaining perimeter at ground floor presents either service yards or a bus station to the surrounding roads.

When one adds the fact that service corridors and blank rear walls to shops constitute the first floor, and three car parking trays make up the remaining storeys the designer deserves sympathy. Nevertheless, the challenge is there and at both Kingston-upon-Thames and Leeds the clients are aware of the civic importance of these huge structures though they reiterate regularly the need to provide profitable shopping centres.

Waverley, Edinburgh: a different problem
Finally among these examples of working with today's
furore over architectural design standards a shopping
centre where, strangely, there were no stylistic
constraints at all. It was the second occasion on which
we worked as design consultants to a Local Authority
and without doubt the traditional path of private
developer procurement would have foundered
on the rocks of commercial expediency.

The project is in one of the most precious cities in
Britain and the site among the most sensitive in that
city. The place is Edinburgh, the site is on its most
famous street, and furthermore it is on the south side
of Princes Street overlooking the thrilling panorama of
the Royal Mile. The North British Hotel, a distinguished
and much loved blackened Victorian pile bounds the
eastern flank, wonderful views of Arthur's Seat over
the North Street Bridge lie to the southeast, the choppy
skyline of the Royal Mile dominates the valley to the
south, sublime views of Edinburgh Castle close the vista
to the southwest, while due west is the full mile length
of the tree-rimmed Princes Street. The Royal Scottish
Academy and the Scott Monument soar above the leafy
canopy on one side and a variegated streetscape of
shops, hotels and offices lines the other.

The site of old Waverley Market is sunk well below
Princes Street, indeed the bottom floor is only a few feet
above the tracks of Waverley Station, some 30 feet (9
metres) below street level. The most important planning
restriction on the site is that under an Act of Parliament,
no less, nothing more than four feet (1.2 metres) high
above Princes Street may be built on the site. The
architectural profession is no place for the faint-hearted.

The memory reels at the negotiations that took
place with the Scottish Royal Fine Arts Commission,
the Cockburn Society, The Scottish Development
Department, the Planning Department and several
individuals whose loud pontifications would lead
the unwary to believe they had made a lifelong study
of planning strategy, shopping centre design and
architectural aesthetics. Suffice it to say that many
private developers could not have endured the
prolonged delays which were promoted by the
objectors and certainly would not have agreed to
proceed with a scheme which had every element
of commercial attraction excised from its external
appearance.

What emerged from this long and difficult exercise
was a decision to treat virtually the whole roof as
an open, accessible plaza through which two large
roof lights projected to take full advantage of the
permitted upstand above the level of Princes Street. In
architectural terms the scheme is a dramatic example of
how, occasionally, the dictum of allowing form to follow
function can have a powerful effect on a building.

It starts with the announcement of 'entrance'.
Remember that nothing higher than four feet could be
built to effect this and it was only after much debate
that the modest pinnacles were allowed to break the
height restriction to give some indication that there
was a building of any kind below ground at that point
in Princes Street. Honour was satisfied by calling them
'sculpture' which, like flag poles and trees, were
deemed not to interrupt the view across the valley
to the Royal Mile.

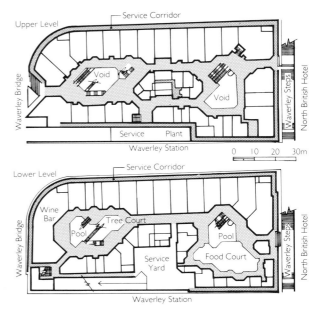

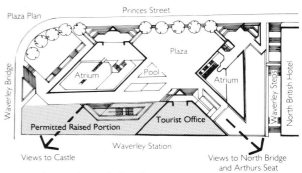

Waverley Market, Edinburgh
*The two trading levels are below the level of Princes Street and
daylight penetrates through two double-glazed planar roof lights.
The speciality centre was the first new building of its type in
Great Britain and the small shop units give a false impression
of the scale. The gross area of 150,000 sq ft is smaller than many
department stores. Note the small service area for lorries and the
2m wide distributor corridor round the perimeter of both levels.*

*The plaza plan indicates the predominant angled views to
Edinburgh Castle and to Arthur's Seat. These diagonals
determined the triangular forms of the raised atria roof and they
in turn echo the 45 degree splay of the escalators and staircases
between the floors. The tone indicates the permitted area for a
height of 15ft (4.6m) above Princes Street.*

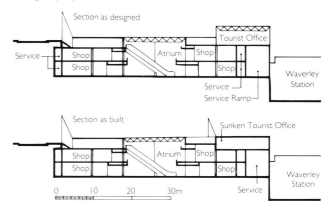

Waverley Market, Edinburgh
*Two sections show first the Tourist Office raised to the permitted
building height of 15ft above Princes Street and secondly the way
we were obliged to sink it into the mass of the main building. The
preferred design was conceived as a fully glazed structure which
would have afforded views of the Royal Mile, masked views down
to Waverley Station and given wind protection to the new plaza.*

Waverley: pedestrian flow as a planning determinant

An important function of circulation in a shopping centre is to ensure that the greatest percentage of shoppers reach all parts of the project to achieve a balanced trading pattern. On most schemes the planning stage quickly identifies one or more areas which need special attention. Waverley was no exception and given the prime points of entry from Princes Street it was apparent that strong downward diagonal pedestrian flows would have to be established if the more remote corners below ground were to trade well.

At the same time we had regard for the best views to the south, and from the main entrance in particular the views southeast to Arthur's Seat and southwest to Edinburgh Castle were clear standouts. They vie to be the most beautiful panoramas in Europe. The resultant 45 degree views from Princes Street were studied for design inspiration and we quickly connected the consonance between the internal requirements and the external potential. So the armature for the design was established and all the detail flowed from that simple geometric notion. Because the design is perceived mainly as a horizontal tapestry and much foreshortened as one walks across the plaza we neither saw the need to clutter it with decorative detail nor dilute the message of the diagonals. The decision seemed to favour clear crystalline materials to complement the hard edged angled forms; this led to the use of granite rather than sandstone.

It is true that sandstone is the predominant building material for walls in medieval Edinburgh but a good many other materials including granite are much in evidence from later periods. Furthermore sandstone is too soft to withstand the heavy foot traffic across the large roof areas. The dark grey Cairngorm granite is no longer commercially available and we were looking for a lighter clearer granite for our image. Eventually we chose a lovely pale grey stone from Portugal. Indeed this shopping centre uses only two external building materials – high quality granite and toughened glass; usually in two layers.

One does, incidentally, discover bizarre cost anomalies when shopping for materials internationally. We started the quest for granite by being surprised that local Scottish quarries had priced themselves out of existence and that Cornish granite could be hauled the length of Britain and fixed more competitively than from quarries a couple of shires away. Only ones lack of enthusiasm for the dullness of Cornish gray granite and abhorrence of Cornish red encouraged a wider look abroad.

At an international stone fair in Lisbon we fell in love with the perola gray from northern Portugal. It was priced 20% below the Cornish granite – fully fixed and in position. To make sure we were not being taken for a ride the Portuguese family quarry firm offered to take us for one. It involved flying 450 miles (725 kilometres) north from Lisbon to Oporto where we transferred to a camper van and bumped our way for two hours up unmetalled roads into the mountains to the east of the city. The granite was there all right, but the thought of cutting it out of those remote hills, lugging it in huge blocks over 450 miles (725 kilometres) of tiny roads to Sintra, sawing it into slabs, cutting it to size, loading it in individual crates, packing it into containers, taking it to Lisbon docks, craning it into ships, sailing it to

Waverley Station and the Old and New Cities, Edinburgh
This aerial perspective shows the relationship of the Waverley Market site to Princes Street and to the view of the Old City across the valley. The diagonal view from the new plaza to the Castle is evident and this view shows the wisdom of severely restricting building on the south side of Princes Street.

Waverley Market Entrance on Princes Street, Edinburgh
The maximum building height above Princes Street was 4ft. The pinnacles were allowed as sculpture.

Waverley Market, Edinburgh
The western court showing the warm internal finishes.

Waverley Plaza from the Scott Monument, Edinburgh

Liverpool, transferring it to lorries, carting it up to Edinburgh, unloading and fixing it in place – all for 20% less than driving up the motorway from Cornwall, struck us as pretty cockeyed economics.

Lessons from Waverley: living with others
Two other matters concerning the design of Waverley Market illustrate how architects must listen, debate and, if necessary, give way on aesthetic issues in spite of their own better judgement – or at least 'better' to them.

Although an Act of Parliament decreed a height limit of four feet (1.2 metres) this was not applicable to the whole site. With great wisdom those who drew up the ruling recognised that a band on the southern rim could be allowed to rise to 15 feet (4.6 metres) without destroying the view of the skyline though the lower height was reimposed at the eastern end to preserve a view of Arthur's Seat. The higher strip of permitted building hid the downward view of the roofs of Waverley Station: a real bonus.

We took advantage of this relaxation to locate the Scottish Tourist Office in a glass box with a serrated roof which would not contrast too starkly with the skyline beyond. After many meetings and modifications the Inspector at the Inquiry agreed with the design approach we took.

However the Scottish Royal Fine Arts Commission insisted that the 15 feet relaxation should be ignored and the four feet limitation prevail across the site. The Commission is the advisory body to the Scottish Development Department whose approval had to be secured because the Edinburgh District Planning Office could not be seen to be approving its own application. To achieve any progress it became politic to push the Tourist Bureau down into the body of the building, seriously disturb the economic viability of the centre, render the facility difficult to find from Princes Street and make its planning, structure and mechanical services cramped and tortuous. The plaza is robbed of a sense of enclosure and protection from wind and although the decision was to the detriment of the scheme acquiescence was the only path to progress.

The second issue is a fascinating insight into the way architectural theory must accommodate retail realities. The design team was readily persuaded that the cool grey granite should pervade the exterior and also that the interior should be one with the external ethos. It, too, should be cool and beautifully poised.

To our concern the message from the development agents came that the interior should be warm, friendly and welcoming. The bleak Edinburgh climate should be left firmly at the doors and the mood inside should be 'warm brown'. Natural timber, red/brown ceramics, luxurious planting and gay bunting should be the order of the day. Again it was a time for pragmatism. Tantrums would have seen our dismissal and rival interior designers taking over. Resignation would have achieved the same result. Calm reflection on the issues showed a good deal of common sense behind the arguments against us so we conceded with all the grace we could muster.

The result is a loss to aesthetic integrity but a gain to commerce. The atmosphere has the warmth that retailing needs. The shop fronts won the National Shopfitting prize for 1985 and the way people use and move about the centre shows that the commercial judgement was right. Architecture however is indubitably the poorer.

Lip service is often given to the idea of designing for people, but in the normal run of their work architects have prime responsibility to satisfy the client who pays them – though some notable prima donnas get through a whole career designing entirely for themselves. The examples in this chapter show, without being too obtuse, that in shopping centre design the developer – client who commissions and pays the fees is but a mouthpiece for the larger client – the townspeople and shoppers who in practice determine whether or not to patronise the development.

A truly professional designer working in this field must help his or her immediate client by seeking the corporate will of the body politic then transmuting it into distinguished physical form. For let there be no mistake, only architects can hold the pencil and theirs is the design that gets built. Architects should recognise that if the centres of the past have been aesthetic failures, they must bear the brunt of the blame. They are keen enough to demand the credit and the praise when the the awards are handed out.

And, as a postscript with a sting in the tail for architects, interior designers and graphic artists are better tuned to public taste and aspirations than architects. It is true that their art is more ephemeral and their wavelength shorter, but looking at the track record no period of graphic or interior design got things so dramatically wrong as did the architectural profession between the years 1960 and 1975.

1. *For the first time I acted not as a designer of components but as an assembler of sections from pattern books of the past – just as Victorian architects would have done.*

2. *Actually it is my favourite elevation on the scheme. The rich brick detailing to the back of the store gives a solid but interesting base. The library windows are simply expressed but bold in form and the design of the car park trays begin the long struggle to come to grips with this difficult building type.*

3. *On the day I was there a sudden rain storm broke over the city and all the windows had to be hurriedly closed to stop the water streaming in from the top.*

4. *Eldon Square is an excellent scheme built some 15 years earlier that had been designed, like Blackburn and Rochdale, in the years when we all forgot about daylight.*

4

CURRENT DESIGN TRENDS

The move to quality

Better packaging

Better shop fronts

Procuring better shop design

Working with interior designers

The limits of an interior designer's skill

Where architects and interior designers overlap

Design trends in the malls

Irregular mall configurations

Pop-out shop fronts

Pilaster and structural bay widths

The return of daylight

Imaginative atrium roof profiles

Using the top lit space

Planting in the malls

Cleaning of roof lights

Glass types in the roof light

Painting the structure of atria and mall roofs

Mirror glass in roof lights

Blinds in roof lights

Cautious attitudes to novel ideas

The trend to mixed use centres

Should the centre be open all hours?

The American view

Creative approaches to minimising vandalism

Benefits of mixed use centres

The types of mixed use: all but housing

Housing: a beneficial use

Shopping as 'Theatre'

The value of water in the malls

Do as Rome does ....

Dealing with vehicles

Multi-storey car parks

Sloping floors and spiral ramps

Parking: the start of the shopping experience

Ways of improving the multi-storey car park

The fifth elevation: roofing the car park

Putting cars in the basement

The American alternative: greening the city

Charges for parking

The service lorry

Basement service

Ground level service

Roof top servicing

Service areas: economic design

Conclusions: the way ahead

4

CURRENT DESIGN TRENDS

From almost every aspect one must be greatly encouraged by the way central area shopping design is going in Britain. 'Almost' because the only worry is the Gaderene rush to out of town. Even that worry has a silver lining because lately there have been encouraging signs that the government has grasped the notion that uncontrolled market forces will ruin us if let run wild.

The move to quality

The most positive aspect of current central area shopping design is the thrust for quality. This phenomenon needs explanation. Twenty-five years ago the game was new and the players few. Most developers were stereotypes of the popular image of flint-eyed, cigar-smoking entrepreneurs. Few of them had two thoughts worth rubbing together on the subject of townscape and the quality of the urban environment. They were money men, risk takers, and from that era came many of the slogans that have on occasion sprinkled this book. Their eyes were attracted like magnets to 'the bottom line'. Most have either passed away or, in advanced years, are living on some exotic isle on their invested profits. It is a fair bet that they would find these comments unacceptable but the evidence is the legacy of townscape they left behind and the overwhelming public condemnation of it.

To give due credit they revolutionised shopping habits in Britain and throughout the world. People may blame them for failures in matters they knew nothing about but they were simply trying to make money, and they saw in the first American malls a prototype that could be adapted to Britain. In the process they brought shoppers in off the streets. No longer need shopping be a drudge with the family trailing round the town in dripping raincoats, walking miles to tick off every item on the shopping list – dodging buses, lorries, cars and anything else on wheels. By 1970 the average family could park the car under cover, do the week's shopping in one or at most two locations in dry, passably clean conditions and in almost certain safety. It is quite silly for academics and aesthetes to say (as they do) that shopping centres are awful and people hate them. Aesthetic quality might be lacking, but people love them. The shopping public is under no compunction to shop where they do not wish. If developers had caught the merest whiff of public resistance they would have developed shopping centres differently or taken their entrepreneural skills elsewhere. If people dislike them why are Brent Cross, Eldon Square, Merseyway and a dozen Arndales to this day still 'wall to wall people' on any Friday or Saturday? Certainly they all need refurbishing but in every case the public patronising them could still shop in the high street if they find the malls distasteful.

Better packaging

But things have changed. Since those days standards of living have risen (in spite of painful recessions and high inflation) and expectation of quality in every aspect of life has also risen. The process started with the goods in the shops themselves: compare any trade catalogue over a 20-year period. As the quality of the product rose so did its packaging because competition intensified and it became increasingly necessary to compete for customers' attention. It is an age-old cycle.

Manchester Arndale Centre
Recently refurbished to include a fast food outlet.

Bolton Arndale Centre
Built in the early 70's.

Greek Crater,
2nd Century BC
The packaging helped
sell the contents.

In the 7th century BC the Greeks, under their wise and far seeing ruler Solon, decided they needed better packaging to compete more effectively for their olive oil export to Turkey so they hit upon the idea of painting the earthenware jars in which it was shipped. So flourished the supreme art of Greek vase painting that went through several styles and metamorphoses over the centuries. The shattered but precious remains are dug up in hundreds at every classic archaeological site and they are lovingly patched up and sent to every museum which has any pretensions to classical scholarship. Would that our present packaging could pass the test of time so well. Will Laura Ashley's wrapping papers be in the British Museum in 2500 AD?

Thus over two or three decades since the 50's the goods became better, the packaging improved and so shopkeepers took ever more care with the window design and window dressing. It is no use having eyecatching goods if the shop front does not attract attention in the first place. This realisation has meant excellent business for the interior design profession. Back in the 60's only the high quality fashion stores had even heard of this unique breed of professional. The vast majority of traders either did the design for the shop front themselves and got a builder to knock it together or commissioned a technical draughtsman to draw up a sketch over the weekend.

Better shop fronts
Either way the architect for the shopping centre who vetted the shop front designs for the developer was presented with much the same conundrum as are

most planning officers every day of the week. How to persuade clients to demand a higher standard of design from their consultants? The problem was different only in that the planning officer could recommend outright refusal of a design whereas the shopping centre architect could only try persuasion. If that failed the architect had to give in because the developer client had probably already decided that he wanted that particular trader in the precinct. He was not going to lose an excellent covenant just because two airy fairy people could not agree on a shop front design – especially when he probably saw nothing wrong with the proposal in the first place.

In those early years we spent weeks trying to raise the standard of design on shop fronts and it is not an exaggeration to say that the only real successes were with small, one unit traders. Few of the big multiples took the least bit of notice. They knew that if the developer and the local council wanted a Boots, a C&A, a Woolworth or a Marks & Spencer there was nothing the consultant architect could do about it. There was unlikely to be any opposition from the planning office which generally took little, if any, notice of design standards inside malls. Indeed it ill behove a planning officer to be seen as the one who had scared off such an important covenant. His political masters would be very upset when they found out.

BDP was fortunate to have as prime developer client an organisation that called itself 'an urban farmer: if we want something good out we've got to put something good in'. We therefore devised a booklet for all tenants which has now long been standard practice. Called 'Notes for Guidance for the Shop Tenants', the booklet not only sets out the technical constraints of the developer shell and the statutory consents that will be required but it also treads the dangerous ground of design quality control. So low were the general standards in the 60's that we fell into the trap of being too dogmatic. We stipulated stall riser heights, fascia depths, preferred materials and lists of acceptable letter faces for shop signs. The guide fulfilled a purpose in that it enabled us to sieve out the worst horrors but in retrospect it produced a blandness which was the opposite of our intent.

Rochdale
shopping centre
Approved shop front.

Very high quality shops were never a problem because the owners have always known that quality sells quality. But these traders rarely came to the provinces. The real difficulty lay with the standard national multiples because they were a ubiquitous presence in every high street and their standard was low.[1.] We badly needed quotable examples of high quality and there we were helped greatly by the rising design standards of shop traders on the Continent.

The earliest positive moves to quality design were made in France. News began to leak back to the UK that some remarkable shopping precincts were being built on the outskirts of Paris and though the exteriors were uniformly disastrous as works of architecture, the interiors were an intriguing Aladdin's cave. Dutifully we trooped over to Paris and, map in hand, we tracked down Parly 2, Velizey 2, Ivry 2, Bobigny 2 (anything with a figure 2 after it) and were enchanted by the elan and variety of interior design ideas in both the malls and the shops themselves.

Procuring better shop design

In the 70's therefore BDP changed its design criteria away from negative restriction to positive encouragement. We photographed the most imaginative shop fronts in France, omitted from the Notes for Guidance all the bits about stall riser heights and so on, and said that the photographs of shop fronts in our 'Notes' represented our idea of design quality. If tenants aimed for that their proposals would receive our approval and we would recommend the planning authorities to do the same.

It worked like a charm. When traders presented a dreadful or simply boring design we referred them to the photographs and asked if they were seriously trying to tell us that their design was as good as those in the brochure.

Some traders tried architects but rapidly found that though architects undergo a rigorous 7-year training in building technology and design they experience

Parly 2, Paris
The quality of design on the exterior was lamentable.

Parly 2, Paris
One of many imaginative designs for shop fronts. Such standards were well ahead of shopping centres in Britian in the 1960's.

virtually no specific lectures on shopfitting and interior design. One can usually tell an architect's interior. Bar a handful who have mastered both arts, the architect's shop will be heavy, over structured, dully lit and the colour scheme will either rely wholly on natural materials or everything in sight will be painted white – with perhaps one wall painted a primary hue or the woodwork stained blue. The lack of finesse in the use of soft materials, decorative features and lighting will be obvious.

Working with interior designers

There goes any remaining credibility with the architectural establishment, but the evidence is there to be seen. The fact is that Fitch, McColl, Conran, Saunders, Crighton and several others saw a gap in the market that architects were not filling and the rest is history.[2] The nearest modern parallel which comes to mind is the art of landscape design. Accepting again that there are one or two highly gifted designers who can span the skills of both architecture and landscaping,

the great majority of us have little feel for the potential of man made landscape and none at all for the botanical or technical aspects that make it possible. Even great masters like Alvar Aalto regularly failed to get the best (or anything at all) out of the landscape potential of their great works – the Town Hall at Saynatsalo and the Technical College at Jyvaskyla are typical examples.

The contrast with the way Eero Saarinen and his proteges Roche and Dinkeloo worked with the great American landscape architect Dan Kiley is an object lesson. Go to the Ford Foundation office block on 43rd Street in New York if in doubt.

Historical parallel is even more persuasive. The Gothic cathedrals are unthinkable without their stained glass and their sculpture – even the sculpted forms of the architectural and structural elements. Try too to imagine the Renaissance and the Baroque without the contribution of the sculpture, the painted plasterwork, the wood carving and the metalwork. How much

Waverley Market, Edinburgh
By the 1980's British shop front design had generally caught up with the best French and American examples.

Ford Foundation, New York
High quality landscape in the atrium by Dan Kiley

St Paul's Cathedral, London

poorer St Paul's would be without the wonderful metal screens of the French ironmaster Tijou, the exquisite wood and stone carving of Grinling Gibbons and the painted plasterwork of Sir William Thorburn. Christopher Wren seemed to have no hang-ups about interior designers.

This current trend for greater collaboration between architects and interior designers is especially important in shopping centres because while the former must be looked to for creative overall design, the organisation of all the building's complex elements and the detailing of its many parts, the latter's contribution is vital as a setting for fashion and a sense of theatre. Neither arena is the natural habitat of the architect (we cannot all be a Vanbrugh or Inigo Jones).

The limits of an interior designer's skill
There is, however, a dangerous trend. Interior design and graphics are in demand and the high profile, charismatic design studios have had much success and contributed greatly to the raising of shop design standards: in fact, they must take the main credit. Some of them have now convinced themselves that architecture is an extension to interior design rather than the other way round. They are busily marketing their firms to handle the total building contract and are hiring in-house architects to do the bricks and mortar bit.

Time will not be wasted describing the chasm that divides the two skills nor trace the quite separate nature and responsibilities of the skills themselves. Nor will an argument be mounted for demarcation for its own sake – there are few subjects which bore and irritate more. The aim here is to stress the importance of collaboration and integration of the two professions, either by merging their entities as in BDP, or by collaborating as equal but separate firms, or by setting up a single project partnership to ensure an integrated design input. What interior designers must do if they want to be accepted as co-designers by architects is to avoid

their present tendency to ask the architect to show them the space to be treated and then by every implication tell him to go away and keep his distance until the job is done. Furthermore a good deal of annoyance could be avoided if some of the more aggressive interior designers would cease publicising shopping centres on which they have worked in such a manner as to give the impression that they conceived the whole thing.[3]

Where architects and interior designers overlap
For good or ill, architects have hair-trigger egos and if collaboration is to be achieved, a good deal of mutual respect for the right quantity and quality of design input and leadership will be needed. At the extremes of each others skill the matter is easy to resolve. In the overall planning and external aspect of the scheme the architect must lead. A creative interior designer will have a view but he or she should not be the dominant voice. When we get to the department store or shop interior the reverse will be the case.

Things become tricky however when the two areas approach each other. In shopping malls and atria the balance should be about equal but even there much will depend on the design ethos being developed. For instance at Ealing we could have brought either the feeling of the exterior and the open town square much more into the malls, in which case the architect should have dominated, or the interior of the malls should have been conceived as an extension of the shop design; in which case the interior designer should have been more prominent.

By contrast at The Lanes in Carlisle the client wanted an exterior ambience to the whole of the internal lanes so that while there was little call for interior design, there was a very strong input from graphic designers who worked on all the directional signing and the logos. The best balance we have so far achieved is at Waverley Market in Edinburgh, where the interior and exterior is a complete amalgam of the skills of architect, interior designer, graphics and landscape architect.

Waverley Market
Edinburgh
Western Court.

Design trends in the malls

First a word about the interface between shop and mall. For two decades architects have fretted under the developer's requirement for a dead straight frontage. The theory was that every shop should have equal prominence and there should be no masking of one by or from another.

Even hanging signs were frowned upon because they hid each other. If architects suggested that the client looked at the arcaded streets of Innsbruck or practically any alley in Hong Kong they were patted on the head.

Furthermore developers and prime retailers insisted that shoppers should be able to see the fascia lettering of the trader from the street as soon as they entered the mall. That of course was a sop to the anchor trader who would have liked to have been at the front of the scheme but was persuaded to go to the back by dramatically lower square foot rents. Shoppers would then be dragged past all the other shops in order to arrive at the famous name.

A final nail in the coffin of an architect who pleaded for the slightest re-entrant angle in the mall was the demand from the client that he would only agree to such a feature if the architect would clean up the excrement that would assuredly be found there each morning. Developers had been to America and seen the latest malls and they were all as straight as stair rods. We who had seen pictures of Place Ville Marie in Montreal had to admit that IM Pei had done straight malls – though some of us thought they looked as dull as hospital corridors.[4]

Furthermore, said the client, if we long-haired, bow-tied Berties were given our head we would design monuments to our egos; if we wanted to see examples of shopping schemes with funny angles and malls shaped like a dog's back leg we should go to Cumbernauld or Portsmouth: empty concrete moonscapes they were.

Place Ville Marie, Montreal

Nathan Street, Hong Kong

*Cumbernauld
New Town Centre*

*Cumbernauld
New Town Centre*

*Faneuil Hall,
Boston*

Hazelton Lanes,
Toronto
One of the first new
built speciality centres.
The malls are only 10
feet wide and barely
any two shops are in
line with each other.
Many frontages
change direction
within one tenancy.
The open court is
an outdoor café in
summer and flooded
for ice skating in the
winter. Exclusive flats
are built above the first
floor shopping level.
The whole development
is very successful
and is being extended.

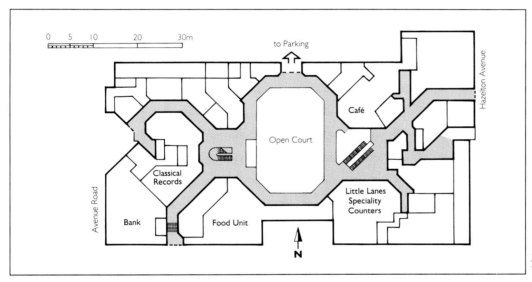

Hazelton Lanes,
Toronto

Irregular mall configurations

It was only with the arrival of the speciality centre that these theories were turned on their head and it was realised that the straightness of the mall had absolutely nothing to do with trading success. Faneuil Hall in Boston was straight but that was because Perry's Quincy Market back in 1776 had been built that way. At first floor level however Rouse and his architect Ben Thompson turned and twisted the narrow shopping alleys like an Arabian casbah. On the far west coast of America Ghiradelli Square had no recognisable mall at all and The Cannery, also in San Francisco, was a maze of galleries in an old warehouse on Fisherman's Wharf. Salt Lake City's Trolley Square broke all the planning rules and by the time North America decided to risk a new building for these specialised centres, rather than converting an old one, they took their courage in both hands and built Hazelton Lanes in Toronto. From stem to stern there is hardly a straight stretch of mall in the scheme. Here are hanging signs and glazed shop fronts projecting right into the line of the mall, so giving greater mystery and a hint of the unexpected.

Pop-out shop fronts

So we come to the latest trend in this fashion conscious world of shopping: the pop-out shop front. Hailed as a

breakthrough, it is actually as old as the hills as a stroll down Burlington or Piccadilly Arcades will show. It is also an amusing confidence trick on tenants. The theory is that traders are offered rent free the facility of using a lightweight glass box (which the developer builds and pays for) projecting out into the mall which of course, when full of goods, quite obscures the next trader as you approach the shop, (it has been decreed that the sacred principle of unfettered view is no longer immutable). Rent on the 'free' area however is only waived until the first rent review whereupon the added square footage is charged at the full inflated Zone A rent.

The first time it was tried as a deliberate gambit in Britain was at Cameron Toll in Edinburgh in 1985. Every shop in the centre opted for the pop-out option with the exception of one giant multiple trader who said he would have nothing to do with such gimmicks. Within two weeks of the opening, with his glittering shop front shining like a new pin, he approached the developer, said that after all he would like the pop-out option. He ripped out his standard solution and installed the amended design – all in time for the opening jamboree. If you can't beat 'em ... So popular is the concept that at The Olympia, East Kilbride, every shop is designed with a pop-out shop front.

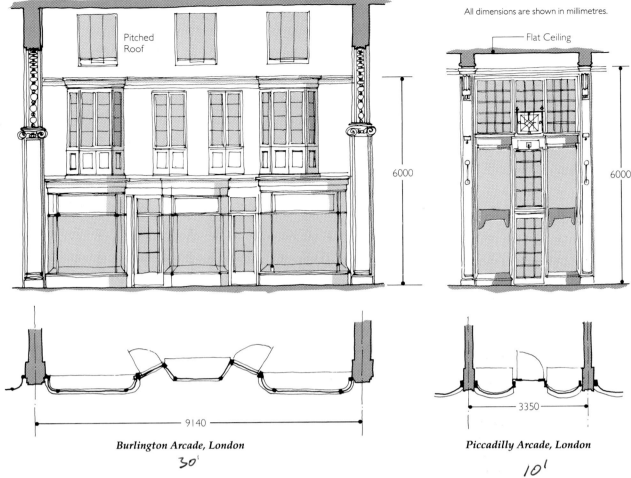

All dimensions are shown in millimetres.

Pitched Roof

Flat Ceiling

6000

6000

9140

3350

Burlington Arcade, London
30'

Piccadilly Arcade, London
10'

Burlington, Piccadilly and Royal Arcades, London
Tall and elegant, the bay size is much narrower than that demanded by retailers in the 1980's. The architectural form is a strong armature to which the shop front, which is allowed to pop out, is subservient.

We still occasionally go through the charade of demonstrating to an anchor store director – Large Space User in the vernacular – by lines on plans that the shop front can be seen from the other end of the scheme. It never seems to dawn on these retailers that when the mall is full of people and it is an exciting melange of projecting signs, hanging banners and seasonal decorations the chances of seeing beyond 100 feet (30 metres) are nil. Furthermore, if the populace of Rochdale, Wigan, Slough, Stockton and a thousand other non-tourist Meccas have not become aware that there is a John Lewis, a C&A, or a Debenhams in town then there is something more seriously wrong with their public relations than will be cured by seeing the fascia from the bus stop on the ring road.

At the other extreme, in the USA, probably the best up-market department store is called Nieman Marcus. They have a handwritten logo that cannot be deciphered beyond fifty paces: they just expect people to know they are there. Indeed, the maximum clamour on this issue comes from the weakest traders.

Pilaster and structural bay widths
Another curious debate that usually takes place between the architect and the client centres round the width of the pilaster between shop fronts. It seems a rather minor subject to get hot under the collar about but be assured that some developers will argue that the

pilaster should be no more than the width of the party wall between shops and they will hold that the level of Zone A rents (the front 20 feet (6.1 metres) depth of the shop) will be affected by the lineal feet of glass showing across the front of the tenancy.

This is demonstrable nonsense. We have designed pilaster widths from 10 inches (250mm) in the old days to 30 inches (800mm) more recently as the schemes have moved progressively upmarket. We have never yet had the gall to suggest the 6 feet (1800mm) that is on show at a superb, high quality centre called Fashion Island in Los Angeles but clearly the criterion is not the width of the pilaster but the quality of its design and materials.

On the subject of pilaster widths the architect and the developer start from opposite ends of the telescope. The architect is trying to provide a characterful framework in which the shops will stand out as individual trading elements, so the more dominant the pilaster the more he or she is able to model it to maximum effect. Twenty-five years ago at Blackburn and Rochdale we succeeded not so much in width but in the projection of the dark-tiled columns whilst competitors were simply exposing the party wall and cladding it with mosaics. Nowadays we favour holding back the face of the party wall but giving it substantial width, modelling it strongly and letting the shop front glazing itself come out into the mall in the pop-out way. At Carlisle the team eventually

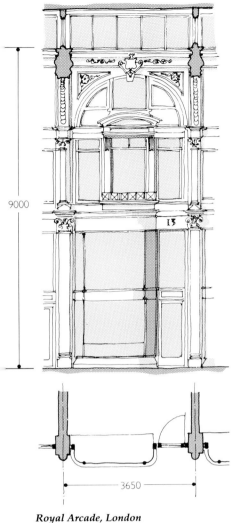

9000

3650

Royal Arcade, London

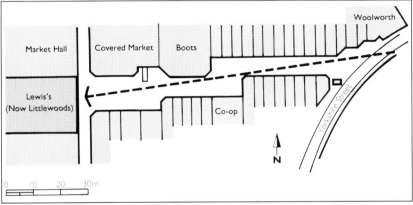

Yorkshire Street, Rochdale

Rochdale shopping centre
A plan showing the sight lines Lewis's insisted on so that their shop front could be seen from Yorkshire Street. The photo at the entrance from Yorkshire Street shows the results. Boots can just be discerned: Lewis's is at least double the distance further on. Note the litter which would give an American developer apoplexy.

settled on 28 inches (700mm) width for the brick pilaster and it clearly is not a millimetre too much. At East Kilbride we are pressing for 3 feet (900mm) but with 6 inches (150mm) slivers of mirror glass on either side of a semi- circular pilaster, so giving a specular reflective flash of interest as one passes by. There are a host of possibilities once the client will concede the fact that the pilaster could be more than the structural minimum and can contribute to the quality of the mall.

A really tricky design problem is the increased grid or dimension that retailers are calling for as their ever larger units face the mall. In the 60's 20 feet (6 metres) was the rule for shop widths and when we went French and had to grapple with metres, six of them were near enough to allow the trade to carry on thinking of it as 20 feet (6 metres).[5] Now the rule is 23ft 6ins (7.2 metres) minimum and many centres go to 24ft 6ins (7.5 metres) or even as wide as 26ft 3ins (8.0 metres).

The problem for architects is one of facade proportion. To be blunt the architecture is too far apart. The columns or pilasters between shops are so widely spread that it is difficult to get any real elegance out of the vertical element.[6]

The return of daylight

Another most welcome trend is the return of daylight to our shopping centres. This is not so much a welcome

return but rather a surprise that it ever departed. For two centuries top lit galleria have been beloved of shoppers and sightseers the world over. European lexicons list hundreds of them. The places where daylight was not let in was where it was not welcome and that only because the designers could not keep the heat out (like the casbahs of Casablanca, or David Street in Old Jerusalem). Precincts with uncovered malls were in places like Southern California and South Africa where the climate was perfect.

In the 40's and early 50's the USA had experimented with windowless factories because they were much cheaper to build and climate control. They lasted just one generation. People would not work in them.

Why, therefore, the first few thousand American and European shopping centres were built with solid roofs is an unsolved puzzle – unless it was to achieve the same economics as windowless factories. There was more excuse for solid roofs in Britain because we built almost exclusively in towns and had to stack cars, lorries and buildings above the ground floor. Glazed domes and barrel vaults were deemed to be unwanted interruptions to layouts above ground level but there can be little excuse for a solid mall roof on a single storey building. Ultimately the public verdict became unequivocal and we experienced the turn of the tide when designing The Lanes at Carlisle.

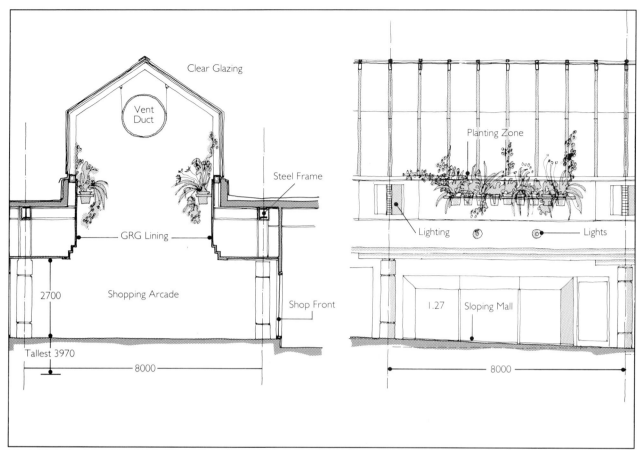

The Olympia, East Kilbride

All dimensions are shown in millimetres.

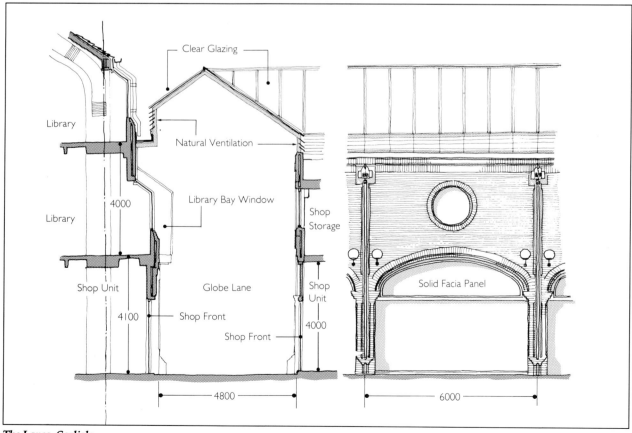

The Lanes, Carlisle

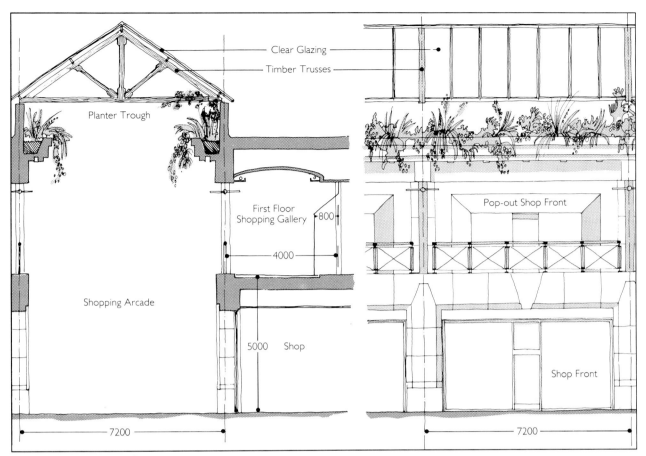

The Buttermarket, Ipswich

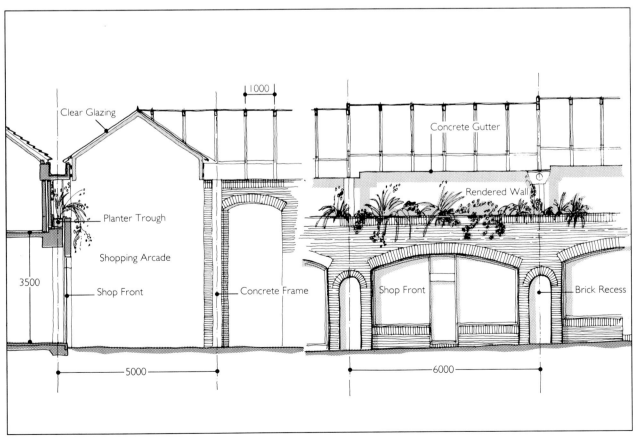

The Bell Centre, Melton Mowbray

David Street, Jerusalem
Daylight is unwelcome only in extreme heat in primitive technologies. On very hot days the squares just inside the gates to the Old City of Jerusalem become deserted, but the narrow vaulted streets with natural vents in the roof remain a hive of trade and industry.

Imaginative atrium roof profiles

Now that we have rediscovered the galleria and the atrium one hopes they will be with us for a long time and there could be a good deal of experimentation with forms. Up to now we have rather tamely roofed our glazed malls with either simple barrel vaults or pitched roofs. Admittedly there is a limit to the number of profiles one can think of when trying to span 20 to 26 feet (6 to 8 metres), but the options become much wider when the malls open out into an atrium.

It is still early days in the rediscovery of daylit space but so far none of our clients have been prepared to think adventurously into profiles which not only make use of modern technology but also reflect in their configuration the ideal requirements of the fire officer. Furthermore profiles could be used which make much easier the problems of window cleaning (both inside and out) machinery maintenance and provide access galleries for adjusting and maintaining light fittings, plant material and temporary seasonal displays.

The creation of space is easy to achieve with a barrel vault or a dome but there is no point in overprovision unless the space has also some quasi-civic, processional or liturgical function. Galleria Vittorio Emmanuele in Milan, the Pantheon in Rome or the vast chancel crossing in St Peter's in Rome – all have their grandeur and fitness for purpose but what about something more adventurous and of our time in shopping centres?

Using the top lit space

A shopping centre is theatre and the space must act as a bonus in retail terms. The idea of hanging or supporting advertising and decorative ephemera in such spaces has much to commend it. This is done very effectively in the atrium of the Queen's Quay Terminal conversion in Toronto where balletic harlequins pirouette in the space. The balloons at the Scarborough Centre near Toronto have the added attraction of a rise and fall motion as hot air from naked flames is forced into them from below.

One of the best ideas comes from St Louis where in the entrance hall to the Botanical Gardens the 50 feet (15 metre) barrel vault is filled with lovely diaphanous awnings stretched alternately as quadrants across the space, each one delicately painted with gigantic flowers. On a much smaller scale ideas abound – flocks of birds, flags, kites, balloons, aeroplanes – in fact anything evocative of the airborne. They all help to make the

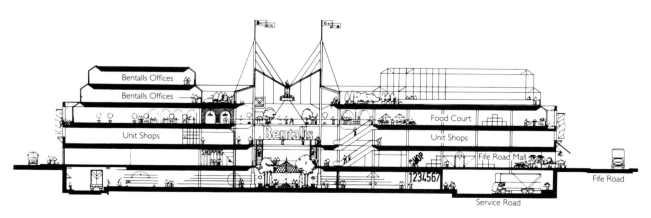

The Bentall Centre, Kingston-upon-Thames, London
The competition design exploring new roof forms: a traditional barrel vault was preferred.

Galleria Vittorio Emanuele

Queens Quay, Toronto
Harlequins dancing in the atrium space.

space more dramatic, meaningful and more easily comprehended. One of the criticisms of the magnificent interior space of the Eaton Centre in Toronto is that in the last analysis it is dull. The flock of 60 Canada Geese called 'Flight Stop' by the sculptor Michael Snow at the Simpson end are not nearly dominant enough in the space. We used the idea at Carlisle and even in the relatively tiny Globe Lane they are not always noticed. The colourful banners in Grapes Lane make a more positive contribution.

Planting in the malls
An immediate beneficiary of the penetration of natural daylight into the malls and courts is the internal landscaping. Trees especially love the high light levels: they were after all designed to be sited in the open air. Some designers, however, seem to be stuck with only two species of plant that relish an internal environment, ficus benjamina and bamboo and the former is now ubiquitous. Planting is discussed from a technical standpoint later and Janet Jack recommends more options before someone decrees that trees are overdone and out of fashion.

Cleaning of roof lights
Remember that two surfaces need to be cleaned (inside and outside) and they have different problems. The exterior will need regular attention – at least once a quarter – but is much easier to solve. A gantry can usually be accommodated and it is amazing what areas can be cleaned with a ladder, a 3m pole and a squeegee. Furthermore, because one is usually looking upwards to the sky with its non-determinant forms, optical cleanliness need not be sought in the way one would expect with ordinary windows.

St Louis Botanical Gardens
Painted awnings enliven the vault.

'Flight Stop' in the Eaton Centre, Toronto

On the other hand, whilst the interior surface need not be cleaned more often than once a year, it is far more difficult to do. All manner of structural, architectural, landscape, lighting and design ephemera may be encountered to compromise the optimum run of gantries and staging. Furthermore, the window cleaner is often reaching above his head so the physical strain is greater. So, whilst the first rule is to remember the need to get at every square metre of glass (and structure) for maintenance, the second is to avoid making the first enquiry of a gantry manufacturer. They are in business to sell gantries.

Far better value for money is to bring in the technical advisers of the National Federation of Master Window Cleaners or one of their member firms. Such people will tell you what can and cannot be done without a gantry. Once the designer is armed with the practical parameters of the problem, there are a number of excellent manufacturers who provide first class mechanical equipment.

Gantries, however, are never a pretty sight and they are usually permanently in view. Far better the mobile 'pea-picker' with an appropriate reach and a multi-jointed jib to get into all sorts of odd corners for tasks other than window cleaning. The best of them collapse to pass through double doors but they need a parking place (not in Zone A of rental values). Consider also the need to transfer them from one level to another.

Glass types in the roof light
Obscure glass is always a disappointment in mall roof lights. Admittedly cast glass, both plain and wired, is a fraction the cost of clear toughened glass but the decorative kaleidoscope of clouds, sunshine and rain is worth an accurate vision of the outside. Obscure glass muddies the image, reduces the sky pattern to an overall pale grey and even when seen on the gargantuan scale of the Eaton Centre it contributes further to the blandness.

Painting the structure of atria and mall roofs
The treatment of the structural members is also an interesting study. There are several permutations and while each has merit, some are more successful than others. For instance at Blackpool we went unashamedly for decorative metal sections but that track leads inevitably to hints, nay accusations, of historicism and pastiche. We also made a much debated decision to paint the metalwork black, not only because the client loved the easier maintenance and absence of cleaning, but because we thought it looked stronger and more rugged against the strong red Accrington brick. White painted metalwork with such a plethora of detail quickly starts looking like a wedding cake or at least the tropical house at Kew Gardens. If that is preferred then the architect must keep the sections of the metal sufficiently robust or the building will appear too diaphanous and effeminate. A good example of this is the Crescent Mall in Dallas where the whole internal appearance is so foppish as to evoke a titter rather than a gasp of admiration.

A few years after the Blackpool Hounds Hill Centre the colours of the metalwork for the atria and malls at Ealing, Waverley and Carlisle were specified. All three structures were simple, functional solutions; one arched, one flat and one pitched. The first two were painted white. In the Ealing atrium the curved sections were placed closer than necessary for strength to create the lace-like quality of a bridal veil. At Waverley the horizontal roof beams were selected for their depth to act as louvres against solar gain and they were painted off-white to bounce light down into the deep recesses of the lower floors. At Carlisle we opted for a very dark green whose strength complimented the external quality details of the lanes themselves. This it certainly does but on balance a light coloured structure is best and in fact at Melton Mowbray – a direct parallel with Carlisle – we opted for a light cream. One's preference is clear; even more so at night when the light coloured metalwork stands out against the dark night sky.

A part opaque, part glass roof is to be avoided. The contrast between dark and light is too great and the glare distracting. The effect is industrial: it is usually done for economy reasons and the solid areas usually finish up as corrugated metal. If one is looking for a quasi nautical effect as were the designers at Baltimores' Harbour Place, New York's Pier 17 or New Orleans' Riverwalk, then the treatment with clear glass panels and aluminium sheet sections is appropriate, but it is not a suitable roof finish for a development in a historic town in Europe. Nor are polycarbonates: the reflections are not true, they scratch too easily and many are still subject to discolouration over time.

There is also the appearance of the glass from within the scheme at night to consider. Whilst one may prefer white tracery to dark lines against the night sky the blackness of the glass itself is gloomy and not conducive to evening trade in the longer shopping hours that may come. Two solutions come to mind.

Mirror glass in roof lights
The first is to use solar glass which, in addition to its mechanical benefits by day, reverses its reflectance by night and acts as a mirror to the interior. Now whether we want to see our architecture and indeed ourselves upside down after nightfall is a matter for discussion. Some feel distinctly uncomfortable in a mirror glass office block after nightfall; one wall becomes completely reflective. To have it on the ceiling in a public space could be deemed 'upsetting'.

Blinds in roof lights
The second solution is to have the equivalent of curtains which give a space a different, enclosed atmosphere after nightfall. Obviously conventional curtaining would not be practical but much could be done with cunningly designed banners. They could hang by day and swivel at night to lie in the plane of the glass and break up areas of unrelieved blackness even if the glass surfaces were not totally cloaked.[7]

Buckminster Fuller got nearer than anyone with the sectionalised blinds designed to pull out in triangles to cover the hexagonal plastic panels which cloaked his famous geodesic dome at Montreal's Expo'67. The notion was sophisticated – like all the notions he had. The mechanism was controlled by photo-electric cells so that by day when the sun shone the blinds closed and they opened as the sun went behind a cloud or set for the night.

Unfortunately although he was a genius and his mind a fertile seed bed of revolutionary ideas, the great majority were either palpably impractical or prohibitively expensive.[8] The blinds at Expo'67 were an example. Whether they ever worked properly is not known but in the third month of the exhibition the system had failed and the dome was a patchwork of screens jammed at various stages of extension.

Hounds Hill Centre, Blackpool

The Crescent, Dallas
This big unroofed amphitheatre is quite unsuitable for lively retailing in Dallas. It is either too chilly for comfort or like a furnace in the summer.

Ealing office atrium

USA Pavilion, Expo 67, Montreal

Cautious attitudes to novel ideas

Partly in parentheses but very germane to the question of retail design trends is the ultimate fate of the USA pavilion at Expo'67. One night some years ago it caught fire and the conflagration was so violent and so total that in minutes the dome was no more. It simply disappeared like a shooting star. Shopping centre design is no place for revolutionary pioneering notions which are by definition untested. If one wants to break new ground the best chance of getting the concept built is to seek a client who has more money than sense and who finds one's ideas irresistible. Of late, banks and microchip manufacturers have rated highly in this category.

Central area developments, on the other hand, are funded in Britain largely by institutions who manage pension or insurance monies or by entrepreneurs whose main object in life is to minimise the already frightening risks that speculative buildings incur.[9] Those who provide the money to build shopping schemes (rarely less than £20m these days) have not only a responsibility to their shareholders and pensioners but they take their responsibility to society seriously. They desperately want the centre to be liked so that people will want to come to it. If the proposal does not look as if it is going to be an excellent investment for the next 125 years (the length of the lease) and if they are in any doubt about both the practicality and the safety of any element in the design they will reject it. Their public liability in every sense is too exposed not to have every angle covered as far as can be assured by the wit of man.

In contrast to Treasury mandarins, who fix the level of investment in the public sector buildings – like schools, hospitals and housing – developers are interested in potential growth in value in their investment. Developers will often take a modest view of profit in the first rent period or a relaxed attitude to high first cost finishes as long as they are satisfied that the rewards will be high in the long term.

That is why centres like Cumbernauld and Milton Keynes could never have been commercially funded in the private sector and why futuristic concepts like the Hammersmith shopping centre in London never had the slightest chance of being built – at least not with the aid of orthodox funding.

The trend to mixed use centres

There is now a trend towards mixed use centres and it will have an important impact on whether centres are open to the public at all times or closed out of trading hours.

Ranking equal with one's pleasure about the trend to higher quality centres, is one's delight about the fashion for mixed use developments. Such a ranking is not shared by developers. The best of them see it as excellent business that quality should rise – so long as it is matched in due proportion by rising value and profits. Mixed development, on the other hand, gives them white knuckles because the question marks behind key words like Management? Covenant? Responsibility? Access? Vandalism? and Legal Agreements? strike terror into their hearts.

To put the matter frankly, the average developer's most ardent and simple aim is to pick the hottest retail spot in town, make it a flytrap for luring customers by day, then transform it into Fort Knox to keep people out at night. Do not be misled by any protestations to the contrary.

Should the centre be open all hours?

Such an aim would be tenable if they were building something – anything – out of town: a zoo; a space centre; a museum; Disneyworld; a shopping centre even. But a central area retail scheme is by definition at the very core of a community. Furthermore it is usually very big; it often covers many blocks of the city and directly affects many other blocks around it. Cities are for people: for all the people that have elected by free will to live there. They are not for developers, for architects, for borough engineers or for any other single sector, no matter how influential; they are not for visitors or tourists either. All these groups have a role to play but towns are primarily for the people who live there.

Therefore any proposal which debars citizens from crossing their town when the shops are shut should be anathema. A number of central area schemes have been built in Britain where, after 6 pm people are forced to walk cold and sodden round bare cliff-like walls to get from the pub to the bus station, or from the cinema to their chosen restaurant. It is like having to walk round the walls of Avila in Spain or Jaiselmer in India to get from one side of the city to the other. Yet for every strongly held view there must be some tempering if it is not to become a dogma. It would be silly to argue the right of public access to every piece of private property. In the shopping world some centres are so small that the inconvenience to the public is slight and the proportionate cost of maintenance and supervision for 24 hour access would be unreasonably high.

In a speciality centre this caveat would certainly apply. Many historical examples illustrate the reasonableness of closing off, say, a market hall or a shopping arcade such as those in Piccadilly, London (though none in Leeds, the most arcaded city in Britain, are locked off at night). Speciality centres usually abound in fragile and highly accessible features like pools, fountains, carts, chairs and tables. Waverley Market in Edinburgh is one such. The centre is small, at 150,000 sq ft (14,000 sq metres) gross it is less than many a department store, and there is good access round the site. At the other extreme it would have been quite wrong to close the Blackburn centre at night because the various phases cover 15 acres (6 hectares). It would have been tantamount to closing the town. Of the centres one has worked on Blackburn, Rochdale, Blackpool, Ealing, and Carlisle are all open; only Waverley is understandably closed at night; Melton Mowbray is gated off quite needlessly. BDP is working on a number of central area schemes where the arguments are still rife. If when built they are closed at night you can conclude that we lost the fight.

The American view

One more thought: whilst discussing the issue with American developers a surprising number take the view that they have 24 hour supervision in the centre anyway so they see no reason to close the centre down – some not even in the small hours of the morning. The St Louis Centre and the Mayfair Centre in Coconut Grove, Miami, are interesting examples. The latter is an exotic confection of pools, fountains, decorative lighting and planting. The potential for vandalism in this, the most crime-ridden city in the USA is boundless but at both midnight and midday one has found it unblemished. Ghiradelli Square in San Francisco is closed for only three and a half hours out of 24 – and that is a highly vulnerable speciality centre. The truth is that it is just simpler to lock citizens out of their centre at night and

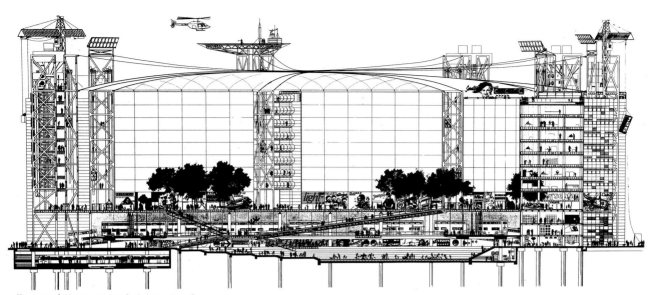

Proposed Hammersmith Centre, London
Shopping developments like this have scant chance of being constructed. Exciting they may be, but Funds will require assurance that they make retail sense and that technically they will be trouble free for 125 years - the normal leasehold period.

developers should be told that it is unacceptable. The bogeyman of institutions refusal to fund open centres is a myth.

Now, (for the developers and clients who are still following) one must not be naive and ignore the difficulties. The problem of vandalism and nuisance must be addressed.

Creative approaches to minimising vandalism
The first priority for an acceptable night time environment (difficulties will never be entirely eliminated) is first class estate management. After that all other measures pale into insignificance. Management is a high art and well worth the diploma status it has now achieved. The best British centres have learnt well from the Americans; people or groups can be picked out from the very moment they enter the precinct on closed circuit TV monitors and high profile management deters all but the most determined vagrant. Graffiti must be removed within minutes of the offence for it is axiomatic that graffiti (like litter) attracts graffiti.

Again the best American centres are exemplary. At the Esplanade Centre in New Orleans they have one employee going round every hour the mall is open with a pot of paint obliterating any mark. The walls of the recess for the telephone booths are washed twice a day and the whole of that area is repainted once a fortnight.

Lastly, since most loitering or nuisance offences occur out of shopping hours and at night, the importance of good lighting. Not the expensive, decorative lighting that is used during shopping hours but the economical high wattage, low voltage systems that are now available. Nobody will by choice seek out a well lit location to commit either a nuisance or a felony. It follows that after first class supervision by far the cheapest and most effective way to control vandalism is high quality lighting.

Benefits of mixed use centres
Matters of accessibility and supervision are all germane to the trend to mixed use centres. A number of factors have converged to bring about this thoroughly

Mayfair in the Grove, Coconut Grove, Miami
This partly uncovered centre is open 24 hours. It abounds with plants, water features and ornaments which one would imagine are highly prone to vandalism.

Carlisle: Scotch Street by night

Housing in The Lanes, Carlisle
The two storey corridors leading to the 27 housing units are accessed by phone entry and are carefully managed by the centre management. They are very popular and so far the developer's nightmare of bath water seeping through his tenants' ceiling and flooding a shop has not materialised.

The Lanes, Carlisle
Plans showing how the 27 housing units fit over the shops on Scotch Street

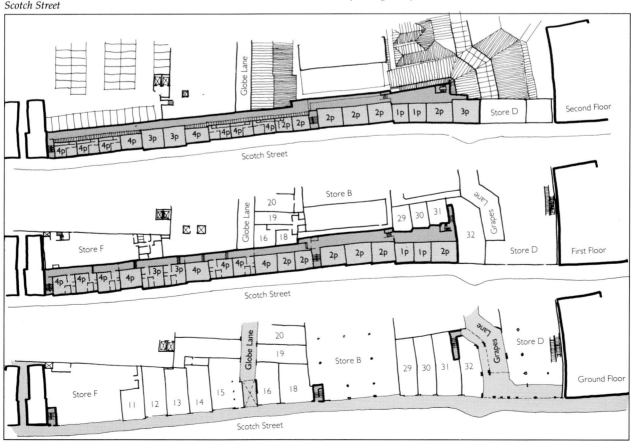

desirable state of affairs and they have their roots in the fact that over recent years the one form of building investment that has out-performed others through boom and slump has been the retail sector. Thus the retail market has been the generator of civic development and since the public sector has lately been severely constrained in the money it can spend, local authorities have been attracted to the idea of extracting 'planning gain' from developers who want to build in their community.

Many towns and cities have therefore switched tack and instead of focusing on money that the Government will not let them spend, they are demanding a range of desirable civic facilities. Many local authorities now care little whether any money changes hands at all and since there are enormous profits to be made out of well-placed developments, there is equity in the idea of spreading these profits to the benefit of the local community. Recent experience of the Leeds Kirkgate Centre is an example. As a condition of building 450,000 sq ft (42,000 sq metres) of shops, the developer is providing a new covered market, a new open market, 2000 car spaces, a new bus station and an infrastructure of roads and services for an adjacent site which will contain many more buildings of community value. Another development we are designing of almost equal area and value is providing nothing but a snooker hall. Both cannot be the best buy for a community.

The types of mixed use: all but housing
The list of uses other than shopping that are now being provided as part of the planning 'gain' is spectacular: theatres, churches, cinemas, car parking, offices, indoor sport of every kind, libraries, fire stations, civic markets and housing. Of that list only the last is seen by most developers as an almost impossible imposition.

The reason is simple: in their eyes all the usual legal and user problems are present but amplified out of all proportion. Housing is a disaster area for institutions largely because the subject is a political football. Founded on the concept that an Englishman's home is his castle and fuelled by the gross injustices of Rachmanism there is now the fatuous assumption in our legislation that the moment tenants, let alone lessees cross the threshold of the front door, the property is theirs to occupy no matter how unsuitable they prove to be.

The subject is difficult enough from a legal standpoint with flying leaseholds, rights of light, rights of access, responsibility for maintenance and so on without the

near impossibility of regaining possession for anything other than failure to pay rent or deliberate vandalism. If the developer wants to redevelop or restructure their property there is at present no means of regaining possession. Yet the developer has a lease for 125 years during which time they will want to undertake a series of fundamental changes to his investment. If sensible legislation could be introduced the architect and planner's dream of life, light and interest to the upper storeys of the scheme could be a reality, day and night.

Housing: a beneficial use
Two examples are relevant. At Ealing the brief stipulated housing but the local authority's ambition was thwarted by the Fund who became a member of the tripartite development consortium. They simply said there had long been a board decision against housing in their portfolio. The problem was overcome by setting aside a separate sector of the site for some 50 units and they were developed and funded separately from the main scheme. Though the accommodation is tiny, the location next to a first class shopping centre with car park, squash club, night club, library, offices and restaurants, has resulted in runaway sales. Selling prices have multiplied fivefold over the cost of building within a four year period. Funds do not turn away profits of that order without very good reason.

The other example is Carlisle where the local authority was the developer. Maisonettes and flats over the shops on Scotch Street were the only way of avoiding storage and cardboard boxes at first floor windows, plus the dereliction of an empty second floor, yet all concerned were clear that three storeys were needed to harmonise the scale of the street. We planned 27 units in a line over the shops and specified phone entry control to attractive landscaped galleries over the shops.

Funds were invited to tender on a predetermined plan and the package had to be accepted as a whole. There was some reluctance owing to the presence of the housing – indeed some chafing at the bit, but tenders were keen, and the project was funded.[10] Even in Carlisle the first turnovers in ownerships are showing very satisfactory increases in capital value.

Again management is the key. It costs money in high quality finishes and security and it is labour intensive, but bad management is at the heart of nearly every housing failure whether public or private. Some 20 years ago we designed two 19 storey tower blocks for the public sector. The local authority managed

Carillon Court housing, Ealing, London
This group of 30 flats and mansionettes was part of the competition brief for the Broadway Centre. Since the Fund would not deal with housing, they were developed by Laing Homes and, though best described as bijou, were selling for £130,000 in 1987.

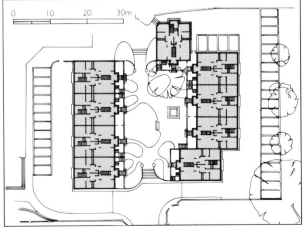

Carillon Court plan

them with monumental ineptitude and the blocks duly became ghettos. For years and to no avail we suggested a management solution based on concierge supervision that works so well in Europe but eventually they were sold for a pittance to a Liverpool builder. He totally refurbished them, instituted good control and management systems, put them on the market at reasonable (but profitable) prices, and sold the first tower of 117 flats in just under a month.

There is a huge market for bachelor business people, childless professionals and the elderly who would love to live right in the city centre with all its facilities at their feet with no need to worry about gardening, bus fares to work, or the expense of a car to get to town. Such living is not for young children, Weimaraners or other strenuous pets: their milieu is outer suburbia or the country.

There is no reason why in town living should not be an integral part of in town shopping, playing and working: ask the tenants of the Embarcadero Centre in San Francisco or thousands of apartment dwellers in Europe. Housing over shops (indeed over anything) needs its own secure entry giving access to private landscaped courts or internal hallways which are the responsibility of the centre management company and the standards should be as high as the shopping malls below. The housing units need pleasant or significant views over the general townscape or the public areas of the shopping centre. Gateway Commons in San Francisco and the housing at Queen's Quay Terminal in Toronto is exemplary.

Avoid overlooking car parks, service decks or roofs peppered with soil pipes and lightwells. If the developer is going to accept the idea of housing it is no use bringing the structure down through the middle of the malls or a shop, and if good quality buyers or tenants are going to be attracted to the scheme do not plan the sitting room balcony in the lee of the vent duct from Wendy's Hamburgers. It is no good pointing to the tower blocks over the Victoria Centre in Nottingham and throwing in the towel. They display a goodly proportion of the ways not to go about solving the problem. What is needed is the will to get the act together. The ingredients have been with us a long time; the recipe is simple.

How do all these current trends help the aim of open centres? Because they each have different patterns of life and movement and many of them demand access when the shops are closed. Unless separate and expensively contrived alternative ways are provided, the natural approach to these other facilities is down the malls. They are the 20th Century streets of our modern town centres. A decision to close The Lanes in Carlisle would be as daft as proposing to put gates at the entrance to The Shambles in York. The only difference between the two is that the property in the former is covered and in one ownership and the latter is not.

In parentheses, the prospect for housing as an integral part of central area developments has recently become much brighter. A newly mandated Tory government seems set on removing some of the legal anomalies which have resulted in the withdrawal of private landlords from rented housing. In the second half of 1988 developers, and even one or two institutions, are actually looking at the possibility of housing as one of the optional mixed uses. Architects now have a responsibility to make sure that layouts are suitable,

house types are carefully researched and, most important, they must remember that the developer is not in town to solve a housing problem. Housing, like the rest of the mixed use catalogue, will only be tolerated as long as it enhances (or at worst does not detract from) the prospect of growth for the investment or increases its sale value.

Shopping as 'theatre'
Now a few thoughts on the fashions and theories of the moment. First for in town centres. The current buzz word is 'theatre' and from this one gathers the notion that shopping should no longer be a grinding necessity but have a market-like atmosphere where people come not only to shop but to meet, talk or just spectate.There is a rather naive view peddled mainly in America that this 'theatre' or 'happening' concept is new. It was however central to the concept of the Greek agora, the Roman Forum, the bazaars of the east, and to all Medieval marketplaces. Acrobats, buskers, actors, preachers, troops of dancers, and bands of every description were the ephemeral but intrinsic appurtenances of the life blood retail activity. It was not discovered on Fisherman's Wharf in San Francisco or the new Covent Garden in London: we had just forgotten about it for over half a century. And very dull trading posts our centres had become.

The prime reason for the recent concept of the food court becoming an essential part of every big or medium sized centre is not people's craving for food but their passion for watching each other. Restaurants nearby can be half empty but the food court will be full. Partly it is a matter of convenience. Food and drink can be bought at a speed which barely causes customers to break step as they pass the counter. The kids can get burgers, mother can carry on slimming with lettuce and diced carrots, while Grandma can relive her Greek childhood with moussaka. All that is true, but the real attraction is watching the passing show: the parade in the mall, the splash of the fountains in the pool, the glass wall climbers gliding through the atrium, the ice skaters whirling round the rink, the gigantic aviary full of birds, the mannequins displaying their clothes, the band reminding us of another, bygone food court – the palm court and its orchestra.

BDP and Donaldsons designed one of the first new speciality centres in Britain at Waverley and the novelty of the idea took time to catch on. What took off from day one, however, was the food court. The units could have been let four times over. People sit gazing at the multiple levels, the thistle fountain, and the fashion shows in the pool; and such is the compulsion of the 'theatre' that even with chairs vacant people will take their pizzas to the pool edge and sit on the broad shallow steps just to be nearer the 'stage' and its action.

The value of water in the malls
Water is mentioned frequently in this chapter; in fact water and 'theatre' are inseparable. Water has a fascination which comes from its life-giving qualities. Since life cannot exist without it water has a basic, physiological attraction which is made irresistible by the ready way it can be turned into a decorative asset. One is forever dismayed by developers' reluctance to use water as a decorative element in shopping centres. The fountains of Rome make many a street crossing and corner a place to meet. Bernini designed most of them and he can take credit for enabling and encouraging more human dialogue than most men in history. When nature puts on a show of waterfalls or waterspouts,

Gateway Commons, San Francisco
Two storey housing over warehouse, shops and parking near the Embarcadero Centre. A village in the sky.

Waverley Market, Edinburgh
People sit by the water even when chairs are empty at the tables.

Trevi Fountain, Rome

they invariably become tourist attractions. Groups of people numbered in hundreds gather every 65 minutes to watch Old Faithful perform in Wyoming's Yellowstone Park – year in – year out: every show a perfect repetition of the last.

The problem with water, developers tell us, is maintenance and vandalism, and there is something (but not much) in what they say. The first problem could be eased greatly if architects would learn to detail pools and fountains so they do not leak into the basements below. Furthermore in Britain there is a dearth of competent fountain specialists who can both correctly specify for the effect required and give good technical advice on how to keep the machinery working properly. The two or three firms that do exist are so overworked that their after-care service is minimal and nothing is more abject than a stagnant, half-empty water feature. Pools the world over have been torn up, flagged or grassed simply because the technical professions were inadequate to solve problems which usually revolve around return outlet blockage and the burnt out pumps which result.

Vandalism or, more correctly in this case, petty nuisance is something that good management can correct. The usually quoted examples are the packet of detergent in the pool causing soap suds all over the mall, or the people who throw wrappings into the water which look unsightly then drift towards the return outlet and block it.

Do as Rome does ....
There seems to be an inbuilt assumption that while one should sweep, hoover and scrub the malls once or twice a day the pools should look after themselves. The Italians have a system. They just empty out and clean the scores of public fountains in Rome every Tuesday morning: it is all part of the street cleaning service. If the streets of a city can be dealt with like that it seems a small thing to ask that it be done in a covered mall which is constantly patrolled by security staff, closed circuit television monitors and maintenance people.

Dealing with vehicles
We have discussed 'front of house' trends; the malls, the new uses for centres and so on. We turn now to the working side; what to do with the motor car and how to deal with the lorries that bring goods to the centre and take trash away from it. The motor car is most poorly dealt with at present so here are some personal views about designing for it.

Many complain bitterly about the vehicle's bid to ruin everything that is fine not only about our cities but our countryside as well. Nevertheless surveys tell us, as if we had not guessed, that motorcars head the list of desired non-essential facilities, leaving holidays (number two) and the rest far behind. Our personalised mobile capsule is here to stay and palliatives like public transport and park and ride, disincentives like meter maids, double yellow lines, towing and clamping will never stop cars entering the cities unless they are completely pedestrianised. The motor car will be an essential design consideration for shopping centres whether in or out of town for the foreseeable future.

We need therefore to give more attention to ways in which the aesthetic constraints imposed by the car can be transferred to design inspiration. In the 50's architects and critics descended upon New Haven, Connecticut, to look at Paul Rudolf's new design for a town centre multi-storey car park which broke new

New Haven, Connecticut, USA
Multi-storey car park, richly modelled in in situ concrete, was prohibitively expensive and rapidly became dirty and forbidding.

ground in elevational expression. The rugged plastic forms of the in situ concrete frame offered an exciting alternative to the rigid orangebox appearance we had grown used to and since it served a department store we asked ourselves why we could not develop the idea for general use. Indeed, some of us had fantasies about extending the modelling to the richness of, say, the Casa Mila or the Guell Park structures by Gaudi in Barcelona. We soon discovered that what might do for Nieman Marcus was not at all what our clients had in mind. The cheapest way of erecting a car park was the only option developers were prepared to entertain, and even in the present climate of concern for the environment, planners and conservationists generally throw up their hands and despair of any decent solution.

Multi-storey car parks

Multi-storey car parks are perhaps the greatest unsolved architectural problem of the 20th century. They brood with arid lifelessness over thousands of towns and city centres. Developers realise that parking is essential to the shopper and in town there is no chance that they will be permitted by planners to develop surface car parks. Even if they were, the cost of land would prohibit it.

The only solution is to go high and with a requirement of one car space to between 250 and 350 sq ft (23 and 33 sq metres) of shopping and with a current minimum cost of £4000 per car space, the total figure is daunting. To spend £4m on a 1000 car parking facility that does not pay its way as an independent element is a big pill for developers to swallow, and with their general disinterest in the external elevations they are certain to be disenchanted by the architect's plea for high quality materials and subtle detailing. It is not much use arguing that for only another £50 per car space the

external elevation could be made decent when the developer is already making a loss. His aim is to keep the cost of parking for an average shopping trip as low as possible to encourage people to come, shop, then leave to make the space available for others. At least that was the aim until recently when the new wave of leisure shopping arrived with its emphasis on spending time in the multi-use complex.

Time was spent in the early days devising clever ways of arranging the parking decks and the access ramps, but designers were driven back inevitably to the cheapest arrangement where staggered trays 52ft 6ins (16m) wide (two 5m deep parking bays with a central 6m wide roadway) cannot be beaten. The staggered trays work well in section because the 32ft 10ins (10m) width of two adjacent bays of cars is just enough to allow a 1 in 7 ramp to rise 4ft 11ins (1.5m) onto the next tray of cars. That in turn means that the trays are 9ft 10ins (3m) floor to floor. With minimum clear heights of 7ft 6ins (2.3m) that leaves room for structure; just sufficient to permit a span of 52ft 6ins with no columns in any of the car parking bays.

The designer must then ensure that the trays are long enough to allow sufficient spaces for cars before the row is interrupted by a ramp. One occasionally sees car parks so short in length that the central parking bays are almost 50% devoted to up and down ramps – of which there must be at least four in a run (two up, two down). They must all move in the same direction because the 19ft 8ins (6m) wide circulation lanes can only take one way traffic. Theoretically there is no limit to the length of a parking tray but in practice it is curtailed by the site size, and this in our tightly-grained towns means that one runs out of site long before needing another set of circulation ramps.

Preston bus station

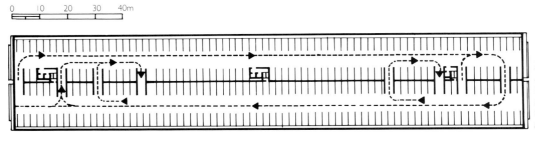

Preston bus station
A rare example of a town centre site being so long that the decks needed two sets of up and down ramps.

This excursion into statistics shows that the pursuit of minimalism produces an architectural straightjacket from which it is hard to escape. Designers find they cannot vary the floor to floor height, and the bay width on the elevations is usually governed by the width of the shop units below. These vary over time but the flavour of the month is 23ft 6ins (7.2m) so that inexorably governs the proportions of the horizontal black slits between columns. It is also worth noting that this scenario of physical constraints produces end elevations with staggered floors which are 4ft 11ins (1.5m) apart at the middle: at least architects can have a bit of fun devising some interesting 'knitting' where the floors meet. More often though, they are so enmeshed with the grinding poverty of the budget that they give up, slap a great blank wall over the whole elevation and propose a big illuminated logo announcing the scheme.

Sloping floors and spiral ramps
Sometimes a variant involving spiral ramps or even sloping floors is proposed. Americans often use the latter. They are cheap because the whole length of the car park can be used for cars with no need for individual ramps. These sloping plate floors however are death to any streetscape and in Britain planners have almost always told the developer to go away and think again. They are also very disorienting to the customer. Since the cars are on one continuous sloping floor it needs to be very extensive in plan to keep the incline small and make the sloped car parking as comfortable as possible. When re-entering the car park it is very important to use the same car deck entrance. Failure to do that will bring the shopper out in the wrong relationship to the parked car and the task of finding it can be frustrating for there is no clear definition of floor level. A colleague in Los Angeles describes the times he has seen ladies with tears streaming down their cheeks running frantically up and down identical floor slopes trying to find their vehicle.

Husbands have been known to be told to stay in the car and watch for the wife's return.

Spiral ramps also are not the easiest things to integrate; not least because they are so big. If one goes in for clever interlaced up and down ramps the overall diameter is much less but then the structure becomes much more expensive than the conventional up-and-down-in-one-plane type. There is no point in trying to cut costs by tightening the diameter beyond an overall dimension of about 100 feet (30m) because most shoppers do not like driving spiral ramps anyway. There is one in Lugano which rises eight floors. The up ramp at one end is not too bad because one is driving slowly looking for indicators for free spaces. The down ramp is another matter. It is very tight and one tends to let rip so that the car goes into a heady spiral and the experience is the nearest equivalent to a bobsleigh run; the Swiss love it.

Parking: the start of the shopping experience
However, restrictions on the cost of multi-storey car parks need not lead to despair. Developers and the design team ought to take the view that when a shopper elects to patronise a centre, the experience of its quality should start from the moment one enters the car park. At present we are a long way from this state of mind. The prevalent attitude is still that the automobile is an inevitable nuisance and nobody will ever sell anything in a car park. Therefore, runs the argument, make the building a cheap, utilitarian concrete bunker, stuff the cars into it as densely as possible and leave shoppers to make their hazardous way across lanes and down vehicle ramps. They run the gauntlet of drivers whose attention is concentrated on trying to grab a space that another chap has spotted or who are dashing to the cash barrier before their time is up – all in a gloom more appropriate to potholing than retail activity. Shoppers grope their way to mean, underlit stairs with never a touch of quality or grace

Blackburn Phase 2 car park

until finally a door is reached marked 'shopping mall'. This opens to reveal the glittery, eyecatching display that is the shopping event. That approach will no longer do.

In spite of protestations there is no truth in the developer assertion that they cannot afford better. There is ample profit in a well-located precinct for quality to be allocated to the multi-storey car park. What is needed is the will. Two specific thoughts lead to conviction about this.

First, standards of mall finish, lighting and special concepts have risen beyond the wildest dreams of those of us who started 25 years ago. The high quality of today's setting attracts quality retailers who sell high quality goods, which attracts high quality shoppers. The formula is both simple and effective and there is no reason why the equation should not be extended to include the car park. Furthermore the quality of the car itself is rising and the age of this highly disposable but very emotive asset is getting younger. The provision of excellent garaging facilities makes the shoppers feel special before they and their families even enter the mall. Such a feeling of well-being can only be good for trade: some smaller up market centres in the USA like the Rodeo Collection in Beverley Hills now have valet parking; it is even to be seen at the giant South Bay Galleria at Redondo Beach in Los Angeles; the ultimate in customer flattery.

There is therefore enough 'fat' in a good development to make quite possible the provision of a multi-storey car park which is excellently designed both outside and in. If this concept were taken seriously then further benefits to the urban fabric could accrue. At a time when flexibility, mobility and adaptability are a la mode for every kind of building from private houses to 'Big Bang' office blocks, multi-storey car parks are just about the only contemporary building type that

can be used for absolutely nothing but what they were designed for; storing cars.

There they stand, huge structures which cannot be adapted for human use because the floor to floor height is too cramped to allow air-conditioning in the deep space. Their long spans make cutting out floors for light wells well nigh impossible and the meagre provisions for vertical circulation is difficult to augment. The car park sits (quite rightly) adjacent to the shopping so the retail provision cannot be expanded in that direction. There are literally thousands of these monuments to constipation cluttering the towns and cities of Britain and the time has come to free them up. Local authorities could start the process by demanding floor to floor heights that would permit a variety of human use and the same high standards should be required of the elevations as for other buildings: different of course, but as carefully wrought as any other elevation.

Ways of improving the multi-storey car park
If such a lead were to be shown by the public sector it might deplete the developer's financial bid but it would release a competitive vying for quality in the car parks. For instance lighting standards (both qualitively and quantitively) should at least double. There should be an upgrading of stairs and lifts so that widths, speeds and finishes become compatible with the malls. Why should a shopper go from an £80,000 panoramic wall-climber in the shopping precinct to a slow-moving latrine in the car park?

All concrete walls and columns ought to be painted, (at the very least), brickwork should be of equivalent quality to the exterior and the graphics be bold, memorable and of high design standards. Common sense suggests a distinctive colour coding and why not a touch of humour to help us remember where we put the car? In the Hansafiertal Centre in Hamburg there are some delightful paintings of different fruits

The Lanes, Carlisle
Metal grilles to multi-storey car park.

Improving a multi-storey car park
Only a handful of designers have given thought to the humanisation of multi-storey car parks or to integrate them into the city fabric – and even fewer have found a client to try out their ideas. Here in Chesterfield is a pointer to much better things. Apart from the interesting design, the most important lesson is that the white painted metalwork is highly effective in masking the cars.

**Horton Plaza,
San Diego**
*The car park levels
are differentiated by
colour and by jolly
logos of various fruits.*

**Ealing Broadway
Centre, London**
*The roof of the multi-
storey car park.*

The Lanes, Carlisle
*The need to hide the
roof top cars from
higher land won the
day for these roofs
at The Lanes. In fact,
just as important and
relevant to every roof
level car park, is the
need to give customers
protection from the
elements.*

on doors, lifts and stairs and the idea is repeated even more boldly in the Horton Plaza in San Diego. 'I'm sure we parked on Pineapple, Daddy' – 'No, silly, that was last Saturday. Today you said you wanted me to park on Cherry'.

When we are released from the tyranny of 'autominima' and adopt a more relaxed long-life loose-fit mentality we can turn our attention to the possibility of designing for vehicular-pedestrian segregation. It is extraordinary how careful to the point of pedantry we can be in keeping cars from pedestrians in precincts and in the street byelaws governing pavement widths and so on. Yet we are prepared to take people from this level of concern into a 1000 car parking structure and mix all those vehicles with at least double that number of people with no attempt to plan for their safety. The only safe places in the whole building where you can take your eye off the cars are in the stairs and lifts – if you can find them. Shoppers should be able to walk from their cars to the malls along walkways quite separate from the carways and these could again be colour coded and differently lit (just like the one in Century City, Los Angeles.)

The fifth elevation: roofing the car park

Another aspect of multi-storey car park design which needs tackling forcefully is the top deck. There are five, not four, elevations to a building and if architecture is to be properly served they should each be carefully considered. Some designers have considered the vertical faces and we now need an attack on the roof. The answer is not necessarily to throw a roof over the whole car deck. The covering certainly hides the cars but its huge form is not likely to be in scale with the rest of the city, and the interior could be joyless.

Developers understandably take the view that if the requisite number of car spaces is provided they have discharged their responsibilities to the scheme. But two considerations still need attention. First, if the centre is built in a city of pitched roofs, whether small like the average industrial town or large like the buildings in a metropolis, any substantial structure with a plan of say 105ft x 260ft (32m x 80m) and a flat skyline is going to look out of place. If it is possible to overlook the top deck and its sea of cars either from another building or from higher land there is no hope of integrating the car park into the grain of the city.

Secondly, with the common method of leaving the top deck open, shoppers parking there are condemned to facing the elements. Whether it is pouring with rain, blowing a gale, snowing or sizzling in a heat wave, the top deck is the place to avoid and small wonder they are deserts of concrete while the lower floors are a log jam of cars manoeuvering in and out of every available space. The situation is particularly irrational when the car park covers the shopping, rather than being in a separate building. When they cover the footprint of the centre, the number of decks are likely to be few. A large centre could readily accommodate 1500 to 2000 cars on three decks and it seems quite unacceptable in both human and town planning terms to propose a flat open top and relegate one third of all carborne visitors to accommodation which is substantially worse than the remainder.

Clearly a covered roof deck adds to the development outlay but the cost can be mitigated. There is no need to take a roof envelope over the whole scheme – nor

is it desirable. If defined pedestrian access is planned between the rows of cars, and roofs are designed to span the cars and the pedestrian ways, then there is no need to roof the vehicular routes. Thus the roofed area is substantially reduced, and the structures become much more modest in size. If the car deck is deep in plan and the lower decks need mechanical smoke extract and sprinkler installation, then the partial roof cover of the top deck will obviate further provision because it is well ventilated.

We looked seriously at the problem of car park roofs at Ealing. The prevailing client concern for quality was favourable to seeking a solution and we built perimeter roofs of low pitch – so low indeed that they made little impact from the ground and they were covered in ribbed metal sheet. We did not win through with proposals to cover the centre parking bays but there is nothing to stop this being done in a future refurbishment.

The Ealing experience stood us in good stead at Carlisle. There the environmental considerations were even more sensitive. The local authority was the developer so it was easier to persuade them to take as great an interest in the exterior as the interior. Finally (and perhaps most important) we had the luck to be tendering Carlisle when rampant inflation had been curbed and a building slump had cut bids to the bone. In fact the full extent of the slated roofs and chunky timber trusses was only assured when tenders came in far below budget. The nature of the client made it easier to put over £1/2m of extra quality into the development whereas the instinctive reaction of a developer would have been to pocket the profit and show a better result to shareholders. Nevertheless we still have some way to go before the idea of making the car park the introduction to the quality of the centre is achieved.

Putting cars in the basement

The designer's ideal solution is left to the last not because it is so obvious but because it is expensive to achieve and therefore to justify. If we really want to produce high quality conditions in car stacks and at the same time solve at a stroke the problem of the elevations then the solution is to put them below ground. Now such a thought among developers threatens to induce apoplexy. Multi-storey car parks are expensive enough but to put them underground doubles the cost per car space: and the more difficult the ground with high water tables, random springs or solid rock, the worse it gets. Excavation, tanking, mechanical ventilation and smoke extract systems and sprinklers are all luxuries the client can do without especially when, by their location and nature, the costs have to be expended at the front end of the project. Millions of pounds must be spent before the rentable parts can even be started. The cash flow is unfavourable to say the least.

In a competitive bid no architect could persuade his client to go for underground parking: it would be suicide to the bid.[11]

Nevertheless, basement car parking is very civilised. The award winning Madrid Dos puts the cars below ground and it is very pleasant to descend from the baking heat of a Spanish August into the cool gloom, which is broken by splashes of bright light and colourful, witty graphics to indicate the entrances up to the shopping malls.

79

Madrid Dos
Basement car park. Witty graphics, high levels of lighting, good colour coding and clear signing all help to take the apprehension out of multi-storey car parking. The addition of pay and display further reduces theft and muggings because wardens constantly patrol the car park.

Madrid Dos
The only truly correct place for servicing is below ground – and the same goes for cars. When the ventilation can be handled naturally like this, everyone benefits.

Madrid Dos
Landscaping is arranged in horizontal trays over the service roads. In maturity the planting appears to cover the entire centre.

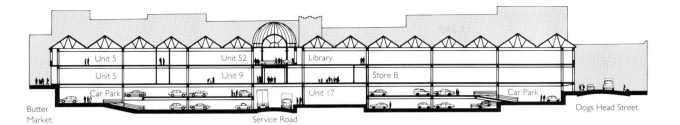

Buttermarket, Ipswich
A cross-section showing basement parking and servicing below the shopping levels. This leaves the roof free for forms which fit naturally into the medieval fabric of the town. It also allows for vertical expansion.

BDP is currently working on a 450 car basement design for the Buttermarket at Ipswich – a circumstance made possible by the client being the landowner and developer. No competition is involved and it affords a rare opportunity to put some of these ideas into practice with a client as dedicated as we are to the quality of the urban scene.

The American alternative: greening the city

To make British architects and planners green with envy some upmarket car parks in the USA put a concrete roof over the top deck of cars and then landscape it. This is a super way of treating the 'fifth elevation' and it brings back high quality open space, greenery and water to the town centre. Certainly it is a luxury and there are to date no built examples over shopping centres, but a glance at the accompanying photographs shows the potential for our cities.

Indeed, one of the first landscaped roofs to a shopping centre is proposed at Bournemouth where the client is supporting our view that the upper and lower gardens

should be continued right over the shopping centre and its car parks so that the town will have more greenery at its heart than ever before. It should be a trendsetter and take a step forward the need to announce the quality of the malls from within the car parks whether they be above or below ground. Some developers overseas are currently building quality into their car parks and British clients can now be taken to a number of very successful instances. An example is a further phase of South Coast Plaza called Crystal Court at Costa Mesa, California, which opened in 1986. There the mall quality – fountains, waterfalls, floor finishes and planting are taken below ground to beautifully finished and maintained car decks. The floor to ceiling height is generous, the bays are colour coded, the floor near the entrance is tiled, and there is a white painted metal suspended ceiling.

Charges for parking

There is yet another aspect of the doom-laden experience that the average urban shopper must endure: the car park charging arrangements. First

Los Colinas, Dallas
A three level car park completely roofed and landscaped. The elevations could perhaps only happen in Dallas, but does anyone truly prefer the standard British concrete egg crate to this?

Bournemouth
A central shopping scheme linking the commercial areas on both sides of the valley. The parkland through the town centre is taken over the top of the precinct.

**Crystal Court,
Costa Mesa**
Mall finishes, planting and water brought down into the basement car park. Note floor tiles and suspended ceiling.

let it be said that although multi-storey car parks are far more expensive than ground level parking there is no financial reason why there should be any charging system at all. One can safely ignore the developer's claim that he or she has to defray the cost of the facility if the entire scheme is to be viable. A number of local authorities make no charge and there is none for instance, at Brent Cross. That is probably the most successful centre in Britain and the decked car parking provision is currently being raised from 5000 to 8000. The only valid reason for making a charge is to deter the all-day office worker or the long-stay non shopper. So what is the most effective method?

Over the years most kinds of pricing mechanism has been tried and, if there is to be any charge at all, pay and display shows the most benefit. This is an arrangement whereby shoppers enter the car park and park wherever there is a free space. After parking they go to one of several machines and buy enough stickers to last the time purchased and the stickers are displayed on the car windscreen. When the shopping is done shoppers simply return to the car and leave. There is no queuing upon entry (unless the car park is full) and certainly no queuing on departure.

The starting point for this preference (as it is throughout this book) is the shopper: the ultimate client. What is their prime requirement and how can that be most reasonably achieved given all the circumstances? The ideal for the shopper is that it be free, but until the local authority is prepared to look upon car parking as at least a partial planning gain and take a proportional cut in premium and until the design itself is ample to cater for multi-purpose use with a basic presumption to overprovision, it is difficult to imagine why developers should voluntarily offer free facilities for people who are not patronising their investment.

Assuming that some money must change hands, the next step is to find the most convenient place for that transaction to take place. It is surely clear beyond question that the best place is at the parked car when the driver is free from stress and the family has safely set off for the shops. Any obligation to pick up evidence of entry time at the entrance and any requirement to mess about making money transactions at the point of departure is a formula for delay and distress.

To pick up a timed ticket at entry demands a minimum driving skill to reach for the proffered ticket (especially on a curved approach) or to get out of the car to do so. Mechanical failure of the dispensing machine causes frustration, queues and backing up onto the highway. To force shoppers to search about in their clothing to find a ticket or money or possibly both to feed a machine on the way out is positively sadistic. If you doubt this, stand unobtrusively near an exit machine and watch the faces of drivers approaching the barrier. And what about a friend of a colleague who found himself wedged under a lifted barrier with a stalled car in front and a line of cars behind? His Volvo finished up with a serrated roof as the bar dropped smartly down in four separate places as he frantically manoeuvered to get out.

Defenders of ticket machines at entrances and exits abound and protagonists continue to rehearse the arguments for them. Nevertheless it is beyond question that if one's concern is for shopper comfort and convenience and if one wishes to avoid queues at the entrance, and even more importantly queues at the exits, then pay and display is the correct answer. Some developers will say that shoppers will hurry out of the centre when they know their time is running out, so missing extra sales. Others will say that it is impossible to ticket cars that have overstayed their time because they have no legal right to do so. The answer to both points is to return to the basic contention that ideally there should be no charge at all. The prime purpose of providing a car park is to get people into the shopping centre. Furthermore what on earth is one trying to achieve by fining people who have stayed in the shops longer than they first estimated? One would not dream of doing that in an out of town centre. Why not take a liberal view of 'overstays'? only the all-day non-shopping parker is a candidate for censure: surely bone fide shoppers can stay as long as they want without threat?

In fact, the only real point at issue is the need to discourage the all-day office worker (though even office workers are very likely to buy something as they move through the centre). The best way to discourage office workers is to open the car park at 9.30 or 10 am. Many shops do not open until those hours whilst offices are all working by 9.00 am A personal preference

The Collection, Beverley Hills, California
High quality underground car park, with valet parking.

would be for a 10.30 am opening and a 7.00 pm close – and that would be the early nights. It seems extraordinarily perverse that the vast office working population should be condemned to going without lunch if they want to shop. If one can devise a situation where the overwhelming percentage of car park users are shoppers the problem is solved. Incidentally the legal point about ticketing is solved at Wakefield by an arrangement between developer and local authority whereby the former provides the labour to ticket the so-called offender and the local authority administers the fine under its statutory powers. The system has some merit in that the developer achieves his aim of keeping the long stayers on the move and the local authority get a bit more money for their grass cutting programme, but the real solution is to make the car parking free for shoppers and very inconvenient by both timing and layout for office workers.

The service lorry

A much more difficult problem to solve than dealing with passenger cars is the question of service lorries. They are much bigger in every dimension, they take acres of space to manoeuvre and they are noisy and very smelly. Some, like rubbish trucks, even smell by virtue of their pay load let alone from diesel fumes. Furthermore, their point of delivery and their point of rubbish removal is at the back or working part of the development. Only the highest standard of management can keep such areas clean and tidy. Service yards will never be RIBA award winners.

Basement service

Profit conscious developers will moan but there really is only one place for the service yard in a downtown scheme and that is below ground. It is an expensive solution because the excavation must be deep (ideally a 16ft 6ins (5m headroom) it must be artificially ventilated and sprinklered, and the access ramps to such a depth take a lot of room (the slope should be 1:12). But what are the alternatives? There are only two: ground level and rooftop.

Ground level service

Ground level is the lesser of the two evils and in some circumstances can be quite acceptable. The trouble is that if there is to be a high quality, lively street elevation

then lorries stopping and delivering to service doors are inimical to the objective. One has to get the lorries off the street and into a service yard which is far enough into the scheme to allow some development of shops on the street frontage. Such a solution presumes that cars are in a separate multi-storey car park, because if the cars cover the scheme then the yard will be covered, and though excavation has been saved one is back with the problem of ventilation, sprinklers and very large spans to give a column free space for manoeuvering. Whatever one does with the service arrangements the scale of opening off the street needs careful design to avoid the nasty 'missing tooth' syndrome.

We saw earlier how we tried to get it right at The Lanes in Carlisle where internal ground level service courtyards were located well inside the site, and we designed arched masonry screens within which were the hinged metal gates for night time security.

Some of the most recent downtown ground level service schemes in the USA offer a solution for which it would be hard to find acceptance in Britain. The developer brings the lorries in off the street, and turns the whole of the ground floor into service yard and storage with dreadful implications for the quality of the street elevations. Access to the shopping is then by ample, beautifully designed atria, again straight off the street and these are placed at either end of the development so that the whole service yard and storage area is sandwiched between them. Once inside shoppers are whisked upstairs to the shopping levels by banks of escalators and only minor traders are placed at ground level before coming to the vertical circulation. The presumption is that the real shopping experience starts at first (American second) floor level. At ground level the pavement is lined with great blank walls or lifeless, contrived display cases.

The disadvantage to its application in Britain is that few developers have yet recovered from some multilevel trading experiments in the 60's. They were all disastrous; with the Elephant & Castle scheme in London heading the list. Actually the reason is not difficult to find. It is all to do with location and pedestrian flow. Assuming that the centre is in the right place (Elephant & Castle was not) make sure

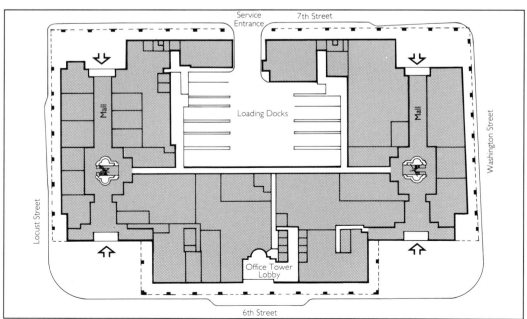

St Louis Centre, St Louis

that at least one of the places most people want to go is the top floor – then make it easy – indeed a thrilling spatial experience to find. That is how the Americans get people to climb 20 feet (6m) above the service yard before they find a single major shop. Alternatively build on a sloping site, bring people in from both levels and you have a multi-level scheme without people knowing how they came to be on the upper level. Preston's St George's Centre and Blackburn are perfect examples.

Historically, multi-level schemes built on flat sites have never traded well and it has been received wisdom for 25 years that multi-level trading only works in the Rows at Chester – and nobody could think why.

Over the years our trips to North America have suggested a reappraisal of objections to three and four storey trading (after all Chicago's Watertower Place trades on seven floors) and the new mammoth Bentall Centre at Kingston-upon-Thames will trade on four levels. That, however, is a long way from saying that there will be no trading at ground level and everyone must be raised 20 feet in the air before they find a shop. Doubters should go to St Louis and San Diego where multi-level trading is placed above the ground level service yards and where the centres attract perpetual crowds (though on a recent trip to St Louis the centre manager told us that they wished the service level had been put below ground).

Roof top servicing

But back to Britain. If ground level servicing has its problems, roof top servicing is virtually insoluble from a visual standpoint. There is no way a designer can integrate the massing and forms of a central area scheme into the fabric of a town of any sort (never mind a town of historic beauty) with 45 ft long, 15 ft high (14m long, 4.5m high) lorries running around its roof. The flat roof may be shielded by perimeter storage accommodation but the views from above will always be of huge service ways and the sheer visual difficulty of dealing with a ramp from ground to first floor level makes one blanch. And all this apart from the near impossibility of keeping the roof leak proof. Flat roofs are notorious at the best of times but when subject to the tearing and torque action of 10 tonne axle loads over the life of the building, then despair is the best way of describing the chances of success.

Service areas: economic design

Having recommended the most expensive solution as the best way of dealing with service vehicles, the designer has then a responsibility to minimise the costs. Much more could be done by close collaboration with the management agents, who are frequently called in only when all the basic decisions have been taken and it is much too late to make major alterations. The size of the basement service area could often be reduced. If one is going to excavate to the depths involved then it is essential to save every cubic metre of dig. Too often architects draw service basements as if they were ground level facilities simply lowered by 20 feet.

It is worth doing a painstaking survey of vehicle frequency and so avoid the cathedrals of empty space that are built. Whatever one does, the service basement is going to be nearly empty for 80% of the working day (quite apart from hours of closure) because deliveries are concentrated between 7.30 and 10.00 am each day. In fact centre managers spend more time trying to prevent fly parking by traders' private cars than they do managing and directing the inflow of service vehicles.

The Ealing service basement will serve as a good example. There we designed a splendid facility with a one-way road system and virtually 100% storage area to the shops above. In a recent check on an average day the 55 shops with a gross rental area of 350,000 sq ft (32,500 sq metres) were visited by 90 vehicles and 24 of those were to the Safeways supermarket. Depending on how you count the cost of development the Ealing basement could not have cost less than £6m nett and was arguably nearer double that when fees, finance and so on are added. The entire team from client to designer could have made considerable savings if the question had ever seriously come up for review. No one person or interest is to blame; it is a corporate matter. Once a month at least 25 people sat down to review progress and discuss policy and they represented every conceivable aspect of the development process. Nobody questioned the enormity of the service basement and the reason is not just inertia. It is to do with the terrific urge to get developments built once there is a planning permission and the money is secured. With interest charges rolling up, and fees being expended and inflation out of control (27% in 1973) it can seem irrelevant even to spend time discussing savings let alone altering all the documentation to implement them.

Nevertheless, it is the architects who have a grasp of the three-dimensional appearance of the plans and they should raise the first alarms and bring things like this to the whole team's notice. If architects in the development world are truly going to serve both their clients and the community they should remember that much quality on the elevations can be afforded for a fraction of the sum necessary to build a service basement.

Basement service roads too do not need to penetrate every corner of the scheme. Tenants will put up with trolleying their stocks quite a long way from the service points, so long as the retail pitch is exactly to their liking. That was a lesson learned at Waverley Market where lorry access to the basement was very restricted. Goods were distributed to all 70 traders via perimeter corridors on two levels and rents did not suffer by a penny a square foot due to the trolleying distances.

Excavation can also be saved by taking the letting agent's advice on whether there needs to be a 1:1 relationship between retail and storage space. If a 1:0.5 relationship will do then the savings could be substantial. As a guide it is safe to assume that on the best pitches the national multiples will want to be represented and that some of them, like electricals, will deal in bulk goods. These traders are likely to want a 1:1 cover and since nobody at the design stage has the slightest idea which traders will take space, it is best to assume 100% storage for the prime shopping pitches. The savings are best made in the remoter parts of the scheme where the rents are lower.

It is axiomatic that it is a waste of money to dig deeper than needed: the lorries are high enough as it is. Do not therefore waste money on badly laid out mechanical and electrical services. The heating and ventilation plant needs carefully locating so that the huge ducts supplying air to the scheme never cross a roadway. A two foot deep ventilation duct over a road means a two foot (600mm) deeper excavation; the lorries will stay the same height. The place for all the ducts is below the 1m high raised service dock (for extract) and above the service dock for the supply ducts and electrical services.

The clear height on the service dock need not be more than 8ft (2.5m) so there should be ample room for people, goods and all mechanical services well within the minimum height of 14ft 9ins (4.5m) clear for the service roads.

One or two practical tips; since no-one will want to spend a penny more on electric lighting than necessary in the service roads, the walls should be as light as possible for good reflection. Plaster is both expensive and impractical because it is easily marked and damaged. Brick is best so keep it light in colour; sand lime bricks will be hard to beat and they are cheap too. The red clays act like blotting paper as far as light is concerned. On the other hand sand lime bricks easily show dirt and are especially prone to black exhaust fumes. A golden rule is to use dark blue brick with black mortar joints to loading bay height and the junction between the dark and the light brick consolidated with a really chunky piece of dark stained softwood. A 8ins x 3ins (200mm x 80mm) section will do; loosely bolted to the wall. Its various lengths can be easily replaced when they get chewed up by badly

driven lorries that would otherwise make indelible scars on the basement walls.

Management is as important in the service areas as anywhere else and the axiom that litter attracts litter is nowhere better demonstrated. Whilst management must not tolerate waste materials on the service docks it is equally the designer's responsibility to allow adequate storage and especially to make sure that compactors are well distributed and of ample capacity. There is plenty of experience in the industry on the proper level of provision and there is no excuse for getting it wrong.

We were fortunate to have worked predominantly with a client who shared our view about the efficacy of basement servicing, and the benefits to the town in getting the noise, smell and visual intrusion of these behemoths below ground. In every case a highly profitable centre resulted. The argument that basement servicing as a principle is prohibitively expensive is nonsense. If there is a significant slope across the site, as we found at Blackburn and Rochdale, the excavation is

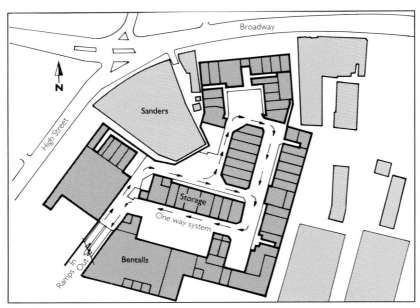

Ealing Broadway, London
– basement level
For long periods in each day the huge underground streets are deserted though the centre management vigorously champions the scheme as built.

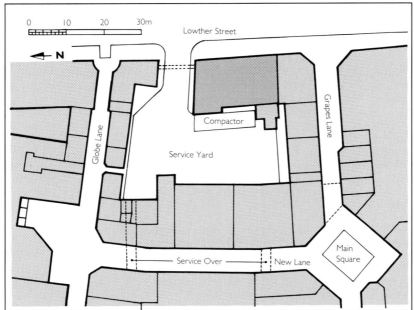

The Lanes, Carlisle
The ground level service yard is cheap and trolleys at ground and first floor level serve 25 shops (including C&A). If the scale of the scheme had justified basement service this ground floor area could have been let very profitably. The scheme is short of good standard units with a depth of 60 to 80 feet.

minimal, and in soft ground the removal of bulk waste can be achieved with remarkable speed. Rock or ground water can make basements uneconomic and it is self-evident that they are more expensive than ground level service yards but if the location is good then every square foot of area should be rent rich and devoted to selling. It can be a waste of money to give space to lorries cruising around service areas at street level. No city surveyor in his right mind is going to let developers serve the scheme straight off the street as they often do in Europe.

Only once were we forced aloft to roof top servicing and that was at the Hounds Hill Centre at Blackpool. There the site was tiny with no space to waste at ground level and one had to concede that it was hard to justify digging a 20 foot deep hole when we ran into sea water at bucket and spade depth.

Conclusions: The way ahead
So what are the main trends and how will shopping centre design develop to the end of the century? From the foregoing discussion it is clear that the industry

(for that is what it is) will operate in a milieu of rising standards and expectations of quality from the great body of the shopping public. This is good news for everyone because with higher quality should come higher profits, and profits are the flywheel to which the architectural context is geared.

The developer's emphasis will always be towards the malls, for that is where the retailer does business. Paradoxically therefore, not too much stress need be laid on the requirement to raise mall and shop front design standards. The pressure is already on in this area. Many of the best designers are already concentrating in this field and it can safely be left to look after itself. A personal preference therefore would be to highlight those elements which so far have not received much attention.

Chief of these is the question of mixed use centres. As developers get more and more involved in the provision of practically the whole spectrum of building types integrated in to their prime retail interest, their civic responsibility for the urban environment will

New Lane, Carlisle
Although vehicular access to the storage area of every shop is a great convenience to retailers, they will in fact trolley goods several hundred feet without materially affecting the level of prime area rents – provided the selling space itself is where they want it. At Carlisle goods are raised to first floor level, trolleyed across bridges and along corridors, then taken down to the shops. In almost every case rents exceeded predictions.

87

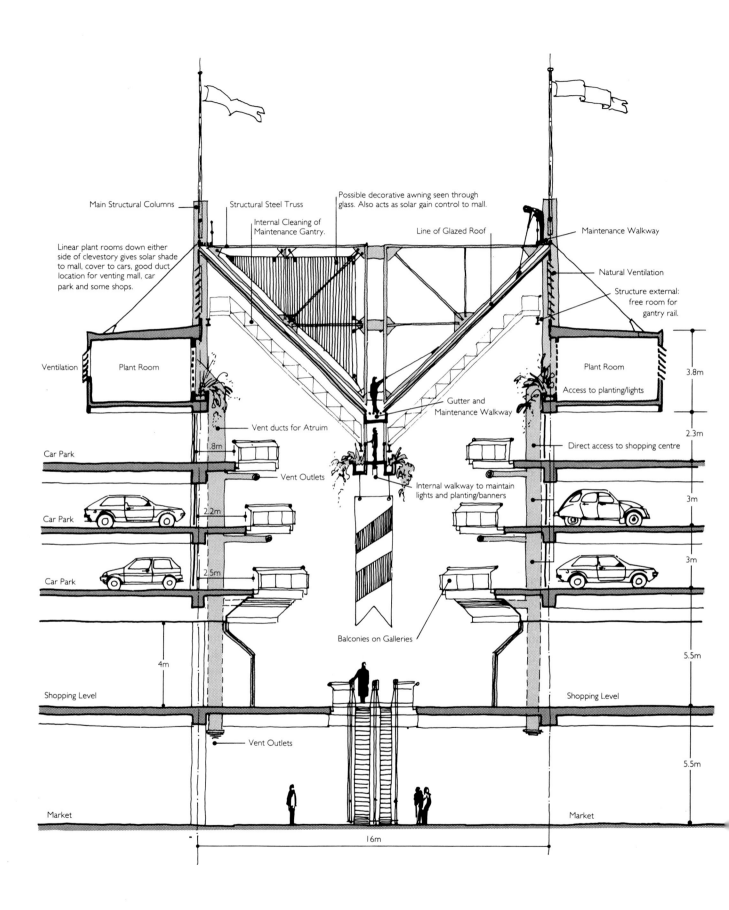

Main Structural Columns

Structural Steel Truss

Possible decorative awning seen through glass. Also acts as solar gain control to mall.

Internal Cleaning of Maintenance Gantry.

Line of Glazed Roof

Maintenance Walkway

Linear plant rooms down either side of clevestory gives solar shade to mall, cover to cars, good duct location for venting mall, car park and some shops.

Natural Ventilation

Structure external: free room for gantry rail.

Ventilation

Plant Room

Plant Room

Access to planting/lights

3.8m

2.3m

Vent ducts for Atruim

Gutter and Maintenance Walkway

Car Park

Direct access to shopping centre

.8m

Vent Outlets

Internal walkway to maintain lights and planting/banners

Car Park

2.2m

3m

Car Park

2.5m

3m

Balconies on Galleries

4m

5.5m

Shopping Level

Shopping Level

Vent Outlets

5.5m

Market

Market

16m

Proposed cross section through a hypothetical major mall showing how radical design thinking can help save maintenance problems and give a new dynamic to major spaces in retail (and other) malls.

increase. Ealing has already been cited as a town centre development rather than a shopping complex. Indeed of the seven different building types on the site the shopping provision and its storage does not come to 50% of the built form. Even more important, the visual impact of the retail component is virtually nil. The service element is underground and shops only appear at ground floor on High Street and The Broadway. The architectural character of Ealing Broadway is given by the offices, the library, the leisure complex, the multi-storey car park and the housing.

This trend means that the whole development team must take on a far deeper civic consciousness than has been the case heretofore. For architects the challenge is immense and worthy of our finest steel. Developers, in spite of themselves, are increasingly becoming responsible for the urban legacy they leave and for the pride (or otherwise) citizens feel for their town.

The 'comprehensive redevelopment' phase as at Blackburn may never return but the architectural impact of urban centre schemes will be profound and this has been demonstrated in the discussions on Ealing Broadway, The Lanes, Carlisle, Leeds Kirkgate and the Buttermarket at Ipswich.

Secondly, and as a corollary to the mixed use trend, will be the 'openness' of our retail centres to the townsfolk; either totally and 24 hours per day, or restricted use in special areas or for unsocial hours.

Thirdly, and again as a corollary of mixed use but

also of rising standards, will be the trend to high management standards. Sloppy, badly cleaned, litter strewn malls will simply fail.

The trend to shopping out of town is considered in the next chapter, so here it is sufficient to say that a town centre is the natural heart of a community and health demands that it be kept in prime condition. Furthermore the majority of British towns have a quality that makes each unique and frequently historically important.

Finite land resources and concern for our countryside is a further disincentive to mindless sprawl. Hence although a few megacentres can be anticipated, an overall retail drift to the suburbs and an abandonment of British (and indeed of European) towns as in the USA is not foreseen. Fourthly, the return to downtown living. Town centres need their quota of urban dwellers for they provide life, interest and a common sense of mutual supervision and security that Jane Jacobs so vividly describes in 'The Death and Life of Great American Cities'.

Fifthly, a determined effort is needed to come to grips with parking the motorcar in urban developments. The design of multi-storey car parks needs re-examination so that the shopping experience starts the moment one turns into the complex. Floor to floor heights, pedestrian movement, environmental standards, lighting, graphics, finishes, weather protection at roof level, elevational quality – and pricing structures (if any) must be reconsidered.

1. *In all but two or three cases it still is as far as the big units are concerned.*

2. *I too once held the view that I would be hanged rather than hand over the cream of the design opportunity to some other profession after sweating blood to produce a series of shapes and spaces for the overall concept. I now believe that there is real stimulus and satisfaction to be gained from working together with another skill that has an altogether different feel for materials, lighting concepts, techniques of joining components and a specialised training in the juxtaposition of colours, tones and textures.*

3. *To avoid this egocentric posturing BDP employs no fewer than fifteen different design professions. Thus, no matter what the job, it is simply credited to the firm and individuals' contributions are recognised by name as seems relevant: it is a supreme benefit of a non-titular style for the firm.*

4. *We were not to know he would never be asked to do another: or if he has it's a state secret.*

5. *But only up to the point of calculating the rent. This is done on an area basis and suddenly square millimetres become an issue.*

6. *Sketches make the point clearer but if the point remains obscure don't lose sleep – I will struggle on alone.*

7. *One day a client is going to give a designer his head along these lines and something stunning will be built. I hope it's me.*

8. *I sat under his tuition for six months at MIT and he got us to make a four foot deep floor of corrugated cardboard tetrahedrons coated with resin. He said it would span 60 feet square and support a Sherman tank. When it got to 20 feet square it had already deflected four feet under its own weight because we could not solve the the problem of movement at the hundreds of joints, so we threw it in the Charles River. The mathematics were impeccable.*

9. *Institutions take the most conservative view of any new fangled idea. Whereas an American mogul might say 'that's neat', 'let's try it', the British fund will say 'that's new, what's wrong with it?' In gloomier moments I have described them as 'anti-panglossian in extremis'.*

10. *Even at Carlisle the Fund refused to pay for the housing though was obliged to accept the houses over shops. The Council therefore paid for the actual house construction, sustained a relatively small loss compared with the selling price, and took a lower share of profit on the scheme as a whole to ensure that no money changed hands.*

11. *Only once in my career did a competition brief from a local authority of a historic city state unequivocally that the car parking must be underground to preserve the scale and richness of the townscape. One competitor correctly judged that, as it is said of everyman, councils too have their price. The team took the risk of defying the brief and they put the cars above the shops and predictably put in a bid that made the others look foolish. They were awarded the contract.*

5

SHOPPING OUT OF TOWN

Mobility the enabler

Concern for a finite countryside

Balancing the claims of town and country

Natural out of town traders

What about the megacentres?

Development will occur where the location is right – in or out of town

Cities as natural organisms

Positive and negative aspects: an American example

5

SHOPPING OUT OF TOWN

Mobility the enabler

The phenomenon of the out of town shopping centre, the out of town business park, leisure centre, university or any other human activity is singular to our age. The reason is simple and a consequence of the invention of the internal combustion engine. Unprecedented personal mobility is one of the most notable contributions of science to the 20th century and it has transformed the environment of the western world to a degree that was unimaginable as recently as the early years of one's father's lifetime.

In the USA, where land seemed limitless and the towns already established were a mindless jumble, it seemed sensible to head out of town, look for some unspoiled land, create a new suburban utopia, and build a new shopping centre to serve it. As we noted in the Introduction the idea took root so strongly that about 28,500 such suburban centres were built and the towns were the losers. In Britain where practically all 600 centres were built in or near the heart of communities, the combined blessing of our strict planning framework, the finiteness of land resources and the high quality of many of our historic cities constrained the flight to suburbia.

Concern for a finite countryside

There is a good deal of concern for the safety of our countryside because it is under threat from many quarters. In the context of shopping it is the giant out of town complex with American style single-storey sprawl and vast tarmacadamed car park that is under the spotlight as we wait to see what a laissez-faire administration will allow. Admittedly the government has protested that it values our meadows, hillsides and green belts, and repeats the axiom that their aim is not to stop development but to make sure it happens in the right place.

Conversely steps are afoot to release thousands of acres of unused or badly utilised agricultural land for development and the constant reference to letting market forces prevail sends shivers down those who have watched market forces at work in many places all over the capitalist world. So what would represent a balanced view of the conflicting opinions?

Balancing the claims of town and country

Firstly every town and city has its own 'scalar rhythm'. Each community of any historical status has attained a size in which it is possible to judge how any new building proposal will affect the urban form. Thus, to be extreme, it would be impossible to put a 150,000 sq ft (14,000 sq metres) Debenhams department store in the middle of Melton Mowbray or Skipton without upsetting the scale and rhythm of the two and three storey buildings on the 20 foot wide plots lining the high street.

The extreme size of a department store has been chosen to make a point. It is extreme however only because neither the economy nor the catchment area of Melton Mowbray or Skipton could attract and support one. What is far more likely is that a superstore of some 30/50,000 sq ft (3,000\5,000 sq metres) with its attendant car parking could seek a site in the town or (more attractively from the operator's point of view) on the edge of town where the land and building costs are far cheaper.

What does a planning officer recommend? Risk wrecking the scale of the town by insisting that the

Inmos Factory, Newport
If out of town shopping is inevitable why should it not be housed in exciting buildings like this rather than tin sheds that planners require to be masked by trees.

Architect: Richard Rogers.

Inmos Factory, Newport
Architect: Richard Rogers.

W H Smith 'Do it All', Preston
Architect: Building Design Partnership.

superstore builds in town or risk injuring the precious countryside by letting it be built out of town?

Carlisle Council faced this problem when they received an application to build a 60,000 sq ft (5,500 sq metre) superstore out of town at the A69 M6 junction in 1980. They took the view that the application should be resisted because they were about to start their own development on 5 acres (2 hectares) right in the heart of the city. As cities go, Carlisle is small with a population of 70,000 but BDP and Donaldsons were retained to see whether an in-town centre with some 250,000 sq ft (23,000 sq metres) of new shopping, including a 50,000 sq ft (4,500 sq metre) supermarket and two 35,000 sq ft (3,250 sq metre) variety stores, could be grafted onto its historic fabric.

At the Inquiry the inspector agreed with Carlisle and supported the refusal on the grounds that the newly reconstructed centre should be allowed to develop its own trading pattern within the community. Once that had been achieved the way could be open to renewed applications for out of town large space users because it was agreed by the planning officer that the urban fabric could not stand the imposition of another huge trading shed in its very heart. The task of designing even one large space user in the city centre was difficult but the new complex was built and it has been well received by both public and traders. More recently the supermarket fraternity has concluded that there is still potential for growth in the Carlisle shopping catchment area, and out of town applications have re-emerged. Asda with 80,000 sq ft (7,500 sq metres) has been built three miles (4.8km) north of the town and further applications have been lodged with the planning office. It will be fascinating to see how the city centre continues to trade and especially to watch the effect of the out of town stores on the inner city Fine Fare superstore.

Natural out of town traders
So far, only one part of the phenomenon has been discussed – the single supermarket. But there are other types of trade which can claim with even greater justification to be more appropriately sited out of the

town centre. White goods, (fridges and cookers) the furniture emporia, and the DIYs can all claim that not only do their turnover and margins prohibit an in town pitch, but the size and nature of their goods are inappropriate to a quality shopping centre in the heart of town.

You do not need to go as far as the USA to see the result. Practically every town in France and in the Swiss valleys sports its ribbon of industrial sheds in a never-never land twixt town and country. The choice has been made: many a sleepy town centre in Languedoc has been preserved but the fields and woodlands have been pushed further from the townsfolk.

The decision is surely right, and even more so in direct proportion to the quality of the town. That is the crucial factor. If civilisation is going to be a continuum then not only must the best buildings of the past be preserved but the new buildings which are built around them, as derelict and second rate buildings are replaced, must be in scale. An 80,000 sq ft supermarket with its 500 car parking garage cannot possibly live agreeably with a row of Queen Anne shops, an early Victorian pub, a mediaeval covered market hall and a 15th century perpendicular windowed church: at least, not with equal architectural prominence in the main street.

If all such large elements are put behind the street frontage as at Carlisle then the rupture in the scale of the town fabric can be masked, but it still leaves the problem of sheer size unresolved. And even if it were one still questions whether it is right to put a DIY and a furniture emporium in a tightly planned town centre when heavy transport is needed to carry the goods to the store and take them away again when they have been sold.

What about the megacentres?
There remains the issue which is confronting many of our biggest cities: the out of town retail centre of giant proportions. They cover scores of acres, accommodate thousands of cars, provide up to and beyond 1,000,000 sq ft (93,000 sq metres) of shopping and offer all-day

Asda superstore, Carlisle

***Serfontana Centre,
Lugano, Switzerland***
Edge of town retail strip.

Tesco, Llanelli

*These two
photographs
demonstrate the
impossibility of
juxtaposing huge
building blocks with
small buildings of
a bygone age. The
banality in Llanelli is
not made acceptable in
Peterborough by better
quality bricks and up-
market roof cladding.
The alien window slots
add insult to injury.
If new buildings
adjoining the old ones
cannot be broken down
in scale or be buried in
the heart of the new
development, then in
towns of architectural
or historic quality they
should be banished to
edge of town – or a
green field site where
they can be built
much cheaper.*

***Queensgate,
Peterborough***

*St Louis Centre,
St Louis*
*If the return to
downtown is going to
succeed in civic and
environmental terms
we must do a lot better
than this. The super
glazed entrances get
all the publicity but
the reality for St Louis
as a city centre is this
bleak metal panelled
goliath.*

Horton Plaza, San Diego
*Shopping and life return to downtown. Perfect climate and Pacific
breezes mean the centre can be left uncovered. A riot of colour and
comic forms lend novelty and attraction. It will be interesting to
see whether it has the permanence that good city centre building
really needs.*

Westside Pavilion, Westwood
*Not downtown in the sense of central Los Angeles, but as central as
one can get in the amorphous suburbs in which it is set.*

enticements for every member of the family with leisure
add-ons from multi-cinemas to waterparks. In 1987
many of our largest cities had at least four proposals
for megacentres on their outskirts. Countrywide about
40 proposals lay on the Minister's desk (for he quite
rightly decided to 'call in' any application for an out
of town retail consent larger than 250,000 sq ft (23,000
sq metres)). One, at Gateshead, has already been built.

Concern for the impact on the environment has been
so acute that in a major speech William Waldegrave,
a Minister of State for the Department of the
Environment, has seen fit to tell the nation that
the Government and his department are alive to
the danger. He has assured us that he is aware that
both the countryside and trade in existing towns
could be destroyed if planning applications were
to go unchecked. He has been told of the concern that
just when the Americans have concluded that two
decades of out of town development have ruined

their city centres we seem about to go down the same
destructive route.

Some of us have been at pains to point out that since
1984 nearly every state of the art centre that British
designers go to study in North America is in-town: The
St Louis Centre, Horton Plaza (San Diego), Westside
Pavilion (Los Angeles), South Bay Galleria (Redondo
Beach), Stamford Plaza (Connecticut) – and, of course,
the much praised speciality centres in Boston, New
York, Baltimore, New Orleans, St Louis and San
Francisco. The glamourous out of town new centres
at Edmonton and Dallas are now the exception rather
than the rule.

Nevertheless nobody but a dyed-in-the-wool
environmentalist seriously believes that all out of
town megacentres should be resisted and there are
several reasons why some are inevitable and why the
Gateshead Metrocentre was not just aberration.

Metrocentre, Gateshead

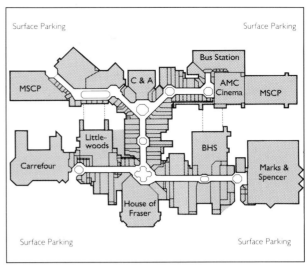

Metrocentre, Gateshead
A vast complex comprising 2.2m sq ft of retail
and leisure with 10,000 cars

Metrocentre, Gateshead

The Point, Milton Keynes
The leisure complex: the ten cinema units are behind this large
structure.

Some traders are actually better located out of town than in, and though they do not form the raison d'etre for a megacentre, they become important ingredients of the trading mix.

Furthermore with the new focus on leisure with shopping and the trend to include waterparks, free form ice rinks and huge multi-cinema units like The Point at Milton Keynes there is an added incompatibility between their size and inward looking orientation, and the small scale outwardly expressed function of unit shops, churches, markets, pubs and houses that go to make a town centre. None of the leisure structures listed need fenestration to illumine their activities, and daylight and sun is positively inimical to cinemas and ice rinks. Multi-screen cinemas work best in substantial numbers of units. Ten auditoria were built at Milton Keynes and AMC's only regret is that they did not build 14. That is a huge windowless hulk, 20 feet (6m) high, with a 'footprint' of over 50,000

sq ft (4,600 sq metres). How does an architect put that down in Windsor without wrecking the place?

More importantly, however, it is clear historically that whenever the great trade routes for the passage of people and goods have crossed or come to a resting place, man has naturally established a trading post. The silk route, the spice route, the pilgrim routes, the military routes have all been the genesis of cities like Istanbul, Venice, Leon, Lyons and dozens more.

We in Britain have now practically completed a huge programme of motorway construction and these roads constitute the first completely new system of transportation since the railways were built. The railways rarely sponsored new trading locations because their prime purpose was to link established settlements. Similarly, the canals which preceded them were built to transport goods cheaply from one industrial town to another.

Motorways, however, not only pass similarly through virgin countryside to get from A to B, but people and goods pass along them in infinitely flexible mobile containers which can stop and start where they please. There is no constraint, as on the railways, to stop only where there are stations to deal with people or at goods yards where there are facilities to handle raw materials or products.

As night follows day therefore, there will be tremendous pressure to build trading centres where motorways cross or terminate. Some are already established: Brent Cross at the foot of the M1, Aztec West and Retail 2000 at the junction of the M4 and M5 are two examples. We will all have views about the way they have been done. Brent Cross for instance will in time get a major face lift but even now, set in its surrealist rabbit warren of roads and awful office buildings it is doing no worse than compound the acretia in which it sits. On the other hand one can only be saddened by the loss of hundreds of acres of soft rolling Gloucestershire farmland at the end of the M4. If megacentres are inevitable we must do better than this.

Whilst ARC's application at Wraysbury on the M4 may not be one of those eventually selected, that degree of unity, breadth of thinking and control of massing is the right approach. The radials out of London must cross the new M25 ring and it should therefore occasion no surprise that at nearly every crossing there is currently a proposal for a megacentre. No purpose can be served by a Canute-like protest that none should be permitted. The pressure over time will be irresistible and the success of the few already established will encourage expansion of those that have proven track record. The developers at Brent Cross, the first and still the largest European centre (before the Metrocentre was opened in 1986), have plans to double its size. What we in Britain must do, therefore, is react positively to the proposals and recognise that the bewildering array of out of town development proposals are in fact a sign of national economic health.

We must set up mechanisms that channel the desire to invest in megacentres that are firstly in the best strategic locations for trade, secondly are not in areas of outstanding natural beauty, and thirdly are not (without the most compelling reasons) in a Green Belt. They must prove as conclusively as we have the statistical techniques to demonstrate, that they will not seriously impair the trade of the settlements in close proximity.

Development will occur where the location is right – in or out of town

One need have no compunction about refusing applications that do not measure up to these criteria. There is no excuse for strangling a city like Boston, USA for twenty years even if one does give it the kiss of life just before it expires. Investment in retail shopping is as certain a profit maker as exists in the entrepreneural field. Throughout the recession of the late 70's and early 80's it was the only development sector to prosper. As long as the location was good, success was assured. Now that we are in an expansion mode and confidence is high developers and funds will go where the opportunities are.

Although we might wish it otherwise, it is no part of the development fraternity's mandate, as they see it, to have a care for the countryside, the historic town, or for the economic health of a community other than the degree to which those aspects affect their own development prospects. The funds have vast sums of money to invest and whilst in public they may protest otherwise, the reality is that if the bottom line predicts the right percentage return they will build. There is nothing amoral in this. The overall responsibility for balance in society lies with the component parts of society itself. Checks and balances must ensure that no one aspect runs amok.

If conservation is sometimes a tourniquet to the life blood of a town, it can alternatively also be a saviour. Local and central government is also often presented as the agent of asphyxia but in towns like Carlisle, Ealing and Ipswich their positive influence led to good planning solutions. Architects have to be monitored as much as anyone and, on the evidence of the last 25 years, the more cerebral, vociferous or egocentric they are, the more they have to be watched.

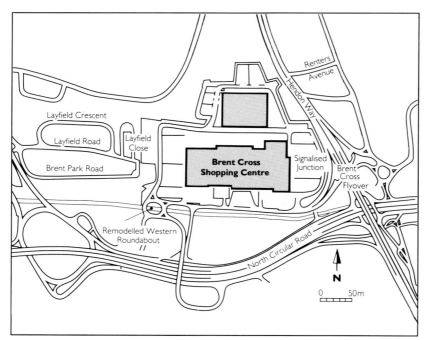

Brent Cross
Plan of roads complex.

Equally, if developers are told firmly that they cannot build in a sylvan glade near a motorway junction, they will happily turn their attention to the town centre because retailers show no sign whatsoever of wanting to leave them. They like to be at the heart of things. Why should they not want to be at the confluence of bus routes or the railway station and be near the central library, the municipal buildings, the main post office, the concert hall, the cathedral, and the historic buildings that attract the tourist? And why should the national multiples like Marks & Spencer want to endanger let alone abandon the billions of pounds worth of investment they have in the high streets of Britain?

Cities as natural organisms

A city centre is a complete functional organism and its natural proclivity ought to be to self-sustaining health: the parallel with our body is striking. Outside influences can be either beneficial, or without discernible effect, or deleterious. Government's responsibility is to ensure that the impact of out of town retail conglomerates fall into the first two categories. In the long term there is no conceivable benefit to society in the latter. The clamour for special attention from any source must be questioned and balance remains the most precious commodity.

So far in Britain we have done fairly well in striking the right economic equation. There is no evidence to suggest that Brent Cross has laid waste to Hendon, Hampstead and Neasdon as was widely predicted at the Public Inquiry. If some new and some existing retail locations within a five mile (8 kilometres) radius of Brent Cross have not done as well in the last few years as they might have hoped, that could as easily be because they are poorly designed or are ripe for refurbishment. Moreover if Brent Cross does undertake a major expansion and a thorough restyling of its external image and existing malls, it will exacerbate the deficiencies of these surrounding suburban centres. This should perturb no-one because competition is the spice of life and the spur to upgrading.

It is too early to judge the permanent impact of the Gateshead Metrocentre on Newcastle. The effect on

Gateshead itself is likely to be significant. The centre there is unloved and the strip shopping must be highly vulnerable. Newcastle, however, is a regional city of great economic importance and civic dignity. It is the home of Eldon Square, one of the most significant shopping centre achievements of the last decade and a serious negative impact would be regrettable. Early indications for the health of the city centre shopping are encouraging. The drop in retail spending in Newcastle has so far been quoted as 'minimal' but it is difficult to know whether retailers in Newcastle are whistling past the graveyard, or whether (as some would have us believe) Metrocentre is not trading as well as expected. A further possibility is that the marked increase in economic activity and in the standard of living has enlarged the shopping pool for retailers to fish.

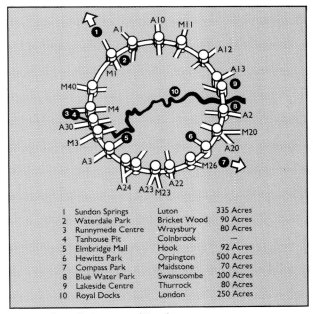

1	Sundon Springs	Luton	335 Acres
2	Waterdale Park	Bricket Wood	90 Acres
3	Runnymede Centre	Wraysbury	80 Acres
4	Tanhouse Pit	Colnbrook	—
5	Elmbridge Mall	Hook	92 Acres
6	Hewitts Park	Orpington	500 Acres
7	Compass Park	Maidstone	70 Acres
8	Blue Water Park	Swanscombe	200 Acres
9	Lakeside Centre	Thurrock	80 Acres
10	Royal Docks	London	250 Acres

Proposed retail ring around London
If they were all built there would be an extra 10m sq ft of shopping.

ARC's proposed centre at Wraysbury on the M4 round London

Prestonwood, Dallas

Valleyview, Dallas

The Galleria, Dallas

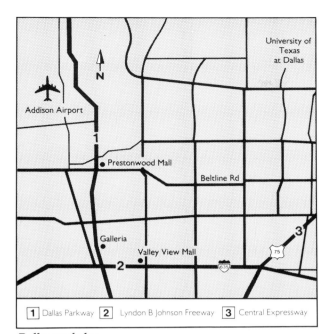

Dallas road plan

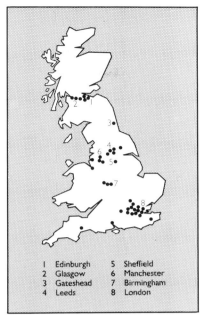

Proposed out of town regional centres in Britain, 1988
A location map was compiled by Hillier Parker of 40 proposals. Most would compete with each other and seriously affect trade in nearby cities. About a quarter of this number however would be beneficial and relieve pressure in city centres.

1	Edinburgh	5	Sheffield
2	Glasgow	6	Manchester
3	Gateshead	7	Birmingham
4	Leeds	8	London

Positive and negative aspects: an American example

Prophets of doom consistently underestimate the flywheeling effect of peace and prosperity. This is nowhere better demonstrated than in the USA and in the heart of capitalist prosperity itself; Dallas. Some years ago developers could see that the affluent were moving to the north and building new homes along Beltline Road – just beyond the Lyndon B Johnson Freeway. So they followed the throng and built 1,250,000 sq ft (116,000 sq metres) of shopping and put at its heart one of the early ice rinks. It was called Prestonwood Mall. Affluence begat affluence and within a few years a competitor called Valleyview Mall was built two miles (3.2 kilometres) to the south right alongside the Freeway. Again the formula worked and so a further centre, Dallas Galleria, was built only 400 yards (350m) to the west of Valleyview with even greater exposure to the Freeway and it, like Prestonwood, chose to have an ice rink at its heart. Predictably the new Galleria hurt Valleyview but, undaunted, the latter refurbished its malls, persuaded Bloomingdales (one of America's best up-market department store chains) to open a store and the centre is again trading excellently. Prestonwood too was hurt by the Galleria ice rink but they fought back, converted their rink to enable ice hockey to be played (impossible at the Galleria) and again the centre has recovered.

It is relevant to add that this amazing retail activity has taken place at a time of great business trauma in Dallas due to the fall in the price of its staple industry – oil. In 1988, 38% of all office space in Dallas was vacant.

The point of recounting this little saga is that here we have three shopping centres built within a few hundred yards of each other and none is less than 1,250,000 sq ft (116,000 sq metres). In other words the smallest is bigger than Gateshead's Metrocentre and, apart from the ice, none of them has the huge leisure ingredient that is seen to be so vital at Gateshead. Location, location, location...

The salutary side of the story is that Dallas has many other malls – and all are well away from the city centre. The retail dilution is complete: downtown is a morgue.

To sum up, when all the factors are taken into account, there will be irrefutable evidence to justify the building of about a dozen Metrocentres in Britain. Where? Well, motorway location and population must be the clue and that suggests one on the Glasgow, Edinburgh axis, another outside Leeds, and at Sheffield, and in the West Country, one or two round both Manchester and Birmingham, say three round the M25 and, of course, Gateshead. None of those, properly located and controlled, would contribute to the death of the cities on which they feed. Indeed, by the addition of large scale leisure and related facilities which could not be located in the adjacent cities without injuring the urban fabric, they could be a positive bonus to the quality of life of the people in that area. They could be a spur to the constant quality upgrading of the retail precincts in the city centres themselves and of the urban spaces and facilities which will bring people back in even greater numbers to city centre living.

6

DEVELOPERS, PLANNERS AND THE ENVIRONMENT LOBBY

The current state of play

The architect's dilemma

A wind of change

The pendulum of power

Architect/planner relationships

The role of environmentalists

The problems for conservationists

The Victorian Society's dilemma

A recent example: Leeds Kirkgate Market

The value of public participation

And a postscript

6

DEVELOPERS, PLANNERS AND THE ENVIRONMENT LOBBY

The current state of play

The very mention of planners and organisations like the Victorian Society within the average developer's hearing is to risk provoking epilepsy. Rather than being seen as people with a statutorily approved care for the environment many developers have them down in a book marked 'opposition to progress' and they see the whole debate as one founded on confrontation.

So comprehensive is the lack of understanding between the two sides that the developer's scorn of planners and environmentalists is fully reciprocated and many in the latter group put developers at the top of their list marked 'vandals'. It is into the middle of this confrontation that the architect is thrust.

Architects are actually forced into a state of schizophrenia by the debate. On the one hand they see themselves as sensitive people who come into the profession because they want to design the best buildings possible and they spend seven years at university learning the process. They are taught that buildings must be seen in a context – both urban and rural – and the more intense of their kind can be seen wandering round the streets of Nimes, Florence and Bath or the sylvan glades of Chatsworth, Osterley and the Tivoli Gardens with sketchbook well-thumbed and Olympus cocked. A sizeable number of architectural students come to realise during these formative years that whilst they have no great talent to create buildings themselves they want passionately to contribute to the environment and so join planning offices or become professionally involved in one of the many environmental groups.

On the other hand, architects working in the development world find themselves employed by people who have a vision of restructuring the commercial heart of a town for financial gain. The jobs are huge, complex and on the face of it they give a designer a heaven sent opportunity to put all he has learnt into practice. He or she quickly perceives, however, that the client has never been to Rheims (other than a fleeting visit to the Roman caves to sample the Taittinger '67) and that visits to Wentworth have been to play golf rather than to study the ground modelling and tree planting techniques of Capability Brown. At project meetings the conversation is full of gratuitous homilies such as 'if this job doesn't tick there is no scheme', 'the bottom line simply isn't good enough' and 'special bricks are very nice but they are damned expensive and I can't sell goods off the external walls'.

The architect's dilemma

At this point the great majority of architects either throw a tantrum and resign or become so disenchanted that they lose the will to carry on: either way they are lost to the debate. Of the remainder they fall into two camps.

The first sees exactly what the developer is driving at, sympathises and designs layouts tailored to the commercial point of view. That group of architects used to be highly regarded by developers and they were employed regularly during the years 1955 to 1970. The current reaction against what they achieved is what this chapter is about.

The second group also sees what the developer wants but sees also the wider context. This (quite small) band of architects is doing a high wire act and is desperate to avoid the tag that they are running with the hare and hunting with the hounds. In fact, of course, that is exactly what they are doing and they daily run the risk either of being banned from the setts of the former or of being torn to shreds by the latter.

A wind of change

The situation is, however, not so desperate as it may seem, for the last two years have seen a refreshing wind of change blowing through the boardrooms of the biggest and best developers. Put simply it is that they have perceived that the public want something better at the heart of their communities than huge, characterless boxes and that, as the standard of living rises, people are demanding and willing to pay for quality.

An earlier chapter analysed what went wrong in the '60s and '70s so here it is sufficient to recall that planners are now mandated to demand a care for the townscape as a comprehensive tapestry. Where once their political masters told them not to scare away the proposed covered mall or the cutprice supermarket, there are now votes in quality and no politician is prepared to defend his or her seat on a reputation of condemnation from the Royal Fine Arts Commission. Twenty years ago he or she could not have told you what the initials stood for.

The pendulum of power

The planning fraternity are now, therefore, flexing their muscles and enjoying a period of influence the like of which they have not enjoyed since the years immediately following the 1947 Planning Act. It is particularly sad that a recent president of the RIBA spent the majority of his term berating planners and what he saw as their 'interference'. No one however who has spent time in both a borough and a county planning office can have other but sympathy for a planner's point of view. The incompetent rubbish, both technically and aesthetically, which pours daily into a planning office has to be seen to be believed. Most days in the planning control department were spent either in hysterics or in despondency trying to decide how to reply to the majority of applications. And the sad fact is that most of the drawings came from fully qualified members of the Royal Institute of British Architects. One should have nothing to do with proposals to

Fusio, Ticino, Italy

Tesserette, Ticino, Italy

Norwich Cathedral, England

Sintra, Portugal

El Escorial, Spain

These sketches made randomly over a number of years, in the heart of communities great and small, tell one consistent story. The sheer size of a building relative to its context is irrelevant providing that its mass is broken down to a scale compatible with the overall grain of the community. Even a relatively banal and repetitious elevation such as the Escorial is acceptable so long as the main building mass is enlivened. While a windowless department store would be ruinous to the urban scene in Sintra, any of the Gothic churches would be a bonus.

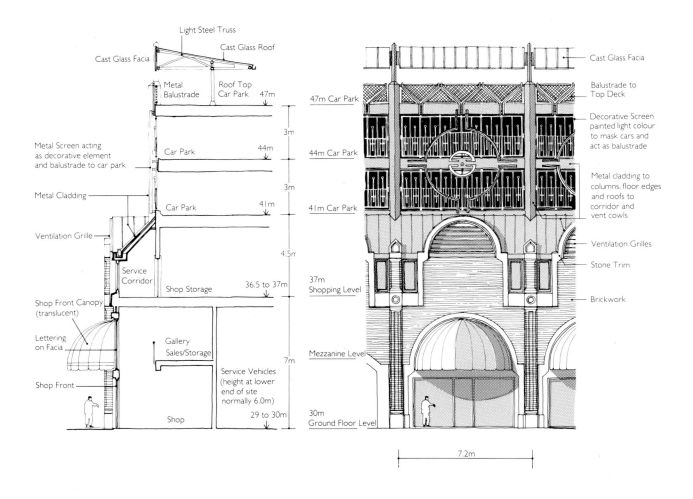

Labels (left diagram):
Light Steel Truss
Cast Glass Roof
Cast Glass Facia
Metal Balustrade
Roof Top Car Park 47m
47m Car Park
3m
Metal Screen acting as decorative element and balustrade to car park
Car Park 44m
44m Car Park
3m
Metal Cladding
Car Park 41m
41m Car Park
4.5m
Ventilation Grille
Service Corridor
Shop Storage
36.5 to 37m
37m Shopping Level
Shop Front Canopy (translucent)
Gallery Sales/Storage
Lettering on Facia
7m
Mezzanine Level
Service Vehicles (height at lower end of site normally 6.0m)
Shop Front
Shop
29 to 30m
30m Ground Floor Level

Labels (right diagram):
Cast Glass Facia
Balustrade to Top Deck
Decorative Screen painted light colour to mask cars and act as balustrade
Metal cladding to columns, floor edges and roofs to corridor and vent cowls
Ventilation Grilles
Stone Trim
Brickwork
7.2m

Kirkgate Centre, Leeds
Section showing the functions behind the elevations. Shops facing the street were requested by planners to ensure commercial vitality.

Kirkgate Centre, Leeds
Elevation of one bay showing how functional requirements were solved on the street facade.

exonerate qualified architects from the need to obtain planning permission. The evidence is that many architects need close monitoring and those who do not have little to fear.

Architect/planner relationships
Architects do though, have grounds for apprehension if they are trying to break new ground aesthetically. They can only hope that the ground rules for productive dialogue will be observed and the first of these is that there should be mutual respect. The planning officer has to remember that the subject of aesthetics is highly subjective and that hopefully he or she is dealing with a creative artist who is also a professional with a client to satisfy and a living to make. The starting point for constructive criticism should be an understanding of what the designer is trying to do, and then making a judgement on the evidence before him as to whether the building is likely to fit into the overall strategy for the community. So long as planners stick to this approach they are on solid ground because their duty to make sure council policy is not violated and their role as advisers to members on quality is being discharged. They must grasp the fact that they are not there to hold the pencil: that is the designer's job. They must also be

on their guard against falling prey to the fantasy that their new found influence confers aesthetic infallibility – an especially tendentious trap in these days of stylistic plurality. The verdict of history will fall with equal severity on planners who rode pet hobbyhorses and architects who peddled zany notions that have little to do with their art.

For their part architects must realise that the planning officer is employed by elected members. They in turn depend for their position on the goodwill of the public and particularly the pressure groups that make up the more vocal sectors of the townsfolk. When therefore planning officers say 'I do not think my members will approve of that ', they are at best accurately reflecting public opinion and unless the architect (and the client) wants to test their disagreement at a Public Inquiry they would be wise to reconsider.

What is sometimes obvious however (and here one cannot but agree with the Past President) is that the planning officers are parading their own views under the shelter of reference to the planning committee. It is particularly tedious to spend hours and many meetings arguing about the depth of re-entrant angles, the

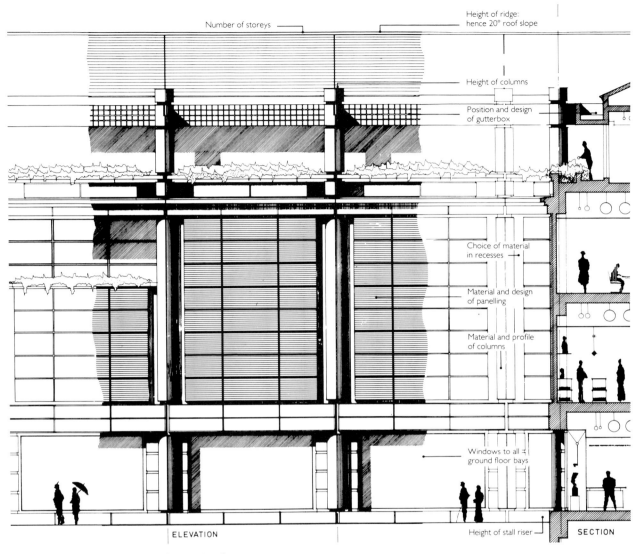

Number of storeys

Height of ridge: hence 20° roof slope

Height of columns

Position and design of gutterbox

Choice of material in recesses

Material and design of panelling

Material and profile of columns

Windows to all ground floor bays

Height of stall riser

ELEVATION

SECTION

Bentall Centre, Kingston-upon-Thames, London
Details which were challenged by the planning department.

projection of a cornice or the profile of a string course. It is all a delicate balance between the planner's tendency to impose his or her subjective prejudices (under threat of recommending a refusal) and a talented architect's desire to create something new, radical and tailored to the client's needs. Whilst much of this is relevant to any type of building it is particularly apposite to shopping centre approvals because time is money. The developers do not want their architects spending hours arguing about the depth of a shadow whilst they are champing at the bit for a planning approval which will provide the key to signing up a Fund, the job starting on site and the prospect of profit becoming a reality.

It is for reasons of haste, bred of the financial imperative, that developer architects seldom draw planners' attention to the Department of the Environment Circular 31/85. This is a specific instruction to technical officers to avoid the subjective ground of aesthetics. Many officers act as if it did not exist and many private architects have never heard of it, let alone read it.

The Circular is worthy of wider knowledge of its message, so here is a verbatim quote of its principal paragraphs, 19, 20 and 21:

19. Planning authorities should recognise that aesthetics is an extremely subjective matter. They should not therefore impose their tastes on developers simply because they believe them to be superior. Developers should not be compelled to conform to the fashion of the moment at the expense of individuality, originality or traditional styles. Nor should they be asked to adopt designs which are unpopular with their customers or clients.

20. Nevertheless control of external appearance can be important especially for instance in environmentally sensitive areas such as national parks, areas of outstanding natural beauty, conservation areas and areas where the quality of environment is of a particularly high standard. Local planning authorities should reject obviously poor designs which are out of scale or character with their surroundings. They should confine concern to those aspects of design which are significant for the aesthetic quality of the area. Only exceptionally should they control design details if the sensitive character of the area or the particular building justifies it. Even where such detailed control is exercised it should not be over fastidious in such matters as, for example, the precise shade of colour of bricks. They

should be closely guided in such matters by their professionally qualified advisers. This is especially important where a building has been designed by an architect for a particular site. Design guides may have a useful role to play provided they are used as guidance and not as detailed rules.

21. Control of external appearance should only be exercised where there is a fully justified reason for doing so. If local planning authorities take proper account of this policy there should be fewer instances of protracted negotiations over the design of projects and a reduction in the number of appeals to the Secretaries of State on matters of design. When such appeals are made the Secretaries of State will be very much guided by the policy advice set out in this circular in determining them.

The role of environmentalists

The first thing to be said about the environment lobby is that the only reason for its existence is the desecration of what was left of our cities after the War. Developers and designers who rail against 'the preservationists' have only themselves to blame. If society had applauded the results of the fashion for comprehensive demolition and rebuilding to the dictat of Modernist visionaries there would be no conservation movement, this chapter would not be necessary and one could have saved a life subscription to the Victorian Society. As in all important matters, however, the most difficult state to achieve is balance. Anyone who has tried wire walking or even riding a bicycle can testify that the whole matter revolves round a continual weight correction to avoid falling off. Balance is a dynamic state – one can never stand still.

Euston Arch, London
Demolished in mid-1960's.

Euston railway station and forecourt
Built on the Euston Arch site.

For about 20 years after 1945, under the banner of building a better Britain, the nation chased a target of 300,000 new houses a year and comprehensive central area redevelopment. The public went along with the technologies and the philosophies which would speed the achievement. Then dawned the realisation of what was happening as the new centres of Plymouth, Birmingham, Liverpool and London were revealed to public gaze. Concern boiled over into outrage as developers sought not only to rebuild bomb shattered sites but to tear down buildings which were a good deal more characterful than the proposed replacement. The senseless demolition of Euston Arch was the watershed and out of its tragic rubble the Victorian Society was reinvigorated.

Now we have the classic pendulum syndrome and we are out of balance again at the opposite end of its swing for there is no doubt that environmentalists have a dilemma on their hands. To their credit must go the fact that they stopped the massacre and the nation owes them a debt. Many of us are supportive and a soft touch for an appeal to save any quality building from the demolition man.

The problems for conservationists

The concern is that many preservationists appear not to know there is a dilemma and that the extremes of their stance are inimical to the progress and the health of communities. We now have people who are opposed to the demolition of anything that is old on the false assumption that it must be good. In fact much that was built – especially in the boom years of the industrial revolution – was junk and should be recognised as such by people of aesthetic sensibility. We are in danger of arriving at the 21st century with our towns (especially our northern towns) museums of mediocrity from which new building is banned on the grounds that nothing built before 1900 can be demolished – whether or not it has economic viability or aesthetic merit.

But the problem is even deeper. We are all sympathetic to the preservation concept behind the idea of 'listed

Durham Cathedral
Clearly to be preserved as long as men have breath.

Falcon Street,
Ipswich
These listed buildings on the other hand are both decrepit and of very modest architectural quality. Their single merit is that they are old. If such buildings are to be preserved in perpetuity our towns will ossify.

buildings' but no one has grappled with the problem of for how long and under what conditions should a building be listed: 50 years? 100 years? 250 years? or, like presumably Durham Cathedral, for as long as we can prop it up. Granted there is a review procedure implicit in an application for what is euphemistically called 'Listed Building Consent' (which actually means permission to knock one down rather than consent to preserve it) but it is never argued that a building should be preserved until some better building more in keeping with society's needs is proposed.

And there lies the crux of the problem. The crisis of confidence in contemporary architecture is so great that a substantial, influential and highly vocal section of society is saying 'Until you come up with something we like we shall be highly critical of any new buildings and we will fight to the death to keep what we have.' Understandable as this view is, it is untenable as a formula for progress. Fortunately the solution, as we have seen, lies in the public's hands. The concerted thrust for quality and the demand for a return to humanity in all the arts is well within the capabilities of the best designers. What the environmentalists must do to make a positive contribution to the process is to develop a far higher standard of critical appraisal not only of new architectural directions but of the historic buildings they were formed to defend.

The Victorian Society's dilemma
This advice is directed especially at the Victorian Society because they have the most acute problem. It lies in the fact firstly that their period is the one when historically the most building was done and the new industrial might of the nation spawned buildings by the million. Secondly, in the nineteenth century standards of aesthetic taste were at their lowest ebb since the dawn of the Renaissance in Britain, so that a high percentage of the work produced was quite awful. Thirdly, since the Victorian age is closest to us it follows that compared with earlier periods, a greater proportion of their buildings still stand.

If, therefore, the Victorian Society do not do a better job of discrimination between the good, the bad and the ugly, they will lose credibility and that would be a tragedy for them, for architects and for society generally.

A recent example: Leeds Kirkgate Market
In Leeds in 1985 a major developer made a proposal for a new scheme to be centred on the old Kirkgate Market Site. The Edwardian market hall designed by Leeming and Leeming is one of the most magnificent structures in Britain and extends in an easterly direction by a series of much lower timber-framed structures which date from 1875. In 1975 a fire destroyed much of the timber structure and the Council erected a lightweight temporary steel framed building to house the market. The remainder of the site was occupied by an open market of squalid appearance and a bus station which is open to the elements apart from glass sided, concrete framed bus stands. Immediately east of this 12 acre (4.9 hectare) conglomerate is Quarry Hill – a 21 acre (8.5 hectare) windswept parcel of land awaiting a user since the demolition of the famous Quarry Hill apartments (beloved of schools of architecture as the pioneer home of the much vaunted Garché system of waste disposal).

Over recent years Leeds City Council received many proposals to redevelop the Kirkgate market site but all foundered on economic grounds. At last a developer came forward with a package that was unique. The developer would place 450,000 sq ft (42,000 sq metres) of new shopping on the site with parking for 2000 cars. In return he would build a new market to replace what was left of the old timber structure and the temporary sheds; lay out a completely new open market with modern toilet, storage and service facilities; replace a decrepit pub with a new one; build a new covered bus station for both national and local buses; incorporate a multi-screen cinema complex and build a children's fantasy world. He would also lay out an infrastructure of roads and services and ground level parking for a further 1000 cars on the Quarry Hill site which not only

Leeds Kirkgate Market site
This Victorian pub of modest aesthetic pretensions on the street side and abject dereliction at the back was held to be of irreplaceable importance by conservationists.

gave bridge access to the car park over the shopping (thereby relieving local roads of vehicular congestion from the new car park) but it also brought into viability the construction on the Quarry Hill site of a new theatre, an exhibition hall, an hotel, offices and a retail/light industry complex.

Apart from the demolition of the sheds already referred to, the development proposed the demolition of the Victorian pub and two blocks of three-storey Victorian buildings lining the southern boundary of the development.

This detail makes the point that in community terms the exchange was the planning gain versus three Victorian buildings – two of which had derelict upper floors.

The vituperative opposition of the Victorian Society to the entire development is well documented, so suffice it to say that their campaign quite missed the real points at issue. They failed to balance what was being lost against what was being gained and in their total condemnation they ignored the architectural problem inherent in the Brief. This centred round the client wanting to maximise his profit not only to attract

Leeds Kirkgate Market
A splendid confection by Leeming and Leeming in 1904.

Westminster buildings adjacent to Leeds Kirkgate Market
This 'spot listed' building will now be integrated into the market scheme.

Kirkgate Centre, Leeds
A study model to explore the possibilities of designing an entrance into the new market complex.

a Fund, but to pay for the extraordinary amount of planning gain. The struggle to achieve the necessary financial balance led inexorably to a 'form follows function' solution with perimeter ground floor servicing to the market and the shops, above which were rear service corridors to the shops and three layers of car parking above that.

It would have been immensely helpful to have had a constructive dialogue towards a design that gave a viable result to the developer, yet broke the building down into lateral blocks which respected the scale of Leeds and worked vertically to enrich the detailing to a standard commensurate with the noble warehouses and commercial buildings with which the city is well

endowed. By concentrating their attack on the need to preserve a quite ordinary pub, a set of sub-standard timber and temporary steel sheds and a row of three-storey semi-derelict offices the Society demeaned its reputation.

The story has a fascinating postscript. Just before detailed planning drawings were submitted the Victorian Society applied for and was granted a Spot Listing of one of the two three-storey office blocks which means in effect that it is now protected under the Listed Building provisions. The Society labours under the illusion that it has won an important victory in that we have now incorporated both buildings into the overall scheme.

We did, however, on many occasions in the design process debate with the planning officers whether to keep or to demolish these buildings. We weighed two things in the balance. First whether we were capable of designing buildings for this frontage which were as good as the Victorian elevations with their fine (but neither outstanding nor unique) brick detailing and elegant window proportions. We believe we are and so did the planning officers. Second, whether new buildings would be a better economic buy than a conversion and whether an equally viable use could be found for refurbished offices compared with new tailormade commercial premises fully integrated into the new precinct. This produced a negative answer and it remains negative.

Upon being told of the Spot Listing we simply took out the studies we had already done and worked them into the planning submission drawings. It is unlikely that anyone will trouble to work out the degree to which some aspect of the total scheme is financially (and therefore qualitively) the poorer for this decision and it is safe to assume that the Victorian Society does not care.

The value of public participation
There are two final points to be made about dealing with the public either through statutory bodies or independent societies. First, top-class designers have nothing to fear and everything to gain by dialogue with people who are authorised to voice an opinion and genuinely interested in central area development. They stand to learn a lot about their aspirations for the town and the cards are so heavily stacked against arrogant intruders, be they designers, developers or agents that the game of trying to ride roughshod over people is not worth a candle. To the overbearing or even insulting

public participant the point has eventually to be put that whilst the architect is prepared to hear what needs to be said and bear all mens censure, the designer in the end has the job of distilling all that is relevant or helpful and of producing a design.

To the planning officers who try too consistently to play the architect one may have to remind them of the limits of both their power and their skill (a fairly ticklish job at the best of times). The planner's skill is quite different from that of the architect and whilst one would shun advice to be rude, a colleague used to be very effective in these situations. When he had tried every permutation with a planner and got nowhere he would push a piece of clean white paper and a pencil across the desk and say 'There, that's what I started with, now you have a go'.

And a postscript.
The second point should strike fear and apprehension into every architect's heart. Planners present a broad back to much criticism concerning the poor standard of design they allow through their net. That may be so but it is worth recalling that the present generation of senior planning officers in charge of departments were trained at a time when it was fashionable to take planning as a postgraduate degree after architecture. Indeed 45% annually came into planning by that route in the 50's and 60's. In 1985 that percentage had dropped to 5% annually. Hence by the end of the century planning and environmental policy is likely to be set by men and women whose first degree is statistics, geography, sociology or economics and who quite simply do not speak the same language as architects. So the news for architects is; if you think there is a communication problem now – just wait.

7

STATE OF THE ART IN NORTH AMERICA

List of shopping centres visited and described

UNITED STATES OF AMERICA

Boston	Copley Place Faneuil Hall Various others	Dallas	The Galleria Prestonwood Valleyview Los Colinas Various Others
Connecticut	Stamford Mall		
New York City	South Street Seaport Trump Tower	Chicago	Water Tower Place
		Minneapolis	The IDS Centre
Philadelphia	The Gallery on Market Street East	Denver	The Tabor Centre
Washington DC	Georgetown Mall Various others	San Diego	Horton Plaza
Baltimore	Columbia New Town Harbourplace The Gallery	La Jolla	University Towne Centre
		San Francisco	Ghiradelli Square The Cannery Pier 39 San Mateo Fashion Mall
Miami	Mayfair in the Grove The Falls Bayside	Los Angeles	Redondo Beach: South Bay Galleria Westwood: Westside Pavilion Newport Beach: Crystal Court, Fashion Island Costa Mesa: South Coast Plaza Santa Monica: Santa Monica Place
New Orleans	Riverwalk Jackson Brewery The Esplanade		
St Louis	St Louis Centre St Louis Station Various others	Beverley Hills	The Beverley Centre Rodeo Drive: The Collection
Houston	The Galleria: Phase 3		

CANADA

Various

7

STATE OF THE ART IN NORTH AMERICA

Various aspects of shopping centres in North America have been referred to to make a particular point in the text and it is now opportune to highlight some of the best of the current crop – that is up to 1988.

As a general point no developer, agent or designer can be said to be up to date and aware of the latest trends until at least one visit to North America has been made. The concept of the shopping mall was born in the USA in the 50's and in spite of flurries of excitement with new malls around Paris and some delightful galleries in Germany, the Americans have forged ahead with newer and newer ideas over the ensuing three decades.

Waves of British developers went across the Atlantic in the 60's and they learnt invaluable lessons. Their interest was exclusively in the interiors and they therefore ignored a vital difference between the American and the British condition. Simply put, it is that almost all American centres were built out of town, surrounded by scores of acres of surface car park, and made no attempt to contribute to the built environment. Conversely Britain developed almost exclusively in town centres and had therefore to stack the cars to save land. The effect on the urban fabric was profound but until very recently was never addressed.

This section must therefore start with a negative point. North America has little to teach Europe about the external quality or the contextual awareness that is needed when building in towns and cities. That is what American designers come to Europe to discover. It is true that in the last 10 years Americans have done some sensitive refurbishments but only very recently has the problem of urban context been tackled.

That said, there are some quite thrilling interiors and it is odd that some of the best have the most banal exteriors. One wonders how designers of such obvious talent could be so unaware of what they were doing to the city.

The only excuse can be that they have such an entrenched tradition of building malls out of town that when required suddenly to build in town they were quite unprepared for the challenge of the exterior. For therein lies a significant point which is worth reiterating: Americans have realised that cities cannot be left to die and are now developing almost exclusively in town.

The following is personalised to the extent that it is restricted to those seen by the author. There are undoubtedly more worth visiting; nevertheless if one were to study all those noted here one would be very adequately appraised of the latest developments in America. The notes are kept concise and we start in the East and work our way over to the West coast.

Copley Place, Boston This is one of the most up-market centres in the USA. It is a large development in the heart of the city and is responsible for the regeneration of a derelict area adjacent to the business district. The architects are the famous The Architects Collaborative (TAC), not noted for retail work, and this is evident in their freshness of approach. Their inexperience shows in matters such as over-generous mall widths, but the high quality finishes and detailing indicate their pedigree. There is a not very successful water and sculpture feature at the centre of the scheme but on the first floor in the side mall, a beautifully detailed restaurant court with a Japanese flavour and first-class landscaping is an object lesson. Two huge new hotels form part of the scheme. The exterior is very disappointing for such well known designers.

Faneuil Hall, Boston The doyen of speciality centres and responsible not only for regenerating Boston's wasted waterfront but for inspiring dozens of other cities to do the same all over the world. Faneuil Hall itself is only the most famous building on the site. It is the adjacent Quincy Market which is the conversion and the three parallel granite-faced warehouses are required study for any student of retail architecture. Now some 15 years old it is well documented in most books on shopping centres. It ensured for Rouse, the developer, and Ben Thompson, the architect, a permanent place in the annals of urban regeneration.

Various, Boston If time permits, a walk along Boston's waterfront will reveal the regeneration of old warehouses into offices, retail workshops, restaurants and leisure activities.

West of Boston is Chestnut Hill with a classic straight mall and a well designed space frame roof which uses cheerful yellows and russet colours to lend warmth and intimacy particularly in the snowbound winters.

Pickering Wharf, north of Boston is now complete as a carefully detailed speciality centre in the New England clapboarded vernacular which is entirely appropriate to its coastal and suburban setting.

Stamford Mall, Connecticut A deceptively simple plan which becomes a rich multi-levelled interior full of exciting angled views from escalators set at 45 degrees to the mall's axis. Nine levels of car parking wrap round four trading levels (with disastrous impact on the elevations) and the centre space has a stepped and dark blue carpeted amphitheatre in which shoppers and children can relax. Stamford Mall is in the heart of a coastal town some 60 miles north of New York and is a good example not only of the USA's return to downtown but of the fact that, properly anchored and with good pedestrian flows from the car parking, shopping centres can trade on many levels.

Copley Place, Boston
Top lit food court at first floor level.

Faneuil Hall, Boston
The glazed side wings extend the restricted depth in Quincy Market.

South Street Seaport, New York City Opened in 1985 the Rouse/Thompson team again regenerated a waterfront slum – this time on East River at Fulton Street on the southern tip of Manhattan. The Fulton Market building was refurbished as a three-level food emporium containing fast food, good restaurants, and a food market. The surrounding old brick buildings were also refurbished and the flywheel effect on the upgrading of property in the area continues. A tricky problem was created by the elevated Franklin Delano Roosevelt Highway separating Fulton Market from the river. Undeterred, the space under the road was paved and people drawn by views of tall ships to a water's edge speciality centre known as Pier 17. A three storey steel frame and metal clad shed, it contrasts markedly with the brick structures nearby. The awnings, bollards, railings, boardwalks and graphics all combine to give a strong nautical theme. Food is on the top level, so ensuring (due to the American penchant for grazing) that the centre trades well on all levels. The centre space is a disappointment. Its two end walls are fully glazed, the paintwork is in dull colours so the glare factor is disturbing. It badly needs top light, the colour scheme rethinking and the softening effect of greenery.

Trump Tower, New York City There are no standard shopping malls in New York, firstly because the initial trend was out of town (the aging Paramas Park in New Jersey was about the best of the bunch) and secondly because land is so expensive in the city no one could afford to assemble sufficient area to promote a scheme. (The same is true of London and most capital cities). However the five storey trading atrium at the base of the office and residential Trump Tower is required viewing for anyone interested in high quality shopping. Clearly all the big money is made aloft so developer Donald Trump could afford to take a relaxed view on the profitability of the shopping. Certainly no stand-alone retail scheme could afford such profligate use of space and such a nonsense shopping layout. The overall effect, however, is quite magnificent. The finishes in a pink/brown marble, bronze tinted mirror and clear glass, brass coloured metalwork and warm blush/white plasterwork give a glow of opulence. It may be all too much for the aesthete but the man in the street (and at least one architect) finds it admirable.

The Gallery on Market Street East, Philadelphia Although there is something in WC Field's acid comments on Philadelphia[1], this scheme does much to redress the balance and the recent 100% expansion confirms its success. The four trading levels depend for success on basement connection to the subway and upper level restricted access to the multi-storey car parks. Top lighting, banners and planting contrast most favourably with the same elements at Pier 17 in New York.

Georgetown Mall, Washington DC The only major mall in the city to date worth detailed examination, it is set in historic Georgetown, trades on three levels and is heavily (too heavily for some) themed in southern plantation style. Decoration abounds from the moment one pushes open the brass clad doors. Etched glass balustrades, patterned, mosaic-like ceramic floor tiles, combination lighting and planting chandeliers, continuous high level cove lighting over shop fascias, elaborate cast metal stair strings and floor edging – all this and much more worth studying. The site has a steep cross fall to give various entrance levels with car parking in the basement.

Various, Washington DC The conversion of the centre courtyard of the Old Post Office into one of the biggest food courts in America is a dramatic sight from the high level approach from Pennsylvania Avenue. Some 14 outlets dispense food under the gallery and customers are prepared to carry food quite a distance to be in the central atrium seating over 600 people. The interior design and use of colour leaves much to be desired. It is the grandiose concept that is interesting.

Though of little interest as a retail mall, Pennsylvania 2000 is a sensitive conversion of perhaps the last remaining historic shops on the Avenue. This alone is welcome in an otherwise rather characterless city. The ground floor shops are now dual aspect and the rear opens onto a glass covered mall. The glass is a monopitch spanning from a new slab office block to (and over) the old pitched roofs of the houses.

Columbia New Town, Maryland The original scheme is now much extended and is notable for its use of the land form to give ground level servicing with pedestrian access contrived across bridges directly into the upper trading level. On the opposite elevation service lorries deliver directly into the ground floor. Shoppers are expected to cross the vehicle route to access the ground floor shopping, though there are footways above the lorries from the upper level of the two storey parking structure. The malls are covered by an extensive space frame which gives an architectural statement to both interior and exterior which is rare in the USA. It is significant that the original carpet finish at first floor level has been replaced by tiles.

Harbourplace, Baltimore Yet another runaway success for Rouse and Ben Thompson. The derelict docklands have been totally rejuvenated by this scheme and the waterfront is now alive with activity – offices, hotels, an exhibition and conference centre, a superb aquarium and a (struggling) fun palace in a converted power station. A forceful mayor overcame local opposition to retail use on the waterfront and the site is a mecca for both townsfolk and millions of visitors. A rather pointless planning restriction prohibited a continuous building around this corner of docklands so the two two storey pavilions, one selling food, the other predominantly of speciality shops are set apart. Like Pier 17 the architecture has a strong nautical theme but Harbourplace is by far the more successful.

The Gallery, Baltimore This scheme opened in 1987 and architecturally is one of the most successful in America. The proportion of the central atrium, the internal landscaping, the design of the detail and particularly the success of the five trading levels all make this an essential visit. Yet again the scheme is downtown; in fact it is just across the road from Harbourplace and is further evidence of the regenerative force of the Rouse concept.

Mayfair in the Grove, Miami Set in the Coconut Grove district on the shore road this is a truly remarkable scheme by European standards. It is both open to the elements and open to the public at all hours – at least it had not closed at midnight and one could discern no way it could easily be locked up; and it is in one of the most crime ridden cities in the USA. The architectural detailing and its excellent integration with extensive and elaborate water features and beautiful landscaping make this centre a must for those wishing to excel in these matters. The Spanish influenced majolica wall tiling, the gay art deco elevations, the creeper-wreathed multi-storey car park, the brilliant Frank Lloyd Wright inspired light fittings and much else is a constant delight. Downtown again, its elevations are the first in this review to make a conscious contribution to the urban scene in which it sits.

The Falls, Miami Like Mayfair in the Grove this scheme defies all British developer ground rules by making the shops subservient to the design concept. The scheme is announced by Bloomingdales, through which one has to pass before opening onto a vista of water cascades and lush planting. The unit shops are strung out around a sizeable lake and the boardwalk malls are all single-sided with views over the water. The timber clapboarded buildings give a very rural feel and while the ambience is pleasant enough one is bound to wonder whether one can court disaster so obviously without consummating it.

Bayside, Miami The latest Rouse waterside scheme had not yet opened on our visit but all the hallmarks of this master developer's hand are in evidence.

Riverwalk, New Orleans This Rouse speciality centre is built on the Mississippi riverbank site of the ill-fated 1984 New Orleans World Fair – which the world ignored. Riverwalk illustrates the fine line that separates disaster from success. The scheme is strung out in linear fashion overlooking the water and at first visit seems to go on for ever. In fact shoppers are cleverly pulled past the many shops and boutiques. There are small incidents in the winding mall and ceiling heights vary constantly until a clear, high and brightly lit section heralds the huge food court. The food content must approach 50% of the total retail area. Again the scheme defies orthodoxy in that it is totally off-pitch to any retail content in New Orleans and must create its own 'pull'. This it seems to be doing but a significant reason for this is worth explaining in case any British developer thinks similarly to fly in the face of experience.

In Britain the public has many alternatives to hanging out in a shopping centre simply for something to do. European cities themselves, the surrounding countryside, the cultural ambience of the arts, radio, television and newspapers are all a richer feast than Americans can sample. Even in New Orleans, once one has covered the Vieux Carre (a very small enclave) and explored the Garden District, the University Campus at Loyola and the pathetically few remaining Louisiana houses of character, the places of interest are all but exhausted. A walk in the countryside is unthinkable – the wet heat, the eternal swamp, the black moccasin snakes, the black widow spiders and the mosquitoes see to that – and there is scant chance of a view because the land is flat as a pancake. A couple of hours with the family in a mall which has 'theatre' can be the equivalent of the British picnic.

Jackson Brewery, New Orleans Adjacent to Jackson Square, the heart of New Orleans, is this renovation of the old brewery and though it has little advantage over the best of Faneuil Hall or the San Francisco wharf schemes it is worth exploring as part of the inevitable visit to the French Quarter. Indeed, the whole riverbank eastwards as far as the French Market is regenerated and transformed from the dereliction of a few years ago.

The Esplanade, New Orleans This is the first out of town scheme to merit a visit and even The Esplanade is built to serve Kinner, a suburb near the airport. The

architects are the best known US retail designers, RTKL, and it is well up to their high standard. Of particular note is the highly stylised and ornamented structure with the columns, capitals and arches giving a rich arcuated feel to the interior – belied by the simple pitched, glazed roofs which are almost completely hidden. In addition, the food court is environmentally one of the best in the USA. Top lit in the main mall space, it is located at the upper of two levels and is both terraced into three levels and allowed to jut out into the line of the main mall to a degree that many would question. The farthest projections certainly block end to end views of the anchor stores. Good lighting, jaunty table canopies and luxuriant planting all contribute to the excitement and the fragmented table layout proves once again how attracted people are to a little corner they can call their own.

St Louis Centre, St Louis Currently voted number one by most European visitors this centre alone is worth the fare to the USA. Reference has already been made to its influence in rejuvenating the heart of St Louis and to the startling (to Europeans) decision to put service and storage at street level and start the three levels of retail above that. What lifts the scheme right into a class of its own however is the classically cool, white-painted interior, with a beautifully proportioned barrel-vaulted mall. RTKL's detailing of balustrades, staircases, profiled floor edges, column heads, balcony projections, temporary 'starter' retail units and, perhaps most significant, the patterned ceramic tiled floor are all outstanding. The only critical note internally must surely be the third floor food court. Huge (700 seats) badly lit by both day and night, as noisy as a works canteen, with horribly uncomfortable chairs, only the overall success of the centre robs the developer of the initiative to rip it out and start again. Externally the scheme is a classic 'curate's egg'. The two mighty glazed entrances are magnificent but the bleak green and grey metal panelled windowless walls between them are a disaster to the grain of a city made so rich by Sullivan's Wainwright Building.

St Louis Station, St Louis Fourteen blocks away from the St Louis Centre is the old railway station which many will remember as the hub of America's rail network. Now the trains have all gone and the city's eminence as a communications node rests with the prestige of TWA who make their home here. In another bold stroke Rouse, this time with architects HOK, converted the station buildings into an Omni Hotel, added more bedrooms in wings under the station roof and the remaining space was converted into a two level speciality centre beneath the vast spans of the old platform roofs. The overall effect is stunning. There is also much characterful detailing in the railway age genre and mall furniture, signs, litter bins and so on are all consistently well handled. A jarring note is struck by the auxiliary metal structure to the new shop units. It is clumsy and painted a gloomy plum colour which subtracts from the filigree elegance of the great trusses above. Floor finishes too are in a lifeless grey tile, but of the trading success of the centre there is no doubt.

Before leaving St Louis a visit to Leclade's Landing is of interest. This nineteen century rundown warehouse area on the west bank of the Mississippi is being refurbished with boutiques, speciality shops and restaurants. It is all part of the rebirth of St Louis which dates from 1964 when Saarinen's superlative 600 ft high arch, the Gateway to the West signalled the start of a new era for the city.

Fulton Market
South Street Seaport,
New York

Columbia New Town,
Baltimore
At this side the shops are
served by trolley only.

Harbourplace,
Baltimore

The Gallery, Baltimore

Mayfair in the Grove, Coconut Grove, Miami

Bayside, Miami

Riverwalk, New Orleans

Jackson Brewery, New Orleans

The Esplanade, New Orleans

St Louis Centre, St Louis

St Louis Station, St Louis

St Louis Station, St Louis

The Galleria: Phase 3, Houston

Plaza of the Americas, Dallas

The IDS Centre, Minneapolis

Los Colinas, Williams Square, Dallas

The Galleria: Phase 3, Houston Houston is the obvious place to go to study the modern office block but it has quite lost its retail lead to Dallas. Nevertheless the trendsetting Galleria with its ice rink and jogging track round the roof has now been extended through Phase 2 (a great bland irrelevance) to Phase 3 which has much more character. A small central court is excellently detailed with both hard and soft landscape and an air of intimacy is captured which contracts strongly with the earlier phases.

Repeated visits confirm the view that the retail environment is adversely affected by a sheet of ice in the middle. One sided trading malls are the inevitable result and when the ice is not in use its flat greyness is cold to retail in every sense of the phrase.

The Galleria; Prestonwood; Valleyview, Dallas These three centres have already been extensively referred to in differing contexts. Here it is sufficient to remark again on the astonishing retail virility and planning ineptitude that allows 4 million square feet of retail space to compete in three centres less than a mile apart out in the suburbs while the city centre dies. With the partial exception of The Galleria none of the three contribute in any positive way externally to their suburban environment.

Los Colinas, Dallas This remarkable suburb is the brainchild of Dallas' greatest property entrepreneur Trammell Crow. Shopping is just beginning to establish a toehold but designers should note two things.

First an attempt to solve the aesthetic problem of a three-level car park by decking out the elevations in Mexican hacienda style and by putting a complete tray over the roof and landscaping it beautifully.

Second at the heart of Williams Square, an SOM designed office complex over ground floor shops is the most successful outdoor sculpture complex designed in modern times. A group of a dozen wild mustangs gallop across an arid desert of flamed pink granite and splash their way over a stream in the centre. The lifelessness of the bronze beasts is belied by the sculpted animation and by the sprays of water that are thrown up below their hooves by small jets. Lights are secreted also in the jets so that by night the illusion of vibrant life is complete. Bernini never did better than this. The sculptor was Robert Glenn.

Various, Dallas Retail downtown in Dallas is all but dead and buried but three schemes should be noted. The Plaza of the Americas has hotel and office blocks linked by an enormous space frame (much like the troubled Omni Centre in Atlanta) and the atrium thus created has a free form ice rink as a centre piece ringed by shops that lack any true retail ambience. Below the great mirrored office block on Main Street is a very well designed fast food operation by RTKL and West End Market is a warehouse conversion into speciality shops and fast food which does exhibit signs of real retail life. Philip Johnson's shopping arcade at The Crescent has already been discussed and it remains a curious anachronism. Other architects have been approached to see whether they can breathe commercial life into it.

Water Tower Place, Chicago Built in 1972 this scheme retains its 'state of the art' rating by the remarkable success of its seven trading levels round a tight atrium (and the seven levels do not start until shoppers have already been coaxed up two banks of escalators) by the

very high quality of the finishes and by one of the best indoor planting schemes to be seen anywhere. Janet Jack describes that aspect in greater detail later.

The IDS Centre, Minneapolis Again an older scheme, but the atrium at the base of the office tower is one of the most satisfactory spaces to be found with its uniquely structured egg-crate roof and hanging balcony. The shops ring the space at two levels, the upper of which links to the first floor walkway system connecting many of the downtown blocks.

Whilst in Minneapolis there are a number of schemes worth checking for their cautionary lessons. They are all speciality centres. Two, Riverplace and St Anthony-on-Main are on the East bank of the Mississippi but their water exposure is lessened by the road cutting them off from the waters edge. They are off the tourist beat and clearly cannot generate enough attraction to survive unaided. The other, the Galtier Centre, is actually in St Paul. The architectural concept is exciting with a high complex glazed atrium and the small centre attempts to trade on four levels. In 1987 it was a sad sight and all but empty.

On the bright side, and back in Minneapolis, the first US mall, the Southdale, still trades excellently and nearby two small speciality centres feeding off strong regional malls, the Bonaventure and the Galleria are trading well. The Bonaventure is a delightful architectural solution with warm timber panelling treated like marquetry on curved walls and balcony edges.

The Tabor Centre, Denver Rouse again: and in the very centre of the city. Indeed the narrow, linear two level scheme stretches over two city blocks and lines one side of the famous 16th Street refurbishment. This town centre thoroughfare is pedestrianised save for electric buses which ply in either direction at two minute intervals and are free. They keep to a tight central line leaving either side for landscape, lighting and, of course, pedestrians. The scheme is a model of its kind, though equalled in design quality by the pedestrianisation of two parallel streets in the centre of Portland, Oregon. The Tabor Centre is a typical Rouse speciality centre with a steel structure, excellent detailing, interesting spaces, a good food court with an imaginative draped ceiling and a Bull Market of little carts at first floor level spanning one of the cross streets. A very interesting scheme, and part of Denver's downtown regeneration, it is still sad that the exterior falls well short of real civic quality: it all has a rather temporary look.

Horton Plaza, San Diego To European eyes the most astonishing scheme in the USA. It is a Hahn development with the Jerde Partnership as architects and its simple aim is to bring life back to the centre of a city which had been abandoned by every element of civic dignity.

Whether it brings back dignity and permanence is open to question but the scheme opts for the same strange solution as the St Louis Centre with ground level service and storage so the three level retail scheme only starts at first floor. Even stranger is the fact that from the north the grandiose, Campadolio-like stair is a good deal easier to spot than the escalators. From the south there is no escalator at all – unless you can find a cunningly concealed elevator you must toil up 20 feet of staircase – no fun with the temperature topping 100 degrees Fahrenheit.

The Tabor Centre, Denver

University Towne Centre, La Jolla

Once aloft one is in a bizarre open world of architectural fantasy. Colour, form, and patterns of circulation seem designed to confuse rather than delight, but the whole confection is saved by the eternal sunshine of southern California. Practically every sacred cow beloved of British developers (and planners) is violated, but it is a huge scheme and four department stores anchor the trade and ensure the scheme's own critical mass. One can only go and marvel at something so comprehensively unfundable by British standards.

University Towne Centre, La Jolla Ten miles north of San Diego and again open to the elements – and open 24 hours per day – is this much more orthodox scheme. It is beautifully laid out with intricate (though generous) malls, thickly planted and all converging on a raised, covered podium for community and sales promotion use. An Ice Capades rink and food court anchors one mall but the whole development, with three major department stores is a delight to wander round.

Hardly 'state of the art' but barely one mile away on the west side of Route 8 is one's own favourite small scheme, La Jolla Village Square. Very cheaply and simply detailed, the cranked mall is top lit with a seried row of north roof lights supported on sturdy timber warren trusses which are stained green. Again the exterior contributes nothing of architectural quality or relevance, but the direct simplicity of the interior is an ideal retail foil and is a good lesson for European designers.

Ghiradelli Square; The Cannery; Pier 39; San Mateo Fashion Mall, San Francisco Sadly for British teams wanting a legitimate business excuse to go to America's loveliest city there are now no 'state of the art' schemes in the San Francisco area. A brilliant new shopping development is urgently required.

Nevertheless, Ghiradelli Square, a converted chocolate factory, and The Cannery (which explains itself) are Mark 1 speciality centres which, together with Boston's Faneuil Hall, started the craze for this genre. Both are classic examples of conservation and refurbishment and both had excellent architects: William Wurster for Ghiradelli and Joseph Esherick for The Cannery. Both also had the full panoply of criteria for success available to them (see the section on Speciality Centres in chapter 12). That one can still go wrong, however, is shown by Pier 39 only half a mile further along Fisherman's Wharf and as the name implies it is built out into the bay. It has been re-marketed at least once and still is nowhere near the trading success of its two rivals.

Reasons for this are not hard to find. First, it is just off prime pitch on the wharf area. Secondly it is a peninsula plan and with no end anchor (other than outdoor comedy shows and a chap diving from an incredible height into what must seem to him a bucket of water) it lacks natural pedestrian flow. Thirdly, an odd decision was taken to develop a central mall at water level which means that service vehicles run in a loop around the exterior.

Thus the whole point of building out into the beautiful bay has been negated as far as the ground floor is concerned, because there is either no view at all or it is seriously compromised by lorries and vans trundling past your restaurant window. Only at first floor level is there any visual appreciation of the fabulous panorama

out to Sausalito, Alcatraz and Oakland. The chunky timber detailing from old railway sleepers is very successful.

The reasons for going to San Mateo Fashion Mall are to study the Ice Capades operation which is well integrated into the shopping without detracting from it and to see the Teflon roofed Bullock department store – one of the few tensile, fabric roofed structures to be seen. The quality of diffuse natural light is very successful and the cost of artificial light has literally been decimated over a normal Bullock operation. Only top-up accent light is used in any part of the single level retail store.

Unfortunately a gallery restaurant had to be closed because heating engineers got the heat build up calculations wrong (or failed to do any). The potential for this type of roof for out of town schemes is considerable. It is cheap, saves running costs on services and offers dramatic internal and external forms which attract custom.

Los Angeles This city has been left to last of the USA schemes because it has more fine schemes than any other and a visit is essential.

South Bay Galleria, Redondo Beach The best of the lot; by RTKL architects and vying for number one spot with the St Louis Centre. The interior is a joyful parade of jolly roof trusses, sensuously curved balconies, luxuriant planting, thrilling fountains, 100% top lighting through intersecting barrel vaults and decorated throughout in a blush white paint which imparts a cool warmth wholly appropriate to southern California. The graphics and the food court are worthy of study in themselves. The exterior is a nonentity which contributes nothing to the already anonymous Hawthorne Boulevard in which it sits.

Westside Pavilion, Westwood Rated highly by most visitors, the Jerde Partnership (of Horton Plaza fame) have restrained themselves to using rather muted colours internally – which in fact err on the muddy side. The plan is a long classic mall with anchors at both ends and a food court pulling custom up through three levels of retail. The 'pull' of a food court in America is astonishing.

The operation at Westside Pavilion is as dismal as that at the St Louis Centre but it too, is also packed. The decor and graphics in the mall are witty with many Post-Modern overtones. From a planning standpoint the scheme is notable for its downtown location (at a busy crossing on Pico Boulevard) for its basement service (one of the few in the USA) and for a determined effort to make a contribution to the urban scene. Admittedly much of the applied detail is a Post-Modern or Art Deco irrelevance, but high marks for the attempt.

Crystal Court, Fashion Island, Newport Beach A recent addition to a large up-market scheme in a wealthy sector. A huge atrium with two retail levels overlooks a central food court into which customers bring food from perimeter units or even from the food units of a large supermarket tucked away below the retail floors and approached directly from the car parks. Enormous sandstone columns rise from floor to roof and the sturdy detailing extends to the shop fronts where pilaster widths sometimes extend to two metres.

Ghiradelli Square, San Francisco
Open to the elements and closed to the public for only a few hours before dawn.

La Jolla Village Square, La Jolla
One of the simplest, cheapest, yet most efficient schemes.

The Cannery, San Francisco
An intimate warren of charming alleyways.

Pier 39, San Francisco
The perception of the gorgeous bay is not fully realised.

Crystal Court, Fashion Island, Newport Beach, Los Angeles

Bullock department store, San Mateo Fashion Mall, San Francisco
The teflon roof is a great energy saver in lighting costs.

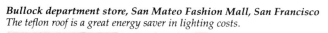

South Coast Plaza, Costa Mesa, Los Angeles
Quality materials and detail at every turn.

Santa Monica Place, Santa Monica, Los Angeles
A self conscious structure.

Santa Monica Place, Santa Monica, Los Angeles
The famous graphic wall 'dies' as soon as the sun moves off the surface.

The Beverley Centre, Beverley Hills

Les Terrasses, Montreal

*Complexe
Desjardins,
Montreal*

Stamford Mall, Stamford, Connecticut

Trump Tower, New York

Georgetown Mall, Washington DC

The Post Office, Washington DC

The Galtier Centre, St Paul, Minneapolis

South Bay Galleria, Redondo Beach, Los Angeles

The Collection, Rodeo Drive, Beverley Hills

Woodbine Centre, Toronto

Children's World, Woodbine Centre, Toronto

South Coast Plaza, Costa Mesa The last phase of this truly vast scheme (with a very good Speciality Centre called South Coast Village Plaza) shows the degree to which America is still ahead of Europe on a number of counts. First the pursuit of quality is relentless. The marble finishes, the detailing, the theatrical light programmed central dome with a star-studded theme, the standard of the shop fronts and, most of all, the design of the basement car park make this scheme an important visit. The car park takes the quality of the shopping experience further than any current scheme on this kind of scale. The mall finishes, planting and water cascades are continued down to the parking level where the foyer from the car park is beautifully finished and the suspended ceiling is extended out of the foyer into the car park itself. The floor to ceiling height is generous, the graphics are good and valet parking is available. No current scheme in Europe matches this.

Santa Monica Place, Santa Monica Important for architects who are expected to treat it seriously because it is designed by a current cult designer, Frank O'Gheary, and because developers, who neither know nor care what he is, think it is badly flawed. O'Gheary's wayward design talent is on view (though his madder escapades have been curtailed) but in every case it gets in the way of the retail intent. Columns and beams form needless geometric patterns, the pedestrian flow is contorted, the food court is in quite the wrong position at one of the entrances and the central space lacks 'personality'. Even the much vaunted wiremesh cloak to the multi-storey car park with the white painted super graphics only works when the sun is in the right direction. When the wall is in shade the lettering disappears and so does the mesh, leaving a typical poor multi-storey car park with every vehicle in full view.

The Beverley Centre, Beverley Hills A three level scheme perched unusually on top of a five level multi-storey car park at the junction of Wilshire and La Cienega Boulevards. The exterior is probably the most brutish design in America relieved only by batteries of escalators falling Pompidou style down from the shopping levels past the parking trays to the sidewalk. The interior is far better, there are interesting views through and around the various levels, though the upper food court is poor.

The scheme is notable for a clutch of 14 cinemas on the top floor, and it is a comment on the current craze for these facilities that AMC currently are planning 12 more on the opposite side of the street. From a trading point of view the Beverly Centre is one of the most successful on the West Coast.

The Collection, Rodeo Drive, Beverley Hills A tiny speciality centre too precious for words. The scheme is on one of the most exclusive streets in America and is littered with famous names. No item in any shop is priced: in fact several do not stoop to a window display. Certain it is that if you have to ask the price of anything, you cannot afford it. The scheme is open to the elements though it can be locked at night. Two retail levels round an open court are brick and marble lined and overlook courtyard cafes and the entrance to the underground valet parking system. The very poor quality brickwork is now almost completely cloaked with luxuriant creeper and the use of bold brick arches over three floor levels imparts a grand sense of scale to what is really a modest building. Full marks too to Roger Vidal, the architect, for creating a street facade which echoes the lively quality of the adjacent elevations.

Los Angeles has dozens of malls but only the ones listed above have elements worth a specific visit. Others such as Foxhills Mall, La Brea Mall, Glendale Galleria, Pasadena Place, Sherway Plaza and the speciality centres of Ports o' Call, Queen Mary Village and Newport Village have ideas worth studying if one happens to be passing. The rest are forgettable.

CANADA After a flurry of retail activity in the 70's Canada has now lost the lead to the USA. This is partly due to the much smaller market. America has expanded not only by 100,000,000 people over 30 years but by a rise in standard of living which is unique in world history. Canada cannot match such growth. Furthermore the eastern, most populous seaboard of Canada has gone through a period of cultural chauvanism with a Canute-like determination to roll back the tide of English influence. English however is the inevitable lingua franca of the international business world and the Francophile myopia has merely resulted in Montreal losing the momentum it gained with Expo '67 and trade has moved to Toronto. From a retail standpoint therefore Montreal's pre-eminence faded in the early 70's and centres like Place Ville Marie, Place Bonaventure, Complexe Desjardins, 2020 and Les Terrasses have not been bettered until very recently.

Toronto then took over the baton and exploded (not too strong a word) onto the retail scene with the world famous Eaton Centre. Even though they look jaded and ready for a thorough upgrading, the basic things are still absolutely right and the great galleria remains as magnificent as Milan's Galleria Vittorio Emmanuele. From the Eaton Centre (perhaps the greatest example of downtown refurbishment in North America) came the connecting ribbon of basement retail developments which link the Sheraton Centre near Simpsons (the southern anchor of the Eaton Centre) through The Atlantic Richfield Plaza, 1st Canadian Place, the Toronto Dominion Centre and into the Royal Bank Plaza. An astonishing achievement which keeps an entire business as well as shopping community out of both the ice of winter and the humid heat of summer. Each has a different character and has much to teach, both good and bad.

Toronto, too, produced the first purpose built speciality centre of real significance and Hazelton Lanes remains required study. It is so successful that in 1987 a doubling of its size was projected. Of special note is the fact that all these schemes are downtown so that the heart of the city remains vibrant. Now a further Renaissance is under way on the shoreline of Lake Ontario. Industrial buildings have been either swept away or converted and the most noted of the latter is Queen's Quay Terminal. This massive warehouse on the water's edge has been gutted and a speciality centre on two levels is topped by offices in the remaining four storeys. Of even greater significance the prodigious strength of the structure permitted the addition of three storeys of high quality housing with internal landscaped courts and a swimming pool that must have the best aspect in Canada. This bold Olympia & York development carries on the remarkable tradition of this firm led by the Reichman family who first startled Canada with 1st Canadian Place, then New York with The World Financial Centre and now London with Canary Wharf.

141

Hazleton Lanes, Toronto

Eaton Centre, Toronto

Eaton Centre, Toronto

Queen's Quay Terminal, Toronto

The Promenade, Toronto

Galleon Hall, West Edmonton Mall, Toronto

West Edmonton Mall, Toronto

Fast Food Hall, West Edmonton Mall, Toronto

And all this is about Toronto downtown. Out of town is the pioneering Yorkville but in the 80's new developments forged ahead with the Woodbine Centre and The Promenade – both north of the city. Woodbine is noted for its integrated Children's World and fairground but has also an excellent top lit food court. The Promenade too has a good food court though a well designed food hall is reputed to be struggling. Of special note is the Health Court where private medical services can be purchased and this could well be an important pointer for Britain with the present crisis in the Department of Health and Social Security.

Finally, in out of town Toronto is the new refurbished Square One on the West side at Missisauga. The unused central open space has been enclosed and the success of the venture has undoubtedly encouraged its British developers, Hammersons, to look radically at their UK flagship at Brent Cross and the rest of their 60's portfolio.

There is little of radical note in the West Coast retail scene in Canada but no review of Canadian shopping would be complete without mention of West Edmonton Mall. This goliath of a centre with 5,000,000 sq ft of retail activity and leisure appurtances from pools, aviaries, zoos, ice rinks, fun fairs and theatres to gargantuan food courts with over 20 outlets is a must for students of shopping centres. Not, one hastens to add, because it should be repeated in Europe, or indeed anywhere else, but because there are hosts of lessons (mostly negative) to be learned. The many facilities abound with ideas which one can take or leave, but the overpowering impact of so vast an agglomeration is not ultimately a satisfactory experience. The exterior architectural quality is uniformly execrable and unforgiveable given so great an opportunity.

1. *'I went to Philadelphia once: it was closed'.*
   'Put on my tombstone all things considered, I'd rather be in Philadelphia'.

8

THE ARCHITECT'S ROLE

Training inadequacies

Understanding developer motivation

Definition of fund and developer involvement

The architect's contribution

The importance of drawing

Footwork: the ability to roll with the punches

Flexibility: the quest for a settled scheme

Ealing: an example of flexibility

The satisfaction of success

The developer's risk: reaction to the untried

Selling the idea: articulacy

The value of seniority: a benefit of growing old

The ability to write

8

THE ARCHITECT'S ROLE

Training inadequacies

There are some simple guidelines for a young architect who wants to succeed in the developer world. Unfortunately no university or college training gives instruction in them. Students are allowed to toil through seven arduous years of study labouring under the illusion that they are the natural leaders of every building procurement team: an ordnance of divine right bestowed by a higher power. The empirical statements of the great iconoclasts of the first generation of modern architects are still deemed to be incontrovertible.

For most designers the shock of discovering their true status in the eyes of developers results in their permanent departure from the field of play. Great innovative design talent is almost always accompanied by an arrogance that is inimical to acceptance by the property development world. For that single reason very few talented architects grace the retail scene. And yet with a minor shift of attitude many good designers could make a significant contribution to the world of retail architecture – with profoundly beneficial effects upon our cities.

Understanding developer motivation

Understanding the client must be the starting point. Developers are not in the business to erect monuments to themselves and to be known as patrons of the arts or the environment. Still less are they interested in their developments being famed as significant works by their chosen designers. There are no Robinson or Fitzwilliam Halls or Sainsbury Centres in the shopping centre world; nor any building like Coventry Cathedral or the Tate extension known almost as well by the name of its architectural creator as for the function it performs.

No architect will ever make a name in the public's perception by working in the retail field even though by definition the buildings have the highest possible profile in public usage. A challenge to the intelligent lay reader to name the architect of any shopping centre in Britain or America (there are nearly 30,000 to go at) would evoke a blank stare, but a modest change in that perception can be brought about with the current trend to higher quality.

Definition of fund and developer involvement

It is fashionable among architects and the general public to attribute 'profit' as the sole aim for developers. It is true that 'the bottom line' will always be pre-eminent but there is a difference between the greed of gambling and responsible risk-taking. Developers and Funds are not synonymous and to help architects understand client motivation in development work a distinction should be drawn between them. The former were once ubiquitous and the famous names of the sixties, Arndale, Ravenseft, Hammersons and so on were the normal channel of shopping centre procurement. Their

aim was to develop land, hold on to it and maximise the profit in the process. The general public would be staggered if they knew the extent to which this select band of great names have property holdings in Great Britain. Generally speaking these companies stopped shopping centre development during the financial crisis and high inflation of the mid-70's. They found safer outlets for their cash and only very recently have some of them surfaced again. They invariably fund their own developments from their vast in-house resources.

Small development companies abound. They are usually led by entrepreneural people who see an opportunity and labour hard to realise it. They have very limited liquidity and need the support of outside capital to finance their ambitions. Their prime motivation is to make a profit from the development by selling it on to an investor – often the Fund who supported them in the enterprise.

The funds are primarily the huge pension and investment funds like Norwich Union, Legal & General and many others. Their motivation is more accurately described as 'growth' rather than 'profit'. They buy investment in property for the life of the lease and they are just as interested in the prospect of growth in value as they are in the first cost. Recently many of them have amassed so much in-house development expertise that they now do development work from scratch and enter developer competitions in their own right. They are formidable competitors because they can assure local authorities of financial stability and of continued commitment to the town. They do not offer an in-and-out get rich quick deal. On the other hand their interest in growth, laudable though it is, makes them conservative and suspicious of any novel idea, so the flamboyant traditional developer can frequently steal a march on them.

So much for the principal players in the game. They are the patrons and a designer's failure to work within the constraints of their perception of financial viability will result not only in dismissal but exclusion from a very tight and exclusive club. Word spreads like wildfire.

The architect's contribution

Architects however should have one attribute that is denied every other member of the team and it is astonishing that so few play to their potential strength. One only has to sit round a table on a development project to realise that all the constituent members are to greater or lesser degrees experts in the field. Everyone talks knowledgeably about land values, Zone A rents, legal boundaries, tenant mix, earnings, bottom lines, yields, pedestrian flows, location, prime pitches, service charges, car park turnover, office rentals, mall finishes, management policy, insurance – the list is endless and they all stick an oar in whether they are pulling in the right direction or catching a crab.

But there is only one person in the room who can draw. Until he or she puts pencil to paper the entire meeting is effectively paralysed. The rest can pontificate and write reports until they are blue in the face, but until the architect suggests how it all might look in either two dimensions or three no real progress will be made. To some degree this is true of every type of commission but in most other fields of design the client body starts with a much higher respect for architects. In projects like schools, universities, public buildings, private housing, hospitals, churches, banks or museums, there is a far greater awareness of the architect's contribution as a pure designer. The first generation of developers took the view that the architect was a mere technical pencil-pusher whose job it was to move the lines around until the client liked the look of it. It was then his or her job to draw it up nicely to get past the planners. In the 80's the architect's contribution can be much more potent.

The importance of drawing
The first and much the most important attribute that the architect must therefore display is the ability to draw with felicity and imagination. The layman might be forgiven the illusion that he thought that was the architect's main talent anyway. Sadly that is often not so. Many young architects have convinced themselves that designing can be done at the Visual Display Unit and that Computer Aided Drafting will lead us to a new world of design excellence. There is not the slightest doubt that CAD will increasingly make more efficient the task of testing the concept and then portraying it accurately for the production process, but the prospect of computers replacing the 6B pencil sketch at a developer's design meeting is so remote that it can be discounted. Time after time meetings have laboured over facts, figures and opinions, the table littered with typed information, then as soon as the architect presents the drawings or (even more impressively) sketches under their very eyes, the written verbiage is ignored. Architects should therefore become so adept at freehand sketching that they can portray any concept the mind can conceive in three dimensions. The pencil should be an extension of the fingers which are directed by the brain.[1]

As a student one visited the studios of many of the great architects and noted two things. First they were all very skilled with a pencil – indeed some were quite brilliant artists. There is nothing about this skill that need put one off. It is a matter of practice and dedication: drawing, sketching anything and everything at any available opportunity. The speed with which one improves depends upon the amount of latent talent but anyone with the visual awareness and basic inbuilt drive to want to be an architect can become fluent with a pencil. The second thing was that the best architects were all avid travellers. They always seemed to be off somewhere with their aesthetic antennae twitching for signals that they tucked away in the recesses of their imagination until the opportunity came to draw on their well of experience. Unquenchable curiosity is an essential prerequisite for a first rate architect.

Footwork: the ability to roll with the punches
The next most important attribute for the shopping centre architect is flexibility of mind and quickness in reacting to changing circumstances. The luminaries of the architectural world all share one priceless asset

King Street, Lancaster

Church Street, Lancaster

Chancery Arcade, Lancaster
These quick watercolour sketches illustrated better than a hundred reports that we had understood the urban quality of Lancaster.

149

which is at the same time an inhibition which robs them of usefulness to the developer. These designers have an ability to conceive a building so completely that the form is, in their mind, a piece of perfectly crafted walk-in sculpture. There is no pejorative 'rear' elevation, the inside and the outside are natural and related design worlds.

That, of course, is the aim of all good architecture but in the shopping world, so complex are the relationships, so fluid are the fashion trends, and so quixotic are the developer's demands for quite fundamental changes to the scheme content, that if a better financial equation presents itself the scheme must be modified. The architect is left to make what sense he can of the fractured massing and the ruined balance of the design. This is not to suggest that good architecture cannot result but it makes it very much harder to achieve. The process can be likened to the art of the juggler. The balls are constantly moving: the art is to keep them at all times under control so that when they 'freeze' they are in a pattern that pleases.

Such a process is not a satisfactory method of working for the perfectionist. He or she wants to be given a specific brief, a carefully defined site and a measured time in which to produce first ideas. That is what the university design programme taught him or her to expect from the client. Such an architect's first proposals usually constitute fairly definitive ideas arising from a meticulously analysed brief for a carefully studied site. They are presented after laborious hours of analysis and synthesis and they are frequently beautifully drawn with copperplate precision.

Flexibility: the quest for a settled scheme
On the other side of the table however, are developer clients who are appalled by such finality. They usually give the architect an idea of the site constraints, but are not too specific on boundaries because they want the architect to help them with the ideal configuration of the scheme. The developer can then decide whether or not to buy in more property. If he gives the architect any idea of content at all, it will be no more than an overall retail square footage (it's a waste of time talking to ninety percent of developers in metres: they will simply ask 'what's that in English?').

So the first sketch the developer wants to see from the architect is a scaled drawing showing what the site could contain. He can then put some rents on the areas, a cost per square foot rate for the building and from that he can tell immediately if there is a scheme worth pursuing. The only purpose of the first set of drawings is to test viability. They have nothing whatsoever to do with the creation of architecture.

Architects as a breed find difficulty in grasping the elementary truth that drawings are not ends in themselves but merely aids to communication. They often fail therefore to strike up a rapport with a developer from the very first drawing. There is, of course, a balance to be struck between the slovenly and the laboured drawing. The one bespeaks the ill kempt mind: the other the pedant. But architects should remember that when developers try to read drawings which are more complex than line diagrams of shopping layouts they are struggling for comprehension. They want to see simple, scaled, freehand plans in bold line and they should give every appearance of being flexible and capable of modification. In spite of appearances to the contrary

developers have a conscience about asking architects to redraw time after time drawings that look to and indeed have taken hours, even days to present. They want to feel relaxed about their ability to change things – even while the building is going up.

Ealing: an example of flexibility
This juggling act at Ealing began in the last week of the competition just as we were finalizing the drawings. Could our scheme, asked Ealing Borough Council, be adjusted to include a 20,000 sq ft (1,900 sq metre) library to centralise the borough's services? We assured them it could:[2] we jacked up the multi-storey car park and slipped the lending, reference, history and children's library together with all the services between the shops and the cars.

We won the competition, got started on the detailed design and within the first month Sainsbury's decided to leave central Ealing and go to west Ealing. They had been trading on the site and a key requirement had been to relocate them in the heart of the scheme. Suddenly we had no supermarket.

Two months elapsed and the developer then reported that he had approached 28 hotel operators and no-one wanted to come to Ealing. The 200-bed hotel and conference centre which had been crucial to the High Street and southern elevations had gone although the facility had been seen as highly desirable, even mandatory, by the Local Authority.

Months went by before a deal was done with another developer with a supermarket frontage on Broadway so Safeway was moved from that location and put where Sainsbury's had been planned: a different size of course. The development was re-planned to suit the newly added development partner and this entailed rerouting and replanning the pedestrian flows, the shops and the whole multi-storey car park system.

Meanwhile the scheme could not be left just one storey high so it was decided that the proposed hotel should be replaced by offices. But how big? For months the development partners dithered over the area to give us as a brief and agonised over the degree of flexibility that should be built into the planning.

Smile if you will, but imagine putting your shirt on building between 75,000 or 150,000 sq ft (7,000 or 14,000 sq metres) of wholly speculative offices costing a minimum of £6,000,000 with inflation running at 1.5% a month and not a prospective tenant on the horizon. And all the time the architect is trying to persuade you to invest more and more money in bay windows, pitched slate roofs, handmade bricks, stone trim to every opening, elm doors and floor to ceiling tiles in the toilets. Many fantasize, but few are called to be real developers …

Then, just when we had given up the idea of a big space user such as a department store, Bentalls decided to move, sell their site on Broadway and come into our scheme with a demand for 50,000 sq ft (4,600 sq metres) on two levels, plus a 5,000 sq ft (460 sq metre) plant room on the roof. Things seemed to be settling down quite nicely, and we had long since started building the basement (actually within 9 months of getting the job and without a working drawing of the ground floor layout) when a leisure operator said he would like to come in at second floor level with 10 squash courts, a gymnasium, saunas, a restaurant and a sports shop.

Central Square, Ealing

Office block atrium, Ealing
More formal sketches that were useful in giving a precise idea of how the space would look.

Meanwhile Saunders department store decided to extend into the scheme, and a 10,000 sq ft (950 sq metre) café-cum-wine bar decided to fill the first floor space round the town court. The housing was replanned with dizzying frequency and the Methodist church and school was in, out, in and then finally out of the scheme. These are just the main changes;[3] dozens of other minor changes were instructed at each post-contract meeting and with the job some five years old an enormous basement nightclub has just been opened. There is intermittent talk of a fast food court overlooking the centre court and the popularity of the centre is leading to questions about adding another tray or two of car parking structure over the library.

At each stage and with each revision, the client wants a quick sketch (at the meeting would be ideal) showing how the modification might work, so that the quantity surveyor can price it and the agent can put a rent on it, so that the client can see if it 'ticks'. If it is not going to make money, forget about it. If it does, get on with it ('don't bother me with the architectural massing problems, just sort it out with the planners and the environment busybodies: that's what I hire you for').

What price rational, finely honed walk-in sculpture? The miracle is not that architecture is at a premium, but that anything worthwhile gets built at all. One could continue, but the litany would be all too familiar to the experienced and tedious to the unsympathetic.

The satisfaction of success

However, if young architects want to be part of this testing, topsy-turvy steeplechase then they should climb into the saddle. If not, they should stick to flat racing and concentrate on trying to get jobs like museums in Germany, banks in the City and concert halls in the provinces. Like both types of horse racing, the two design worlds demand supreme skills at their apogee. One is not inferior in nature to the other. They are simply utterly different.[4] For the good of our urban environment far more young architects must grapple with the problems of shopping centre design and match in their own terms the aesthetic quality of the best one-off buildings.

The developer's risk: reaction to the untried

It is impossible to overstate the gravity and the extent to which developers are exposed during the design stage of a big central area scheme. The risk factor is both daunting to them and incomprehensible and certainly unacceptable to those of non-entrepreneural character. A great deal of the renowned developer bombast and pomposity is faked: they are actually scared stiff. Most of all they want to be surrounded in their enterprise by people with experience; people they trust. The idea of a young designer straight from school with no building experience to his or her credit guiding the fortunes of this hair-raising gamble is unnerving.

Interestingly, developers have no such qualms about young interior designers. They treat their art as ephemeral, they come into play much later in the action, and they are enthusiastic about the concept of rapid change and fashion of which youth is the touchstone. Architecture is different; by the time one has satisfied the Building Regulations, the Fire Officer, the Codes of Practice and all the Statutory Undertakers one has willy nilly got a building that will stay up a very long time and cost a lot of money to demolish. Architects are trained to abide by these constraints, but many spend their careers trying to join the ranks

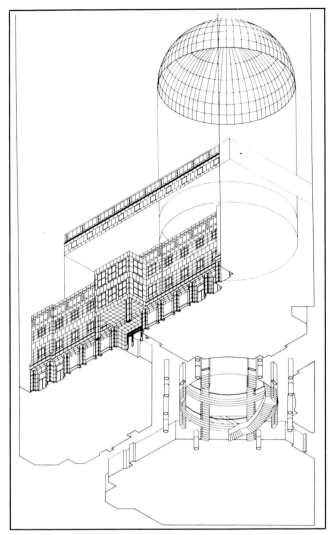

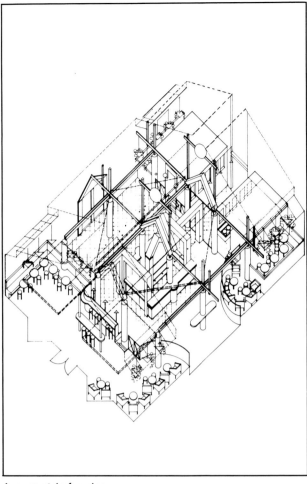

Axonometric drawing
Ingenious, yes, teasing perhaps, but as much use in communicating to the development world as to the worm from whose viewpoint these type of drawings are constructed.

of those who fill the pages of expensive magazines, with exquisitely poised small buildings in remote sites. But the vast body of built work is put up in the heart of towns. On the evidence much of it is designed by people who long ago lost their idealism and they make buildings out of arrangements of spaces whose sole advantage is that they will make a great deal of money.

Selling the idea: articulacy

The next most important attribute for the development architect is articulacy. That is not to imply garrulity but an ability to 'sell' ideas in words to clients first, then to the statutory authorities and finally to the public. Many architects remain perpetually bewildered by the inability of people to read drawings.[5] They tend to retreat into an ivory tower of lofty scorn and cannot accept that plans are a cipher for actuality and as incomprehensible to the average layman as a doctor's prescription. Simple straightforward English is a priceless gift and worth a hundred weird 'exploded' axonometrics looking up into the building from a worm's eye view eight feet below ground. That sort of drawing, much loved by the architectural avant garde, especially when coloured up in pastel tints that have no relation to actuality, is just architect 'in' talk. As a means of communication to a shop developer and the general public it is useless.

A corollary to articulacy is persuasiveness. Almost without exception successful developers exhibit symptoms of papal infallibility and most of their opinions are expressed with an incontrovertible finality that would be comic if it were not so exasperating. Comic because the likelihood is that one has just come from a meeting where a rival developer put forward a diametrically opposite view with the same assumption that its verity is sculpted in granite. Exasperating because one groans inwardly at the prospect of the long hours ahead redrawing, explaining and rehearsing the arguments that must be gone through.

The value of seniority: a benefit of growing old

A word in parentheses to the architect who seeks acceptance in this sphere of work. Whenever possible architects should field a very senior person in these design meetings. There are two reasons. The first is the obvious one that seniority signifies experience; experience is the mother of confidence and confidence is a prerequisite of persuasiveness.

The second reason is not immediately so clear. The development team and the agency world operate on the basis of directors or partners running jobs with the aid of a secretary and (at most) a junior who is there to learn the ropes and who will certainly push off to pastures new if he or she is not promoted to senior level with a speed that would be unthinkable in a design office. In short, everyone round the design table is very experienced, very senior and they show impatience when the architect sends 'a youngster' just two years out of school and working on his first central area job. It happens so frequently that it reveals again how little most architectural practices understand the commercial world with its worrying exposure to faulty judgement and financial catastrophe.

On almost any type of work other than central area developments the architect can plod his or her way logically through the stages of the excellent RIBA Plan of Work with its reliable signposting through the various activities. Young qualified architects can hold their own quite well with such a good guide and they can concentrate on design brilliance and integrity within that framework. But in addition to these talents there is a highly desirable list of attributes which need to be displayed at developer design meetings. They are, in order, confidence, experience, swiftness of mind, flexibility and the ability to deliver design ideas with speed: all these attributes ripen with age.

The ability to write
Finally in a list of skills for the architect comes fluency and persuasiveness with the written word. An ability to spell is a bonus, but beyond price is the talent to get thoughts down on paper quickly and with clarity.

Pedantry is boring, flippancy can be mistaken for superficiality and a tangled verbosity is a certain switch-off to busy businessmen who usually have an attention span limited to one side of a sheet of A4 paper.

One regards with some irony the advice often given to A-level students that if they would like to be an architect the key subject to study is maths, closely followed by physics, then perhaps chemistry or another science. In fact for the practice of any branch of architecture with the exception of research or teaching other architects, the sciences are of precious little help in the execution of the work other than imparting a logical, analytical approach to the whole process of design.

An equally deep study of language can instil the same discipline of thought, and in the process the student cannot avoid hours of practice in putting these thoughts down on paper. Similarly history, geography, English, economics, and art appreciation are all invaluable in this respect. Art itself is an indispensable study for architects no matter which branch of the profession they wish to enter. Of the entire design and building procurement team they are the only ones specifically concerned for the visual impact of the finished product. If they cannot or will not speak for the design and contextual quality of the product then surely no one else will. Then heaven help us all.

1. Nothing tells me quicker that I am talking nonsense than when my hand seizes up at a meeting and I cannot draw what I am talking about.

2. Actually the Developer said we could. 'I tell 'em we can plait fog at interviews – then work out how to do it later' he said, 'then we renegotiate...'

3. Developers usually maintain that they never change their minds: 'I just have a better idea'.

4. When I need a total contrast to entrepreneural development I throw myself into designing my own house developments in the Lake District, a wild fowl sanctuary for Sir Peter Scott, choir stalls, Chapter House Gates, or a new refectory for Liverpool Cathedral where I am architect to the Dean & Chapter. It is as different an experience as Bach is from Berloiz.

5. I fortunately had that lesson forcefully brought to my notice as a Second Year student. I was proudly showing an aunt of mine a sheet of plans and elevations of a three-bedroom bungalow. She studied them carefully and then said 'I like this one better than that'. I glanced to see if she was teasing, but in all honesty she had been trying to read the one she did not like as an elevation. It was the ground floor plan.

9

REFURBISHMENT

Reasons for renewal

What to do with concrete

Enlivening big strong forms externally

The importance of management

An example of faulty management

Lessons from the example

The size of the problem: special considerations in Britain

Covering the malls

Restyling the floor finishes

Introducing new uses

Backstage refurbishment

The right rate for the job

9

REFURBISHMENT

Reasons for renewal

From a number of standpoints it is clear that many of our shopping centres are ripe for renewal. This is not surprising, if only because shopping is fashion and fashion changes. Furthermore, since the urban shopping centre as conceived in the 50's was a new building type and came to fruition in what many people consider to be the nadir of the modern architectural movement, it is natural to want to have another go at it.

It is easy to be wise after the event, but architects in practice in the first two decades after the Second World War were snared by two dragging anchors. The first was the scant resources in both money and materials, so that using quality building materials both internally and (especially for shopping centres) externally, was a virtual impossibility. The second was that older architects were trained in an era when gods with feet of clay were pre-eminent as teachers. Many of us fell for the egocentric fallacies of men like Le Corbusier, whose influencial forms, materials and textures were well reviewed in the 1987 Hayward Gallery on London's South Bank retrospective exhibition and whose influence is well attested in the horrid concrete bunker in which the exhibition was housed.

Thus if the exteriors were not bland, faceless rectangles and designed by architects of little talent, they tended to be attempts by serious designers to import strong forms to give life and meaning to the functions within. That is a laudable aim and some very powerful architecture resulted. The trouble was that the forms were expressed in concrete left raw off the shutter as The New Brutalists had taught and the depressing result was further compounded by unworkable commercial plan forms.

What to do with concrete

This chain of events is mentioned again in the context of refurbishment to make a constructive point. Namely for the many who have sympathy for what that generation of architects was trying to do, an immediate, simple and relatively inexpensive improvement to the concrete exterior of these buildings would be to paint them. There will be howls of protest from paid-up Brutalists who still labour under the delusion that raw concrete is beautiful, but they would be dramatically outvoted both now and in perpetuity by public opinion.

Much more to the point is the question of maintenance and there are still those who believe that paint is but a three to five year job. They are quite wrong. A new generation of exterior masonry paint is available which has a 20 year life: quite long enough to be acceptable as an exterior finish, especially when one considers the alternative of leaving the blackened concrete.[1]

One's aversion to fairfaced concrete (a grotesque misnomer if ever there was one) as a finished material

Tricorn Centre, Portsmouth
Shopping centres like this gave 1960's developments a bad reputation. The buildings are forbidding and few shops let at profitable rents.

has already been described, and the first generation of grubby bridges over the M1 were cautionary examples. A number of architects like BDP and YRM therefore tiled their elevations firstly with white glazed tiles like Blackburn shopping centre and the Manchester Magistrates Court and then with earth-coloured tiles with an all-through body and glaze at Rochdale shopping centre. To this day the forms look crisp and clean and they will be an acceptable backdrop for many generations of refurbishment.

Indeed the only reasons for not persevering with the potential of this material are firstly the public clamour for brickwork with its infinite possibilities, and secondly because whilst tiling is a perfectly sound technique, it is only as good as the specification, the detailing and the operatives. In our litigious days, failure by any one of these three elements could well result in claims and problems we could do without. One would therefore hesitate to recommend tiling or any other applied material such as glass mosaic or render to the exterior of concrete walls.

Enlivening big strong forms externally
With the basic material enlivened or made acceptable three more transient measures could be undertaken

Kajima tower block, Shinjuku, Tokyo
This 70 storey tower block is completely painted in a soft brown colour. Until you get within a yard of the panels they look like sandstone.

Base of Kajima tower, Shinjuku, Tokyo
A detail of the painted concrete at the base of the tower.

157

Manchester Magistrates Court
White tiled exterior. Architect: YRM.

London University
Wall laced with straggling Virginia creeper. The concrete is soot-stained and the creeper makes it look cracked.

with dramatic benefit – two by day and one by night. First much more use could be made of foliage and sensitive landscaping even when the buildings follow the site boundary. Good landscape consultants are necessary to ensure the plants will survive city conditions and trees, bushes and creepers should be predominantly evergreen. There is nothing more forlorn than a concrete wall laced with straggling Virginia creeper tendrils throughout the winter (the walls contrive to look cracked as well as dirty). More about this in the section on landscape in chapter 12.

Secondly we in Britain are not yet as vibrant and bold as the continentals when it comes to external graphics. Piccadilly Circus is always with us, of course, but Italy, Germany and Switzerland especially have some excellent examples of high quality signing which looks good either by day or night. The silhouette of free standing signs are usually a lesser joy during daylight because one cannot avoid seeing the support structure but good graphics would enliven many a dull wall surface in our early town centre schemes.

Thirdly, and wholly a night-time bonus, is floodlighting and accent lighting. Since Architecture Year in 1984 especially, many public buildings have benefited from an increasingly sophisticated use of this technique: 'painting' the building with light. Even very modest elevations can be transformed by selective highlighting and there is a novelty about the result because the light by night almost inevitably comes from the ground (or at best from adjacent rooftops) as distinct from the sky by day. Shadows and the play of light and shade are inverted, so giving a quite different appearance to the formal composition of the elevations.

Energy costs are high but there is no need to have the lights on throughout all the hours of darkness. It is well too to remember that light discourages mischief makers: flood lighting has always played a vital role in reducing crime to both people and property, quite apart from its positive role in attracting law abiding citizens: ask the Dean of any great cathedral.

The exterior has been dealt with first because remedial measures fall directly into the province of the architect. For the developer or fund wishing to protect its investment, however, attention is bound to be concentrated on the interior where the customers and shops are, and where the profits are made.

The importance of management

Interestingly the most important aspect of the internal refurbishment is not the quality of the finished product, but the way the process is managed. Some early refurbishments were disasters from this point of view. It was not sufficiently appreciated that there is a world of difference between refurbishment and a new normal building where a contract to construct is agreed with a contractor and the site in law then becomes his until that contract is fulfilled. The implication is that the builder is free to go about fulfilling his contract in whatever manner or sequence he elects as long as it is in accord with the contract.

When builders are refurbishing a shopping centre they must grasp the essential point that the whole design and building team is operating on a live patient. The traders are the working parts of the body and the people flowing to those working parts are the blood stream that keeps the whole thing alive whilst the operation is in process. Cut that flow off and you really are in trouble.

It follows that everything that is proposed and carried out should be done in collaboration with the tenants' association so that they understand before the event why a course of action has to take place. The developer must get the traders' input into the best way of achieving the result. Arbitary action will almost always be misinterpreted. Experienced national multiples apart, small traders will naturally approach the impending changes with deep suspicion. They have been trading in the centre for years, and are doing reasonably well, but they have no great resources to fall back on, to weather a dramatic fall-off in trade whilst the public parts are knocked about. Their inexperience affords no certainty that the restyled malls will attract new trade, yet they know with absolute certainty that the landlord is going to be looking for greatly enhanced rents when the process is complete.

Canterbury Cathedral by floodlight

Waverley Market by night

An example of faulty management

The prime ingredient for a successful refurbishment is first-class management and public relations. The relaunch could be soured for months if the disruption is bungled. One redevelopment scheme in Britain was completed by a developer who thinks to this day that the process was well handled. There follows an extended quote of one of the trader's opinion of the experience:

'From the beginning of the operation tenants were desirous of benefits but apprehensive about the consequential costs to them of work being carried out on such a large scale. It was apparent at the outset that the developers were going to have difficulties unless they appreciated and tailored their approach and communication to the differing needs of private and multiple tenants. This they failed to do and the first consequence was the considerable delay they experienced in getting the Deed of Variation approved – culminating in a threat to abort the whole scheme.

'A new Tenants Association was formed to co-ordinate the interests of all tenants and obtain from the developer and their agents information which had been singularly difficult to extract. Unfortunately the Association failed to get co-operation from a substantial number of tenants, especially the multiples.

'The developer did send representatives to association meetings and also issued newsletters recording the progress of the works, but tenants soon realised that when it was a matter of getting remedial action procrastination prevailed.

'A concrete floor screed was laid in the mall and there was an incredible amount of dust which penetrated the shops and ruined items of stock. The application of a sealer would have obviated this but complaints fell on deaf ears.

'New floor tiling proceeded during trading hours with very serious restriction of pedestrian flow. The work continued during normal trading hours despite frequent protestations.

'Our side of the mall was ordered to be closed because sub-contractors had left the area 'unsafe' for pedestrians. We issued an ultimatum that if closure was carried out we would summon the press to photograph the fiasco. The Clerk of Works was brought on site to board up the danger area.

'Our shop was flooded by an expansion joint leak after heavy rain. Stock was damaged. We made serious complaints about frequent water penetration from this faulty joint which had been disturbed by roofing work. They brought no response whatsoever.

'At approximately 6.15 pm many shops on the ground floor were inches deep in water from a fractured pipe which supplied the sprinkler systems. A steel girder had apparently been dropped on this plastic pipe which was lying exposed in a large earth cavity beneath the ramp at the main entrance. No-one was available who had knowledge of the stop-tap arrangements. The water was eventually turned off by the Fire Service who then proceeded to use plywood 'ploughs' to push the water back into the cavity where the pipe was. It later transpired that these were sumps into which the water could have drained spontaneously if only someone had been available to indicate their existence. No word of

explanation or apology was ever given to us about this event.

'Further obstruction to our side of the mall and the ground floor entrance to the mall was limited to space for only one person at a time during the afternoon.

'The developer's agent and insurer called to discuss the water damage to our floor tiles. One year later we still await the repairs that have been repeatedly promised.

'On Friday morning (one of our busiest days) there was a complete obstruction to the mall entrance because of electric work on the automatic doors.

Conclusions
'The failure to honour the terms of the Deed of Variation, the ignoring of complaints, the lip service and unfulfilled promises destroyed any trust which had been built up between the developer and the tenants.

'The complete lack of co-ordination and sensible planning in the programme of works, the lack of supervision of sub-contractors, the repeated failure of communication resulting in the resident Clerk of Works not even knowing when operations were taking place, and the total disregard for the interests of the tenants and their problems were almost beyond belief.

'The failure to inform tenants of the appointment of a centre manager and a complete breakdown in communications between him and the agents was another unfortunate episode during this trying time. His authoritarian and dictatorial attitude to tenants resulted in a petition signed by 77 tenants being sent to the developer for action.'

Lessons from the example

There is much more in the documentation but it demonstrates two things. First, good public relations with the tenants and first-class management are essential if a litany of complaint is to be avoided. From such a diary it is difficult to remember that the aims of both tenant and developer are identical – to create an environment where goods can be marketed and optimum profit made. One gets the impression that one side is actually trying to cancel out the efforts of the other.

The second clear message is the importance of the management of the floor surface renewal. Most of the complaints centre round problems of inaccessibility caused by floor laying obstructions. If shoppers cannot get to the shops, the trader might as well go home.

The size of the problem: special considerations in Britain

Nevertheless, in spite of the hazards, shopping centres must be brought up to date if they are to remain competitive. Refurbishment is certainly today's buzzword in shopping centre design. It has been reliably calculated that at least 30% of all retail work in the USA – a multi-billion dollar industry – is concerned with refurbishment. While such a figure is a significant pointer for Britain it should be remembered that refurbishment is very much more complicated here. There are several reasons. The first is that since the majority of our centres are built in towns and were therefore more complex to build than had they been built on a green field site they consequently will be technically difficult to alter. Secondly the British Landlord and Tenant Act is more onerous on the landlord than its American equivalent and it is not easy to negotiate for any change in the condition of your property if you start from a weak position.

A third factor is that many developers negotiated a full repairing lease with the tenant in an attempt to off-load as much responsibility as possible for the property.[2] Such a lease proves to be a sword of Damocles over the landlord when he wants to refurbish. How do you negotiate to alter someone's property when they say they have just spent any exorbitant figure that comes into their head on maintenance or some upgrading of their own? Willing though the developer may be to pay compensation he certainly does not relish being held over a barrel.

A fourth consideration is the failure of British developers to embrace the American concept of turnover rents. The term needs explanation. The British property world took a fundamentally wrong position on rents from the beginning of the shopping boom. In their efforts to secure predictable income, and therefore guaranteed growth, from their investment they instructed agents to quote 'rack rent' levels which means maximum current rents for the location. That is a formula for confrontation because if the trader does badly the landlord's rent is secure, and if the trader defaults in his or her payments that is legal grounds for repossession.

In the USA landlord and tenants agree a base rent which the former feels is the lowest he can accept to protect the investment, and which the latter feels confident they will be able to meet even if trade is not as good as their best expectations. This is the base turnover rent. There is then an 'open book' agreement between the two parties in which the trader's turnover is made known in detail to the landlord (sometimes these days by direct computer link from the trader's till to the management's accountancy office) and the parties share in agreed proportion any profit on turnover above the base figure.

We will not labour over the fine detail but the psychology should be obvious. The developer has a lease-long vested interest in the trader's success and it is of concern to both parties to see that conditions at every level are optimised. The relevance of turnover rents to refurbishment and to the management of the process is profound. Both sides have a direct financial incentive to make sure that trade disruption is reduced to the absolute minimum. Only one major developer (Capital & County) in Britain has consistently championed turnover rents and its chairman extols the virtues on numerous occasions. His is deservedly a successful company but why he remains a lone voice among his peers is a mystery.

Another important point for the developer team to grasp is that it is probably 15 years since the centre was built, and that since 'retail is fashion' one is looking to restyle the centre in as thorough and consistent a way as possible. It is no good thinking the centre can be dragged into the 1990's screaming 'good news!' on the back of a wash and brush up job.

Covering the malls

From a technical point of view one of the trickiest problems will stem from a decision to cover the malls or to replace solid roofs with daylight. Not only will structural difficulties be encountered but, even more significantly, the fire officer will almost certainly throw the book at the new proposals. And a pretty weighty tome it is. The rules have changed radically over the years and covering the malls will not only impose new restrictions, the mere alterations will enable the authorities to require all round statutory upgrading. More than usual, therefore, it is very wise to take the fire officer's and building inspector's recommendations along with one's earliest thoughts.

Tricky though covering may be, it is certainly the surest way of changing radically the whole ethos of the scheme. If shopping is to be 'theatre' (to quote the Americans) then the best way of enjoying the show is to get out of the weather – in Britain at least. At the same time people like to be conscious of the elements and of night and day. Glazing is therefore an essential component of covered malls and meeting places.[3]

Interestingly, though putting a new roof over a mall may seem a terribly disruptive operation, the technical

St Louis Centre, St Louis
The superb design of the floorscape of both main mall and galleries. There are many lessons for designers here – including technical problems with some of the tiles themselves.

161

St Louis Centre,
St Louis
Excellent hard and
soft landscaping
at the forecourt to
the two principal
entrances off 7th
street.

difficulties do not extend with equal severity to the management. Once one has decided what to do and how to do it, the builder erects a solid but temporary platform at high level and gets on with the job. The nuisance to the traders and shoppers below is minimal so long as the scaffold is erected out of trading hours and the props are sensitively (even imaginatively) located.

Restyling the floor finishes
On the other hand a restyled floor finish is a certain requirement and, whilst the technical problems are easy to solve, it is quite impossible to resurface a mall without causing a good deal of upset for at least some of the time to everyone using the place. Almost hourly liaison and consultation with tenants is imperative if trade is not to suffer dramatically.[4]

It is amusing to recall the change of opinions over a thirty year time span. High quality, precast and hydraulically pressed 3ft by 2ft (900mmx 600mm) concrete slabs, 2" (50mm) thick were the order of the day in the late 50's. Then someone tried quarry tiles, but they chipped and dirt stuck in the joints; and before you knew it terrazzo swept the board. It was smooth, non-slip, easy to clean, chewing gum would not stick or could easily be frozen and chipped off – and it was vandal-proof.

Now, in Britain in 1989, to even suggest terrazzo for mall floors is to risk being written off as out of date. Ceramics are the fashion – yes, those things that crack, that cannot be produced in rich vibrant colours if they are to be non-slip, that are difficult to lay, whose joints cannot be properly cleaned and whose overall surface is so uneven that it ruins the brushes of nearly every scrubbing machine known to mankind. There must be a Latin tag to cover the turnaround in fashion.

The argument runs, however, that ceramics have a character feel and look which can never be matched by terrazzo. They are simply different. Indeed some of the best recent floors in American centres are works of art and a pleasure to study in their own right. And, to hazard a prediction, before the decade is out we will be back to terrazzo but this time utilising much more fully its potential for rich pattern making. It is all part of the thrust for quality and novelty.

Since quality is in fashion it brings into sharp focus the particular skills of the interior designer, the illustrator and the graphic artist. If architects think they can get along without collaborating with these specialists, their myopia will deny them the highest flights of panache. The architect's contribution is incontrovertably responsible for the overall balance and content of the development within the cityscape, but the sheer gloss, and downright excitement of the internal design is the special realm of these supportive skills. Architects may try to dismiss them: the developer certainly will not. The accompanying photographs illustrate a number of examples where their specialised talents have contributed marvellously to the architectural 'armature' that was presented.

Introducing new uses
Turning to more clearly architectural matters, refurbishment is now often the catalyst for introducing new uses – even building types – into the centre. Their problems and their impact may be dramatic, but the end result is a more fully utilised centre and much overall benefit. For instance now that first floor trading is looked upon as a realistic option it is encouraging to see how often a food court is the spark which ignites a whole further level of trading and therefore of rental income.

Refurbishment also offers the chance of righting some original wrongs. Few of us always get the escalators going the right way, always put in the right number of lifts, never kill a shopping frontage by putting a ramp so that shoppers cannot see the shop windows: never make a public staircase too steep and never make the main entrance to the shopping experience look like the vomitory to a subway.[5]

This is a cue to pay tribute to developers in the context of claims and to say what a pleasure it usually is to work with entrepreneurs. Because they are that rare breed of risk takers and because they know that they too sometimes get things horribly wrong, they are acutely aware that consultants also make errors of judgement. As long as they are satisfied that you did your best, took all reasonable precautions and consulted all relevant opinion they take the view that some mistakes are to be expected and the way to settle them quickly is to get round a table to sort the problems out.

Whiteleys department store, London
Interior design contribution.

Waverley Market, Edinburgh
Interior design contribution.

It is a refreshing change from the sanctimonious, holier than thou approach taken by many other client bodies, both public and private, whose reflex action to a problem is to try to determine who is going to pay to put it right before a remedial finger is lifted; lawyers love them.

Backstage refurbishment

The refurbishment of public parts of centres has been highlighted because it is through the obvious value–added benefit of a restyled centre that the developer hopes to revitalise trade, raise the rents and hence maintain the value of his investment. It must not be overlooked however that many 'backstage' areas could well be overhauled and produce marked financial benefits. BDP, for instance, undertake energy audits where we seek to eliminate waste, use energy to better effect and enhance comfort levels without undue financial penalty. Servicing arrangements, sizes of yards, numbers and vintage of compactors, graphic signing to the service ways, management facilities and the efficient use of security staff are all fertile fields for imaginative input from designers who have the developer's interests at heart. In short, refurbishment is an opportunity to make more money by saving it.

The right rate for the job

Finally, and for consultants, a word about fees. In addition to the special chapter on this subject it is well to remember that refurbishment is specialised and time consuming – and therefore expensive. If you can agree a time scale it removes the risk to the consultant, but the client may feel exposed and vulnerable. If it is to be a percentage fee do not fall into the trap of quoting the rate for new work. The task is far more complicated than that and the interior designer's scales are much better geared to the frustrations and challenges of measuring, pulling down, remeasuring and designing to fit a location than anything in the RIBA booklet.

Of course judgement should be tempered with the thought that these are not small jobs: nor is it a simple paint job. Any worthwhile refurbishment of a 250,000 sq ft (23,000 sq metre) fifteen or twenty year old centre is likely to cost at least between £3m and £5m, so fees as well as design input will be substantial.

In a well judged fee agreement which is fair to both sides there should be ample scope to give a superlative service. The only thing that will inhibit excellent design is limited talent.

---

1. *I first came across its use in Japan where the 70 storey Kajima tower block in Shinjuku is painted a soft brown colour from top to toe. Until you get within a yard of the painted precast concrete wall panels they look like sandstone.*

2. *The reason why most American 'strip centres' (a row or cluster of single owner shops on Main Street) are so tawdry compared with conventional malls is that they are 'let nett, nett, nett.' The owner simply wants a regular rent and takes no responsibility for repairs, renewals, rates, taxes – nothing.*

3. *I speak from experience of trying vainly to achieve equal success with open squares and solid roofed malls.*

4. *Remember that dust is by far and away the most consistent complaint from tenants. Thousands of pounds worth of stock can be ruined by one hour's thoughtless grinding or drilling.*

5. *I have got that list, and a lot more, wrong in my time and it is a special delight to be asked to put them right without going through the nightmare of a claim for negligence.*

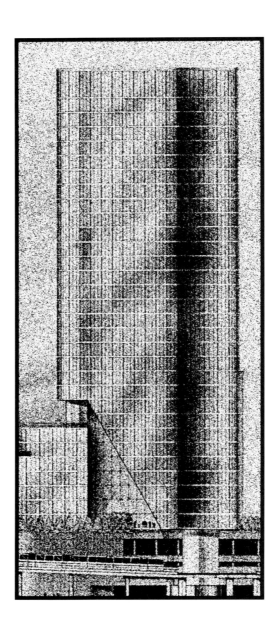

10

DEVELOPMENT COMPETITIONS

An explanation of the terminology

The reality: a near-lottery

The cost of development competitions

Getting better value out of the competition system

Ways to eliminate wasted design

A practical example at Lancaster

Choose a development team: not a scheme

Standards of submitted material

Drawings

Models

Brochures

Promoter's duty: good manners and bad

Bournemouth: a good example

Direct appointment: avoiding a developer competition

No opportunity for young, small offices?

10

DEVELOPMENT COMPETITIONS

An explanation of the terminology

First a word of explanation. Development competitions differ significantly from the open type of competition with which all architects are familiar. The latter are fairly rare events in Britain and they cover all types of building other than commercial retail centres. Usually the promoter calls the RIBA for advice and the Institute gives help in organising the competition, picking the jury and making sure that the whole event is conducted within their guidelines. Usually there are four or five premiated designs; the first prize gets the job and the prize money is rolled into the overall fee for the project.

Development competitions are quite different. Because in Britain the local authority is the best agent for central area land assembly – through either existing ownership or Compulsory Purchase powers – it is usually they who act as promoters. They place advertisements in the property press to the effect that they wish to see a certain tract of land developed for retail purposes and other uses. They invite developers to express interest and to send with their application a note of their track record and financial standing so that interviews may be held with a view to forming a short list for further negotiation. Interviews usually cut the numbers to four or five developers (often in two stages) then the final group set to work to produce detailed proposals and a winner is chosen. So much for the facts.

The reality: a near-lottery

The actuality is so fraught with hazard and uncertainty that there is no more fertile ground for the production of double-talk than these development competitions. Developers rail against them and say they will never enter another (usually the day after they have heard they have lost one) yet they put their names in by the score (literally) for the next big scheme that is announced. Architects swear they are fed up with competitions and deplore the wasted effort: there is no 'second prize'. Yet they hare around the developer circuit urging them to retain them either 'at cost' or for no fee at all.

Local authorities love them: legendary names promising their very own community the earth is intoxicating; the gladiatorial contest for their fair hand is titillating. The only guaranteed statement which appears in every brief is the one about how critical quality will be to success in the competition. In fact the financial offer is of paramount importance. The council has a duty to get the best possible price for its land and if it fails to do so it can be challenged by audit. It can give reasons why it does not want to accept the highest offer but in practice the advice of the treasurer is difficult to ignore. Design quality is very subjective and of dubious vote-catching potential, and councillors feel that the evidence of hard cash and the best deal done is bound to influence the electorate. As a result, out of scores of competitions we can count on the fingers of one hand the times that the best financial offer did not prevail.

The cost of development competitions

Regardless, then, of their vagaries, development competitions are here to stay. The lure and the challenge is too compelling. Yet the waste of time and skill is prodigious. The money that is lavished upon many of the big competitions is quite indefensible, especially when it is manifestly evident that the result, based on the highest financial offer, has time and again not been in the best interests of the community.

It is all too common knowledge to developers and of all too little interest to local authorities who sit in judgement that any substantial development competition (say a £20m scheme) will cost each of the competing teams at least £50,000 and frequently nearer £100,000, depending on how one quantifies the expenditure.

In a recent competition BDP work alone cost £85,000 so the total client and team costs would be well in excess of £125,000. The brochure cost £30,000 (printing alone £16,000) and the model another £14,000. Three hundred brochures were printed so at £100 a copy it was galling to see councillors screwing them up into a ball and jamming them into the pockets of their black leather jackets. Without question this competition through all its phases cost the combined development teams a minimum of £600,000. And that is cost: not profit.

Every major development competition involves sums of this order; local authorities bear absolutely no financial responsibility and display a disinterest in the consequences that can only come from years of inurement to personal monetary risk. A number of people have proposed radical changes to eliminate such senseless waste but none has found general acceptance. Further, so long as the rewards for developing in the best locations are so lucrative and so long as designers are prepared to work competitions on a 'glad or sad' speculative basis there is little prospect of fundamental change.

It should also be said that land owners, be they private or public, would be silly to forego the financial benefits of competition. Developers who make a tongue in cheek protestation that they could give a far better service if the landowner would negotiate solely with them are usually hoping that the treasurer is naive enough not to know that he or she can auction competing teams up by millions of pounds in the final stages of the competition. There is no doubt that a landowner of a prime site is sitting on a licence to print money both personally and for the developer who puts exactly the right kind of retail accommodation on it.

So what is the practical way of alleviating the worst excesses? Much money is made by developers and funds, much money flows into the coffers of local authorities and the eventual fee rewards to the successful teams of architects, engineers, surveyors, lawyers and agents are highly attractive. Yet the end result is not good enough. By and large the quality of the urban form, and the detailed design of our post-war town centres is poor. They are the subject of universal condemnation. The system does not deliver an acceptable quality of urban environment.

Getting better value out of the competition system

Let us start at the beginning: at the point where a landowner decides to offer a parcel of land on the open market. Unless the landowner is unusually knowledgeable and resourceful the first thing he or she should do is to appoint an advisory team. Experience of a development at Kingston-upon-Thames was exemplary in this respect. The client appointed internationally known estate consultants, architects and surveyors to prepare to their approval a comprehensive brief. Once written the brief became largely irrelevant for it had fulfilled its initial purpose of concentrating the mind to ascertain exactly what the clients wanted to see on the site as distinct from how much they were going to get for it. The competition was then announced and the expected spate of suitors applied. The process was then one of making sure that only the teams with a track record and a balance of experience proceeded to a 'long short list' and subsequently by interview to the final short list where design ideas were called for.

Qualitively, however, this method does little to ensure that the best design wins, for at the end of the day the highest bid is still the most potent factor. Indeed, although our developer won the day we were left in no doubt that our design had not been the decisive factor. The private landowner was under the same accountability pressures as the local authority because he has shareholders to answer to – and their interest in design quality is minimal.

Ways to eliminate wasted design

To cut down abortive design costs one or two consultants have put forward the view that the developer team could be chosen by outline sketch schemes supported only by bids from developers on the percentage return or yield they would seek if appointed. The flaw here is that it does not give the landowner the benefit of competition on specific items, the most important of which is the premium offered. If a developer really wants a particular scheme (to balance a portfolio, to give workload for staff, because the building content ideally matches a funding structure, because he feels he has very attractive pre-lets and so on) he will bid some extraordinary figures. It is unrealistic to deprive the landowner of this benefit.

A practical example at Lancaster

If there is to be a competition there is a lot to be said for the bidding to be based on an established scheme. BDP's experience at Lancaster is an example.

The local authority appointed the design and estate consultancy team it favoured (pointers as to how this should be done come later) and together they drew up a scheme which suited them as to the content and quality. Actually they offered two sites together; one throwing up a negative value because of its civic content, the other a very attractive proposition in

the best retail location in town. Outline planning permission was obtained from council for the proposals and in a sensitive city like Lancaster great care was taken to get the support of environmentalists, both local and national, at the level of the Royal Fine Arts Commission.

The local authority retained development control of the less desirable retail site and it was written into the brief for the bids that the council's consultants were to be retained. In other words the council was effectively the developer and was simply seeking funds. Because the council needed funds to progress the less valuable site it was obliged to go down the traditional developer route for the 'good' site. Bids were called for on the basis of a prepared design but latitude was given to vary the scheme content and layout if a better plan occurred to the developer. On this site BDP was retained as the design consultants to the council, but to avoid a conflict of interest were debarred from acting for any of the competing developers. They were each to choose their own designers and agents.

Thus in respect of the council developed site there was no abortive work done because the design was settled directly between client and architect before bids were called for. In respect of the developer competition site, abortive design was minimised because developers could compete on a scheme already prepared and it was entirely up to them whether they wanted to instruct their own chosen architect to prepare an alternative – and risk it being disqualified if the council or their advisers (BDP and Donaldsons) disliked or advised against it.[1]

Choose a development team: not a scheme

Whatever method promoters choose to adopt in selecting a development team they need generally to change their tactics if quality is to be an increasing component of the criteria. The selected design will bear little resemblance to the final scheme so it is much more important to select the right team rather then the most seductive scheme. The former one is stuck with: the latter one can change.

Promoters are universally lax in doing their homework on the competing teams. A bland (even misleading) catalogue of previous experience is not enough.[2] The promoter must grasp that a process is being started which will last a minimum of five years, probably nearer seven or eight: design development; outline planning; public inquiry; listed building consent; road closures; detail planning; production drawings; tenders; building; shopfitting; letting. A huge range of professional skills will be needed on the job – and all applied with the patience of a saint and the negotiating powers of Machiavelli.

In short, people will be crucial to a successful scheme, quite apart from the money bid. The key questions therefore are:

What is the experience of the team fielded for interview?

Which of them will lead the team?

How committed are the leader and other key members to other projects?

Does the personality and the type of work done by the team appeal to the promoter? (The prospect of working intimately for 5 to 10 years with someone you dislike is hardly attractive).

How extensive are the total resources of the firm and how will it cope? [3]

Then the promoter should embark on a tour and do two things:

1 visit the jobs the team say they have designed and see how they work and whether they look well;

2 especially if the client is a local authority promoter, meet the opposite numbers in those authorities where the team, both developer and designers, have worked and ask about commitment, fulfilment of promises, and attitudes when the going got rough.

Standards of submitted material

The question of the submission of drawings, reports and models is a difficult one to resolve satisfactorily but here are a few guide lines and proposals. Since this is by far the most expensive part of the competition process the first requirement is that the promoter prepares the clearest possible brief. Failure to do this will result in a mass of questions from competitors, abortive designing, addendum briefs, extensions of time, and at worst, and by no means uncommon, dissimilar schemes. It is the promoters responsibility to ensure that apples can be compared with apples.

Take all possible steps to limit presentation material and content to the minimum so that the promoter, to whom this is often a novel experience, is not blinded by showmanship. The promoter should understand that he or she is not choosing a finished scheme – as one tries to do in a traditional architectural competition. The aim is to choose the most appropriate concept for the town, and a team. The scheme which gets built will differ radically from the winning design, simply because retail accommodation is both fickle and susceptible to fashion. Until designs are tested against the market

there is no way of knowing what the best permutation of spaces and traders will be – and that comes much later in the process.

Drawings

The drawings should thus cover plans, sections and elevations. On very large schemes plans at 1:500 will be sufficient but 1:200 enables designers to show their experience in detail planning far better, even though the details will alter. Sections and elevations should be to a minimum scale of 1:200 because 1:500 allows too little indication of detailed form. There is a good case for making 1:200 also the largest scale for elevations. 1:100 elevations are very time-consuming and there is an irresistible temptation to fill the sheet with detail. Drawing brick courses and tile patterns is a pleasant and brainless therapy for young architects, but at £25 per hour it does not advance the cause of the competition one iota – on the other hand one sheet of details at 1:20 or 1:10 enables the designer to show a thorough grasp of the sort of quality detail he or she has in mind.

Competitors should be allowed to colour the drawings and project shadows. On plans colour is a great help to legibility and is quicker, cheaper and clearer than hatching. On elevations the competitor is better able to express the three dimensional qualities of the design – and it forces him or her to come clean about the colour of the proposed brick, stone, slate, glass or metal cladding.

Models

Models are a vexed question. Architects love them because they are the next best thing to seeing the completed building. The bigger the scale and the more explicit the detail, the more stimulating the ego trip. The promoter also adores them. The flattery done is highly persuasive but almost wholly misleading because as

Competition model for the Isle of Dogs development
Far too complex and expensive for its purpose.

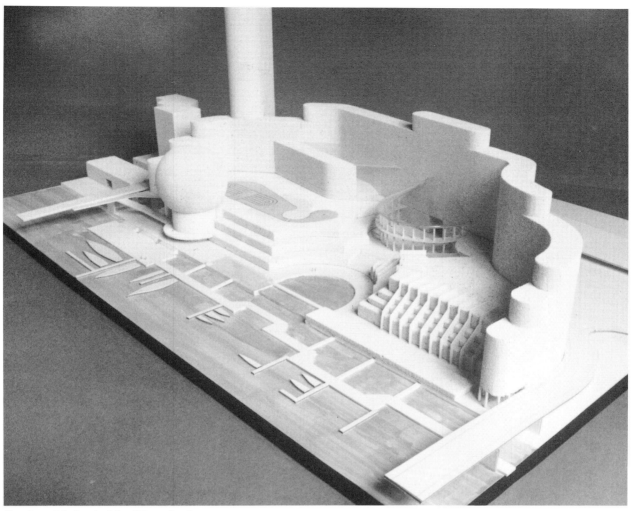

Sketch models for the Isle of Dogs development
Models made out of readily carved polystyrene are quite adequate to illustrate the forms.

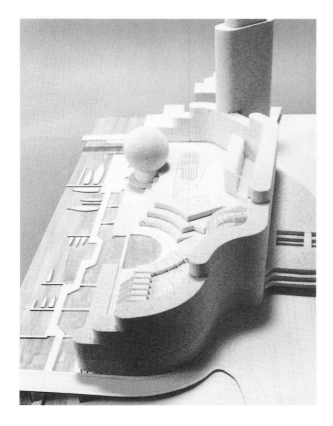

we saw earlier, the prospect of getting a development that looks just like that is nil. But someone has to foot the bill for this tantalizing exercise in deception and all concerned should be clear that no detailed model of a major scheme can be produced to a scale of 1:200 upwards for less than £10,000. BDP has frequently produced models costing £20,000.

A further disadvantage of a detailed model is that it takes away about a month of creative thinking time from the competitors and therefore from the promoter. The reason for this is that complex models take about six weeks to produce and though there can be some overlap with the production of design information, the model maker must have a complete and fixed set of drawings as soon as possible.

Nevertheless, models are the only way to demonstrate the competitor's sensitivity to the urban fabric into which over 90% of British schemes must fit. Models therefore should not just be permitted, but required. However, since material, colour and detail can quite adequately be shown on drawings models should be restricted to monochrome, natural timber, sprayed white or a neutral colour – and preferably restricted to 1:500 and never bigger than 1:200.[4]

Brochures

Brochures as they are currently conceived should be banned. Developers and their designers are at present on a tread-mill they dare not step off. Full colour is 'de rigeur' for plans, sections, elevations, perspectives, comparative photographs of other schemes, charts, photographs of the model, and sometimes even the text. The cost is quite out of proportion to its value.

Anyone who understands printing knows that full colour brochures make financial sense only when the print run is over 10,000. Travel brochures are the perfect example: so cheap individually they can be given away. Developers face an agonizing choice. Either make up by hand about a dozen brochures as called for by the promoter with photographic colour reductions of the competition drawings and hand colour the charts and diagrams, or go for a limited print run of say 250 on the thesis firstly that the promoter is sure to call for another dozen or so (especially if he or she wins) and secondly it would be nice to have some for publicity purposes for future schemes.

The first prediction is a racing certainty and there are few occupations more frustrating than making up by hand a further score of brochures when one knows full well that the cost of the individual hand produced brochures is so high that beyond about 25 it would have been progressively cheaper to have had them printed professionally. And printed brochures look so much better.

As with models, highly finished glossy brochures also take away time that could be better used for creative thought (or shortening the competition time so that

Brochure illustration for the Isle of Dogs development
Again, far too elaborate and expensive for its purpose.

busy professionals can get on with other work). Three full weeks should be allowed for a full colour brochure and it goes without saying that the process can only start when the finished art work is to hand. At least, it should go without saying, but it is surprising how often the final submitted drawings differ from the brochure, simply because the design team had a better idea after printing started.[5]

The expectation of usefulness to support future competitive submissions is almost wholly illusory. 'Almost' because if one wins, the first few weeks after appointment generally produces new ideas that soon begin to make the splendid 'concept for the future' look like an archive document from the past. The whole urge is to produce an amended document as soon as possible so that the agents can trawl the retail world to solicit expressions of interest.

If you lose the competition the trauma is so great, the blow to self-esteem so profound and the embarrassment of showing a failed submission so acute that such brochures rarely see the light of day again.

Brochures should therefore be restricted to simple black and white A4 documents in standard spiral bindings. They should comprise a description of the scheme, its context, the proposed method of procurement, a bar chart of programme times, the team members and any black and white explanatory sketches with which the designer would like to amplify the scheme. A pocket at the back should contain dyeline prints of the drawings: again black and white only. The financial bid is always in a separate sealed letter.

To the argument that every councillor or board member would like to have his or her own full colour documentation the response should be 'rubbish'. It is the duty of the technical advisers to educate them on the cost implications, persuade them to be at the full scheme presentation, then tell them where the original drawings and the model can be viewed.

Promoter's duty: good manners – and bad
It is also appropriate to mention here two matters frequently overlooked by promoters and which give great offence to competitors. When a promoter is the recipient of many thousands of pounds worth of free design ideas, agency advice and cost implications, it might be assumed that excellent presentation conditions would be good manners at least, beneficial to the promoter at best.

Not a bit of it. Colleagues and competitors have lost count of the times the windows could not be blacked out, there were no plugs for electrical equipment, there were no display boards on which to pin drawings and, most common, the room was too small to allow either the drawings to be pinned up or the number of people on both sides to be seated.

We recall a submission for a scheme costing well into nine figures which had from our team alone 35 drawings and two models, one of which was 7ft by 3ft (2.1m x 0.9m). Ten people from our side were needed to explain all aspects of the scheme: the promoter brought a further ten. We requested facilities for two projectors and two screens. There were five shortlisted teams with similar complex submissions to explain over a stipulated time period of one and a half hours each. The room allocated for the presentation measured 20ft sq x 8ft high (6m x 2.4m). A ten minute interval was allowed

between presentations during which every vestige of the last scheme had to be removed before the succeeding presentation could be mounted.

Imagine the chaos. We were the fourth team in to bat. The air was rancid with over five hours of previous occupation. The jury was tired and dazed with the labour of trying to choose between projects of such enormity. The previous teams were understandably drained with the effort of presentation at the peak of awareness for an hour and a half and were slow to demount their drawings. The new team, all tense and edgy, was anxious to get on with displaying their work properly and the tiny room was full of false bon homie, since, because everyone knows everyone in the development world, corny jokes are the only way to relieve tension.

To the question, 'Why did the jury not spread the interviews over two or three days to give everyone adequate time to present and assimilate three months work costing well over £200,000 each for a job costing £200,000,000?' the answer was 'the jury are terribly busy men'.

You smile understandingly through bared teeth. A desire to grasp them warmly by the throat is all but irresistible. (An essential part of the test is keeping your temper...).

Secondly you would think that when a promoter has had the benefit of several hundred thousand pounds worth of free advice from the cream of the development world he or she would have the grace to put on an exhibition of the competing schemes so that all may see and some may learn. At a very minimum it would be a courtesy to the competitors who have laboured hard. Again, such ocurrences are rare: indeed with private promoters they are, in our experience, non-existent.

Bournemouth: a good example
Not all is gloom, however: witness an admirably arranged competition by Bournemouth District Council and Grosvenor Estates. The competition itself was unusual, indeed unique to date, in that the joint developers approached the RIBA and asked them to propose six firms of architects with flair and experience to be invited to compete on a carefully worded brief (which prohibited models among other things) so that the promoters might choose an architect not a developer.

The promoters generated an immediate aura of goodwill by offering an honorarium of £10,000 to each competitor: the winner to merge his or her winnings into the fee agreement.[6] Bournemouth then granted a reasonable time span of three months for the competition and notified all competitors of the list of architects involved. That avoided the silly charade in most competitions where promoters try to keep the matter secret. It usually takes about 24 hours for competitors to ring around and find out who is involved.

For the presentation ample sized rooms were made available, and each competitor was sent a plan of the room some days before the event. The time of the presentation was notified as was the duration permitted. The jury moved between the rooms so competitors were not embarrassed by having to make idle chatter to other teams in a waiting room. Times were rigidly adhered to (one garrulous competitor was told his time was up when he had barely completed his introduction) and only permitted material was allowed (another competitor tried to show a model and was told to take it out of the room). The 45 minute interviews were completed in the day. Winner and losers were notified within 24 hours and by the end of the week the losers and the winner had received their honorarium. There was then a public exhibition of the drawings. It really is very simple.[7]

Direct appointment: avoiding a developer competition
Even better for architects, of course, are the occasions on which local authorities decide to be their own developer as at The Lanes in Carlisle and Waverley Market in Edinburgh. In these cases the local authority either chooses an agent to help select an architect or goes it alone and selects both consultants by interview. Either way the result is that there is no drawn scheme competition, the traditional developer is eliminated and the landowner pockets the developer's profit. Developers are understandably less than enthusiastic about this method. The consultants and local authority pool their experience to get the right scheme, then this is put to the funding market for competitive bids on the yield required and the degree to which the fund will support the scheme.

These rather technical terms simply express what financial return the funding agency expects to receive for putting up the money to build the scheme. The total needed is far in excess of the cost of building because to that sum must be added fees for all the professionals involved (usually around 15%), the cost of lending the money, and the cost of acquiring land and property – which the local authority will usually acquire through its compulsory purchase powers and recover the money from the Fund. Funds differ markedly in the degree to which they will put money into a town. They take a view about the strength of the local economy, its potential within the region, and the degree to which they may have other risk investments there. In one case two financial tenders were comparable but the underbidder said that in addition to the total cost of funding (about £15m) he would be willing to put up to £23m in the town if necessary, so giving the local authority a comfortable feeling that there was a £8m contingency available if for any reason the scheme over -spent or was extended. The highest yield bidder would only go up to £17m. The underbidder got the job.

This route presumes a highly competent and experienced consultant team who work well together. The local authority is likely to lean heavily upon their guidance. Unhappily for entrepreneurially-minded councils this format has, at the time of writing, been frowned upon by central government. One would have thought that with the current market-orientated self-help, get-on-your-bike style of government this kind of local initiative which acts clearly to the benefit of the community in that the entire profits are retained for its use, would be encouraged. It is also a very unwise restriction because there is room for many types of development procurement and they each have a place and a 'best buy' situation.

No opportunity for young, small offices?
An important question is raised by this chapter. Since there are some 4500 architectural practices in the United Kingdom and the average size is five, what chance is there for brilliant young designers to break through? All the scenarios seem geared to the operation of large practices: what about the small office?

Here there is a real dilemma. As noted earlier developers and Funds are in the risk business but they are not gamblers or they would take to horseracing. In fact their whole aim is to narrow the risk to nil and opt for safety so they are monumentally disinterested in taking a flier with an inexperienced architect. They are in fact a good deal more interested in who is going to lead the design team from the firm they have selected than is the local authority or landowner who sets up the competition. The idea of a young Utzon winning an opera house competition in Australia with a set of wispy 6B pencil sketches is not a scenario for a central area scheme. Too much money, too many shareholders, too many careers are at stake. The developer cannot wriggle out of trouble with a lottery as they did in Sydney.

Then the schemes are large and need large scale human resources. A shopping scheme would swamp most offices.

Finally, since developers are in the risk business they try to share that risk, and until the Fund is on board the person who is spending the most money is the architect. On scale fees (or on any arrangement) the architect will probably earn up to 35% of his or her fee by taking the scheme up to detail planning submission stage and that means several hundred thousand pounds on a scheme of any significance – before a Fund is in sight. A developer will therefore try to get the designers to work for nothing or, if squeezed, at cost. That may pay the rent, the wages and the telephone bill but it certainly will not keep the practice afloat as a business unless there are other schemes in the office in full fee earning mode. A small office simply cannot cope with that kind of treatment: they would go under while waiting for their first real fee-based cheque – and the developer knows that.

Paradoxically the big, well-established and highly respected developers understand this dilemma to the extent that they will pay quite liberally in these early stages, but at the same time they will only use the big, highly experienced practices. The small practitioner is usually left with the small developer who is also limited in resources, so they play a cat and mouse game with each other; both cry poverty until one or the other cracks.

For all these reasons one must conclude that shopping centres are in the main big office business. The most fruitful way of bright designers with small offices becoming involved is when they form single project partnerships with big offices full of people and financial resource. BDP's work with Douglas Stephen at the Brunel Centre in Swindon, with Ostick and Williams at Castle Court in Belfast and with Jeremy Dixon on the Royal Opera House seem excellent pointers.

So the competition system staggers on and is wide open to abuse. Sometimes the promoter takes the best financial deal possible at a final 'Dutch Auction' then ruthlessly pinches ideas from the other submitted schemes. The most unscrupulous developer will promise the earth to get appointed – the 'plaiting fog' ploy.

Whilst it will never be totally immune from unfairness and abuse these suggestions move some way to removing the roughest edges. At the very least and with all its faults no developer competition has led to as scurrilous events as those surrounding the Vienna

United Nations Industrial Development Organisation competition of 1971[8] or the bizarre result of the two competitions on the north and south side of Trafalgar Square in 1985 – all three held under the august auspices of the architectural establishment: one of them under the rules of the International Union of Architects.

1. In the event the winning team elected not to alter the designs for 'the Council's site', they altered the detailed layout of 'the developer's site' but kept the strategy, produced a design of sensitivity and offered the best financial bid by a very substantial margin.

2. I recently sat through an interview where one of the competing designers ran through a very impressive list of jobs and he correctly guessed that the promoter would fail to observe that only one very small job was completed and the rest were proposals – some from previously failed competitions.

3. When the job gets above £10m – and most central area schemes are well in excess of that, the total architect, engineering and surveying skills are likely to involve at least 30 people. A recent £50m BDP scheme committed over 60 multi-discipline staff at its peak.

4. That at least would have eliminated the 12ft by 7ft model from one of our competitors at Ealing. It could not be manoeuvred into the municipal building.

5. Again, 'better idea' sounds better than 'we changed our minds' at the interview.

6. Why indeed should promoters who have selected what they deem to be the top half-dozen developers expect them to pour out ideas on their behalf for no recompense? The effrontery of the proposition can only be measured by the fact that the same people would expect the clock to start ticking immediately they asked advice from their accountant, lawyer or consultant paediatrician.

7. The sad postscript is we now learn that Bournemouth Council has decided not to proceed with the scheme so adding to the dismal parade of competition experiences.

8. Because my firm was involved in the Vienna competition I will let your blood chill to the following narrative. In 1971 the United Nations sponsored a huge international competition. The project was to provide world headquarters for the UN Industrial Development Organisation and the International Atomic Energy Authority. It was also to create a conference centre for the city of Vienna. The scheme attracted 273 entries from all over the world and the first indication of impending trouble came right at the start when a Dutch architect told me that his firm was not entering because their information was that 'an Austrian firm had to win it'. I told him that we had faith in the International Union of Architects under whose guidance the competition had been organised.

An international jury was set up and the results were announced: 1st Cesar Pelli (USA): 2nd BDP (UK): 3rd a firm from West Germany: 4th Staber (Austria). Delighted, we went to Vienna to pick up our prizes. It was the highest placing for a British firm in an international competition this century.

In Vienna the four premiated firms were told that the jury had not been fully satisfied with any design and had decided to offer each contestant a commission lasting three months to develop their scheme in much greater detail. This we all agreed to do and a prestigious technical committee was appointed to help the original jury to re-judge the resulted. This time the jury awarded the project to BDP (UK) by a vote of 8 to 1. Even more delighted we set off again to Vienna to receive the commission and start work. There then ensued a strange hiatus during which ceremonies were postponed and no information was forthcoming about awarding the contract. The British Embassy found it quite impossible to penetrate the veil of secrecy.

Then suddenly one evening Chancellor Kreisky came on Austrian television to announce that the winner was the Austrian competitor, Staber. We were in our hotel room. We had received a total of £25,000 in prize money and spent £100,000 on our effort.

11

FEES – GLAD OR SAD

Architects and fees

The 'share the risk with me' ploy

Speculative work is inimical to quality

What sharing the risk does not mean

The input from other professions

Agents and speculative work

Should architects give freely of their design skill?

Between winning the job and getting it funded: a trying time

Ground rules for negotiation

Who to put on the job

What level of remuneration?

When to get onto the fully agreed fee basis

What to charge for competitions

Payment for the control of shop front design

Why a fee?

What to charge for shop front monitoring

11

FEES – GLAD OR SAD

Architects and fees

Here is a separate chapter on the subject of fees because architects find it one of the most difficult aspects of commercial design work. There are two principal reasons. The first is that by their very nature, architects find the subject of fees somewhat distasteful. Traditionally they have been shielded from bargaining for their reward by a mandatory fee scale laid down by the RIBA. As soon as the subject of money cropped up architects used to send the client a copy of the RIBA's little purple booklet with a cover note saying that scale so and so would apply. Clients usually agreed without demur. Mandatory fees were abolished in 1982 and architects must now quote against a specific service and in competition if necessary with other architects.

In fact so intense is some architects' aversion to the discussion of fees – and the more 'artistic' the architect the more acute the aversion – that many ultimate controversies and lawsuits have been caused because the architect did not even remember to make a fee agreement before the job started on site.

The second reason is that most clients would, in the first months of the project, like the architect to give his or her services free until they know that the job is firm. That process can take years, always many weeks or months.

Most of this chapter discusses the period up to the commission becoming firm because it is a most difficult time for both parties. During this period there is no job, the developer is wholly at risk, yet there is a mountain of work to be done if the project is to be landed – and by far the greatest proportion of that work falls upon the architect.

There is no need to describe the fee agreement for the job proper because that is well covered in the various professional institutes' fee manuals and these are readily available. Both clients and consultants might however welcome some discussion of fees in the grey areas before the client has enough confidence to commit him or herself contractually to the designers.

Until the government ruled that the RIBA should abandon its mandatory fee scale and offer scales for guidance only, most top class practices never did work speculatively. They had a very good answer to developers who propositioned them by saying that they dare not risk the disciplinary consequences by breaking the Code of Practice. Many well-established practices held to this line throughout the 60's and 70's and they were able to refer potential clients to some very well publicised cases where practices had been disciplined by the RIBA.

Granted the Code was often honoured more in the breach than in its intent, because as long as some money changed hands the RIBA found itself powerless to act. Although the sum might be derisory it was difficult to prove that the service had not been appropriately minimal.

The 'share the risk with me' ploy

A number of practices however fell for the developer's argument that they were prepared to take a risk and the architect should share that risk. The reward for success was profit for the developer and a job for the architect. They did not add that when the job was firm the developer was then practically certain to suggest a fee cutting arrangement, usually on the grounds that the job was so big, repetitive and simple that it could be done practically in one's sleep. Anyway hadn't the architect already done most of the design on a glad or sad basis? It is now history that because so few reputable design practices succumbed to this line of attack so little of shopping design merit was built in those early decades.

Developers who were berated by the adage that 'if you pay peanuts you get monkeys' were quite unmoved because they only wanted monkeys in the first place. A whole generation of developer was allowed to get away with the belief that there would always be plenty of architects around who would be prepared to defy their professional code.[1]

Ironically, in those early days designers could get involved in this glad or sad process with a good deal less financial exposure than they can at present. Discounting for a moment the profound impact of inflation on office costs since the 60's, developers rarely used to find themselves in the enormous competitions which are now current. The process was more one of land assembly and testing alternative designs to see whether a scheme could be cobbled together. A slick and facile designer could not only make himself invaluable to a developer but he could do literally dozens of alternative scenarios at very little cost. Presentations, brochures, models and so on were not an issue. They came much later when the job was all but landed and a final presentation had to be made to the local Council.

Indeed this is a process that is prevalent in North America to this day. Because local authorities lack British powers of land assembly they rarely get involved in offering significant parcels for tender. Developers are left to assemble plots themselves and then propose a scheme which has been worked out with designers of their choice. American architects compete for developer's work but they are spared the agonising competition process so prevalant in Britain.

Speculative work is inimical to quality

Since the late 70's the scene has changed radically in the

UK. Local authorities still seek the best financial deal and the developer competition is demonstrably the best way to squeeze the optimum. It would not be too bad for the architect if it stopped there, but another dimension has arrived to muddy the pure waters of financial gain. Every official and unofficial organ of community concern now wants the town centre to look good as well as work efficiently . That should be (and is) the best news architects have heard for years. We are thrilled to bits to see the now ubiquitous paragraph in the brief about 'the highest standards of design' being required. But, even if we put aside the cynicism with which it is usually ignored in favour of the maximum financial offer, few developers have cottoned on to the flip side of the 'monkeys' adage, which is that high quality design takes time and is very costly. Only fellow architects will fully identify with the truth of this. The evidence of quality architecture down the ages is clear: great buildings do not just happen.

When, therefore, a developer wants an architect to work for nothing in the competition stages of a job a number of things need to be borne in mind.

What sharing the risk does not mean
The first is that when the developer tries the one about 'share the risk with me' remember that he is proposing no such thing. What is meant is 'share the risk of losing with me'. That is certainly true but if your team wins, all you will get out of it is your fee at whatever percentage you can negotiate. That fee, if it is anywhere near the RIBA Advisory Scale will enable you to do your job diligently and professionally (and the client will quite rightly expect that). But it in no sense offers you a share of the profit a developer is expecting for having risked his shirt. That is the privilege of the entrepreneur and if the architect wants to join these ranks he or she is now free to do so – but that is another subject.

The input from other professions
Now, it may well be protested that other professions – engineers and quantity surveyors – will often work for nothing so why not the architect? The answer is simple: the amount of work they do during the competition is small as a percentage of their total service and eventual fee. For example on a competition for a £30m development the architect is likely to spend a minimum of £30,000 at cost with the partner time thrown in free. If the engineers of all disciplines spend more than £5,000 their input has probably been needlessly extravagant. Similarly the quantity surveyor's input will be small on a hourly basis – but absolutely vital in qualitive terms. The section on 'Cost and the Quantity Surveyor' in chapter 12 elaborates the reasons, so here it is sufficient to say that upon the QS rests the responsibility for the level of the developer's bid for the site. But the hours spent are minimal.

Agents and speculative work
It may also be protested that the agents will do months of work speculatively. Here the reply is different and the issues more complex. Agents do indeed spend much time researching the field to give their best judgement, and the good ones spend many hours with the architects at the concept stage. Their task is to make sure the space utilisation gives the best possible value for money so that rents can be maximised and the developer bid can outdo the rivals. Since the financial offer is usually the winning factor, the accuracy of the QS cost and the agent's income cannot be over-estimated.

Even when there is no competition involved agents have sometimes spent years trying to demonstrate to developers that a scheme is worthwhile. The first thing that needs to be said, therefore, is that these highly professional skills are expended by very experienced people and it is quite unjust to expect them to be given freely. Given the level of remuneration for successful schemes, it might be argued that these speculative endeavours should be offered at 'cost', but to give them away is to denigrate the value of the service.

The same considerations affect the architect and a number of factors make it even more vital that the element of free, speculative work be minimised. The RIBA fee scale has always been finely honed to give proper reward for work done at each stage of the job. At no point in the course of the project does it produce a dollop of money quite out of proportion to the effort expended though it is true to say that the 35% of the fee for the design stage gives a high enough profit to enable the firm to fund the very high time expenditure in the production and the supervision stage. The fees on Ealing Broadway for instance ran into millions, but in the working drawing period nearly 60 people worked on the job for months on end. Thus even if the fee agreement specified quarterly payments, the fact that they are in arrears means that the design profession had to fund up to £750,000 in fees before each quarter's payment.

In contrast the agent's fees come at long intervals but in huge sums relative to the very small numbers of staff working on the job – frequently just one or two senior people and attendant overheads. If they can pace their internal cash flow properly, the bonanza day can tide them over many a fallow month. For instance, the fund raising fee is between 0.75% to 1% of the money raised. On £30m that is £300,000 and if the job is prime and Funds are sniffing around eagerly it is a very attractive reward for the work involved.

Again the best agents now offer a project coordination service and this is an essential part of their expertise – especially in the early stages of the project. The fee for this service is usually 1.5% of the total project cost including all on-costs (except, of course, their own fee). This fee is much more truly earned in the sense of hours expended, especially on long, complex jobs, and they can only be expended by people at partner or very senior level. Nevertheless, the actual numbers of staff employed are minimal – usually not more than a partner and an assistant.

Next comes the letting fee. If the scheme is good tenants are clambering for a pitch and some schemes are in danger of being 100% pre-let before a sod is dug. 'In danger' because no sensible agent would completely pre-let a first-class scheme. He or she pre-lets only enough to attract a Fund and keeps good units back to squeeze the market for what it will stand as the job nears completion. The letting fee is 10% so that on a city centre scheme on a prime location with a rent roll of £3m per annum the reward for the time spent is high. It is justified by the many stillborn schemes the agents try to promote and the costs they incur trying to let schemes that are reluctant trading pitches. Moreover competition among agents is strong and they frequently have to accept a letting fee of 7.5% or even less.

Finally the management fee. Again if the scheme is good the rent reviews produce golden days. On a recent scheme of ours the Zone A rents went up 300% after five years. Fees are charged on the increase of the rent achieved: the management work remains the same. Most big agents (and many smaller ones) offer a management fee for managing the completed scheme. This, at 10-12% of the service charge, gives them a continuing interest in the well-being of the scheme and a regular income for the life of the scheme – or at least for the length of the negotiated management commission.

This discursion into a fellow profession's fee structure will be helpful to demonstrate the different basis of reward and makes the point that agents have a number of avenues down which they seek recompense. They should certainly be paid for the very expert and responsible advice they give at concept stage but it gives them more freedom to 'take a view' about the various fee possibilities. A good profit through an unexpectedly easy negotiation on one aspect can enable them to take a relaxed stance and be very competitive on another.

In contrast, the design professions have only one chance to get the fee right. Clients want a single, all-in fee including all expenses and that must hold to the end of the project. No prospect of a continuing commission and only under extreme circumstances a chance to renegotiate. Designers should therefore not only reject the developer euphemism 'share the risk with me' but also reject the rhetoric 'the agent is taking a risk with me: why can't you?'[2]

Should architects give freely of their design skill?
The second aspect that canny architects need to reflect upon in the 'glad or sad' proposition is that they are not being asked to donate to the cause some aspect of their talent that is run of the mill. They are being asked to contribute their most priceless asset: design brilliance and experience. And we have seen that no other member of the team can offer such a skill.

There is no aspect of architectural practice that demands more specialised competence and tolerance than shopping centre design. If the architect is asked to give his or her talents for nothing it is firstly a patent commentary on the respect in which those qualities are held by the client and, secondly, bear in mind that once he or she has contributed these skills, an unscrupulous client can sack him or her and go to any Tom, Dick or Harry who offers a cut fee service for the non-specialised side of the job.[3]

Between winning the job and getting it funded: a trying time
Consider too the position after the developer competition has been won. In terms of risk very little has changed for the client. All the client has is the sole right to enter into detailed negotiation for the project with the local authority or private landlord. Unless the developer is a Fund or sufficiently endowed to produce the cash, the next most urgent task is to raise the money to get the job under way. To do that in the money market the most critical evidence of intent is planning permission: not just outline but detailed planning permission.

Here we come to a real two-way bind. On the one hand the developer is at risk until planning permission has been obtained but once it is he suddenly reaps a vastly enhanced and marketable asset – and designers can be sure the client has no intention of sharing it other than by way of paying the fee already negotiated.

On the other hand, the road to achieving this windfall added value can be so difficult as to make Pilgrim's Progress look like an evening stroll. The process can take years: many months at a minimum. That, of course, is why the suggested fee up to the beginning of working drawings is 35% of the total, and the greater part of it needs to be expended to satisfy some local authorities. An example will illustrate the client's problem. If the development is worth £30m and the architect's fee at 5.5% is £1.65m, then 35% of that is nearly £580,000. Detailed planning permission will certainly take the architect to within £180,000 of that sum so the client's liability to the architect alone (to say nothing of the other design consultants and legal fees) is £400,000, and he or she still has nothing in hand to say that the job is viable, the key tenants are lined up and that statutory permission to proceed has been given. It is hardly surprising therefore that developers seek to minimise their exposure at the designer's expense.

Having described the problem, some hints towards a solution might be helpful, though these thoughts come from personal experience and from the standpoint of a multi-discipline practice which can offer all the design skills.[4]

Ground rules for negotiation
In the fee negotiation process the first point to make is that inflexibility and pedantry will get nowhere in the development world. There is a balance to be struck between architects who say they will not put pencil to paper without a fee being agreed and those who will go for months without remuneration. The former are either lying or are destined to do very little shopping work and the latter are wide open to unprincipled developers and the resultant work invariably speaks volumes for the lack of respect in which they are held by their clients.

Who to put on the job
In this entrepreneural area the architect has first to determine what sort of developer he or she is dealing with and would be well advised to avoid the cowboys who litter the scene, (although a great many fell away in the big shake-out when the secondary banking scene collapsed in 1974). That done, it is perfectly reasonable for the experienced architect principal to do some rough sketches to let the developer take a view as to whether the job is worth pursuing. 'Principal' because that is where the skill and experience lie and it should ensure speed and economy. It is no good putting the job into the drawing office to let youngsters play about with it. Their inexperience will slow them down, they will take weeks to arrive at a half-baked solution, make mistakes and run up salary and overhead costs. Meanwhile, the developer is expecting some first thoughts within days. Young professionals need to learn the ropes, of course, and they should watch and be taken to meetings, but there is no other stage which needs the principal's attention so critically as these early days.

It is difficult to judge how long to persevere with the initial exploratory sketches on a no-fee basis and when to make it clear that the clock is ticking so far as fees are concerned. If the first sketch holes out in one, it is a fluke. The reality is that you are generally up to option five or six before you, as architect, let alone the client, feel happy with the proposal. Yet while architects are freely laying out their most priceless asset, the client is still unconvinced that there is a job worth pursuing. In the last analysis it is a matter of judgement and mutual respect. If the developer feels the architect is getting nowhere then the relationship should be cut and if the architect feels he or she is being presumed upon and being led into an unreasonable commitment he or she should bring matters to a head by either resigning or by insisting on some sort of payment.

What level of remuneration?
But what kind of payment? The watershed comes the moment the job has to be put into the drawing office. The implication is that a scheme has been established that looks worth pursuing and needs properly drawing, presenting and costing. It is then reasonable to ask for payment on a 'cost' basis and views will differ widely on what constitutes 'cost'. Hourly rates must be negotiated with the client and the architect must estimate the calibre and mix of team members. If a lump sum quote is called for to take the design to one or more recognisable stages then the time must be estimated and the architect would do well to allow a contingency for overrun time, the costs of items like special presentations and the high cost of front end computer time. Expenses should always be extra and at nett cost. Cash flow is crucial and a regular schedule of payments on a monthly basis should be agreed.

The resulting sum, however it is calculated, is going to be substantially less than the 35% of fee which is due at the end of RIBA Stage D – and some would say the point at which detailed planning approval is sought. The difference between whatever sum is negotiated and the 35% of fee entitlement is the limit to which an architect should go in helping the developer to establish a scheme – in the euphemism, 'sharing the risk'.

When to get onto the fully agreed fee basis
However, the moment detailed planning approval is obtained the status of the scheme changes dramatically. The greatly enhanced market value it enjoys should be recognised by the developer by a lump sum payment to bring the fee entitlement up to the 35% of the fee for the whole job or some lesser percentage if both sides agree that RIBA Stage D has not been fully reached.

Getting the developer to pay to this level of entitlement will not be easy because we have to remember that he still has not secured the funding and must therefore use his own money to pay the designers. Nevertheless, with a detailed planning approval he has something in hand which is extremely valuable – against which he can borrow: the consultant has nothing. In the game of 'who should fund who?' the onus is now clearly on the developer to pay up.

If the developer sells on the scheme with full planning approval[5] then a further lump sum payment should be negotiated because the designer's skill was essential to obtaining that approval. He or she is then deprived of the prospect of profit from the remainder of the scheme stages and is forced to redeploy staff. That sum is firmly in the realm of 'quantum meruit': Latin for 'what you can get'.

This whole scenario is relevant to jobs where the developer is dealing with an architect for a job which is starting from scratch and not subject to the traditional developer competition.

What to charge for competitions
We have seen how the architect's role in the competition and the proportion of effort he or she puts into it is high compared to anyone else – the client included. Therefore some remuneration is due and an architect should have nothing to do with a no-fee proposal. What he or she can get depends almost wholly on their reputation as an experienced retail architect and as a winner. Although it is true that competitions are 'a percentage game' and you can never win them all, some firms do have a high batting average and their services are eagerly sought by developers. It also depends on the architect's attraction to a particular scheme. After all hundreds of us go in regularly for RIBA approved competitions with no remuneration at all for other than the three premiated designs – and that for a competition system which is currently discredited to a degree never approached by the 'developer' competition method.[6]

Nevertheless remember the enormous, and largely wasteful, cost of presentation. That is not an area for compromise. If the client wants to play the developer game he or she must bear the burden of these costs. This, is not as big a problem to most practices as it is to BDP because, again, we do everything in-house and it is easy to become inveigled into providing things like brochures and models, whereas practices without graphic and model facilities simply leave it to the client to decide whom to employ and how much to pay.

In short, for the competition stage, try to estimate the effort needed to help the client win, discuss it and negotiate the best deal you can.

Payment for the control of shop front design
This may seem a minor point, but the frequency with which it crops up with developers, agents, project coordinators and architects shows there is a real lack of mutual understanding. It concerns the architect's role in the design of shop fronts and both architects and client show varying degrees of expertise in dealing with the remuneration side of the matter.

We occasionally still meet a developer who tries to argue that the project architect should provide a shop front design control service within the overall fee that has been negotiated. What the developer actually means is that the architect should provide the service free because he knows very well that the agreed fee is based on the contract value of the scheme. That certainly does not include the shop fronts because the developer only provides the shell. The tenant provides the shop front and pays a designer to design it.

Tenants rarely commission the designers of the main scheme and that for two reasons. The first is psychological and due to the fact that the tenant and landlord often have a confrontational relationship and this is extended (however unfairly) to the landlord's architect. The tenants feel they want their own person.

The second reason was covered in the chapter on Current Design Trends. It is that until lately the skill of the interior designer has been quite separate from that of the architect and they inhabited different worlds. Before 1980 there were virtually no architectural firms with an interior design unit capable of producing a top class shop front and interior. Britain has for years been well behind the French and the Americans in this field, and it has taken the recent crop of well-known interior design firms to challenge architects out of their lethargy.

Why a fee?
One could then ask whether the role of the project architect in the control of shop fronts is so significant that the work justifies a fee. It is, and here are the reasons.

Rochdale shopping centre
Examples of shop front designs taken from the 'Notes for Guidance of Tenants'.

Consider first the situation if the project architect were to perform no function. The shop front designer would be left entirely to his or her own devices, the developer would have no one to monitor his interests in how the shell is modified, what materials are proposed or how the mall will look. The tenant's designer would have to negotiate with the statutory bodies, especially the planning officer, and in no time at all the developer would have lost control of the visual appearance of his investment.

The only way to keep a grip on the situation is for the developer's architect to write the document previously called 'Notes for Guidance to Tenants'. This has an objective and a subjective section and the former has a non-specific and a specific application to the tenant.

The objective section takes the tenant's designer through the maze of statutory undertakers who are relevant to the scheme and describes the provisions which apply to the centre as a whole and to their shop in particular. It can be a lengthy document. The subjective section describes the qualitative standards that are being sought and we convey this by photographic examples of excellent shop fronts.

The developer's architect's job is then to draw a unique set of plans, sections and elevations for each tenancy on which must be shown and dimensioned every physical feature and constraint– beams, pipes, trunking and so on that the tenant's designer must cater for.

The experienced national multiple trader has no problem. He has hundreds of outlets country wide, employs either in-house designers or a name of national renown. By implication his aim is at one with the developer; customer attraction through quality. The problem comes with the single outlet speciality trader (the type every shopper in the country seems to want – until they don't see the big multiple that is in the next town: then they moan like a Lancashire wake). It can take a dozen meetings before some of these smaller traders can be persuaded to employ a proper designer (as distinct from the owner's son who is doing an HNC course in graphics at the local polytechnic), read the 'Notes for Guidance', and produce something worthwhile.

What to charge for shop front monitoring
But how does one charge for all this. One can only

suggest a kind of rough justice. That a service is provided to every tenant is beyond question, but a percentage fee is impracticable because one has to ask, a percentage of what? A timecharge would be advantageous to the national multiple because experience often enables him or her to succeed first time. On the other hand the single outlet small trader simply could not afford the hours we spend with him. It is therefore common practice to agree a lump sum per unit then multiply that figure by the number of units. The quantum will depend largely on developer/architect relationships, negotiating skill and, very important, the architectural complexity of the basic shell structure of the scheme. In BDP we currently pitch it at somewhere between £350 and £500 per unit. Just recently a small developer refused to pay us anything so we refused to give a shop front monitoring service. Submissions from the first batch of tenants concentrated his mind wonderfully: we quickly agreed a fee.

It is strange how emotive such a small issue can be although the real reason developers question architects closely on these fees springs from the difficulty they themselves have in getting recompense from the tenants. The solution is for them to build it into their own fee costs at viability stage (after all £500 x say 60 units = £30,000 is hardly going to sink a project worth £30,000,000 on which the design and surveying fees will be 15%) or build the extra into the Zone A rental for the unit. Why bother the tenant with the knowledge of the issue?

Fees which are the most difficult to negotiate have been discussed in detail, not because a reputable developer [7] is unwilling to pay anything, but because the early stages are a difficult time and both sides are trying desperately to land the commission.

Once the job is certain (a fund is secured and detailed planning permission has been obtained) it should all be plain sailing. The various professional institutes all have quite clear advisory scales and these will be the starting point for any negotiations. And negotiations there will inevitably be, if only for the reason that schemes vary enormously in size and complexity. It is just vitally important for the architects to remember that if they agree to cut the fee they should be very clear, and so should the client, what reduction in service is going to be made. As someone has rightly said about the business world 'there are no free dinners'.

1. It was a belief well founded. If free dinners were on offer for the number of times I have been told by a prospective client that he could go elsewhere for a free design service I would not go hungry from Christmas to All Fool's Day.

2. Contrary to the impression the aforegoing may have given, there is no hint of envy in my pen as I write (if there was it is my own fault for being an architect rather than an estate agent). The clever agents just make sure they are with good developers who are hungry for the job. Architects should do likewise.

3. Of course the protestations will be loud and justified from the admirable members of the British Council of Shopping Centres who would be appalled at such behaviour. But I speak from experience.

4. This latter attribute has drawbacks because with all the design skills in-house the developer's fee liability cannot be spread among several firms. So BDP makes a (willing) rod for its own back and must be strong enough to fund all the professions that are appointed.

5. A very rare occurrence – indeed I know of no occasion in BDP on the retail side.

6. I for instance work up a significantly greater head of steam for a competition on the Thames Embankment than I do for an off pitch shopping centre in Bootle. Catch me on a good day for the former and I may be quite cheap.

7. It is unfortunate that one still has to specify the adjective 'reputable' with the clear inference that there is another sort of developer. Indeed there is and we have dealt with our full quota of them in years gone by. If this book does nothing more useful than warn the unwary of these sometimes genial, sometimes offhand, sometimes steely eyed rogues, it will have been well worth the cover price.

12

TECHNICAL CONSIDERATIONS

Speciality centres

Food courts

Design for fire (in association with Stuart Boott)

Cost and the quantity surveyor (in association with Roy Taylor)

Landscape in shopping centres (in association with Janet Jack)

TECHNICAL CONSIDERATIONS

Speciality centres

A book on shopping centres would not be complete without mention of this offspring of the mainstream design of retail malls. Back in 1979 speciality centres were a buzz word and most self-respecting developers would have you believe they had a couple on the drawing boards. They had been to the USA again to see what new developments had taken place since the first generation schemes in the 60's and had come back glowing with the fantasy world of little schemes in tourist traps like Boston and San Francisco. What most of them did not realise was that by the beginning of the 80's the Americans had built several hundred of them, and had had at least a 50% failure rate. The good ones were super but the misfits a disaster.

Ronald Gammie and the author wrote an article on 'Speciality Centres' for the Estates Gazette (Volume 251, July 1979) and nearly ten years later it is still relevant. The analysis is fairly detailed so here it will be sufficient to make the main points again and add some recent experience.

The Americans pioneered the genre in 1964 by converting a chocolate factory owned by the Ghiradelli family in San Francisco into a conglomerate of small boutiques and little restaurants and pavement cafes. It was an immediate success and quickly spawned copies.

In essence a speciality centre is characterized by modest size. Few are bigger than 160,000 sq ft (15,000 sq metres) and many are as small as 20,000 sq ft (6,000 sq metres). Secondly, the authentic speciality centre will have no large department store, supermarket or any discount operation. Thirdly the units are small, up-market and usually unique or one-time traders. Fourthly, there will be a heavy emphasis on food; restaurants and 'food experiences' of great variety. In fact at least 25% of the retail space will be processed food, frequently nearer 40%.

This latter statistic gives the first clue to the uniquely American character of speciality centres. Americans are great eaters-out. The current figure is rising and they are well on the way to spending $1 in $2 on food in a restaurant (it was $1 in $3 in 1979). Their smaller families, high wages, a high proportion of working women (at increasingly close to equal pay with men) all tend to encourage leisure activities, especially since with fewer children there is no longer any need to shop weekly for huge quantities of food. Americans therefore now have more time for leisure and will visit such a centre to browse among the shops then wander into their favourite restaurant. Such a visit can quite easily last four hours, double the time spent in a regional mall for necessities.

Thus, although tourist Meccas will always be the surest formula for success in speciality centres, these added factors of American lifestyle enable them to consider their use well off the tourist track, located in a high income area and set close to a regional mall which

Harbourplace, Baltimore
One of the most successful speciality centres ever built.

is already trading well. Classic examples are still The Willows at Concord and South Coast Plaza Village at Costa Mesa; both in California. Each is in a well-to-do area and very close to excellent road networks. Even in Britain, prosperous as never before, it is hard to envisage such a development and there is certainly no successful example built to date on this side of the Atlantic.

Indeed, experience indicates that there is no reason to revise the established criteria which must be satisfied if a speciality centre it to succeed. They must have a combination of as many as possible of the following:

1 be in a high volume well-established regional centre;

2 be near a motorway exit;

3 have 'water exposure';

4 be in an upper income area;

5 be in a resort/tourist area;

6 be part of a mixed use development;

7 be an historic landmark.

In the USA the range of speciality centres is very instructive. The 'classics' are Ghiradelli Square, The Cannery, Pier 39 in San Francisco, Faneuil Hall in Boston, Trolley Square in Salt Lake City, Harbourplace in Baltimore and, more recently, South St Seaport in New York, The Tabor Centre in Denver, Riverwalk in New Orleans and Bayside in Miami. With the exception of Trolley Square and The Tabor Centre they are all waterfront developments with the lure of the sea and tourist and historical attractions thrown in for good measure. Even so, Pier 39 had many reversals before it settled down. Speciality centres in other, inland, locations rely heavily on unique American patterns of life. In addition to those already mentioned many inland American cities are cultural deserts and the landscape round about is scenically little better. (A Sunday afternoon car ride gets you nowhere). If you are not a live sport addict, radio and television are of an abysmal standard – the ultimate riposte to a defence of commercially sponsored media. All in all a swinging, well-designed speciality centre can sound a jolly good place to be if you live in Detroit or Milwaukee.

In Europe practically all seven criteria must be in evidence if success is to be guaranteed. There are simply too many alternatives for social intercourse. In Paris, for example, there are a group of four speciality centres all within a mile of each other and the secret is that three of them are on the Champs Elysees and the other is in the Rue de Rivoli. It would be difficult to think of locations of higher tourist exposure and even there the Gallery des Elysees Du Louvre succeeds explicitly because it concentrates solely on antiques and is therefore the ultimate speciality centre.

In Britain the only undoubted success is the remodeled Covent Garden in London. In the heart of the historic city, near the opera and theatreland, surrounded by fine restaurants, high cost housing and warehouse conversions for yuppie businesses, it has everything but water exposure, although the Thames is only three blocks away. Several other centres have opened in Manchester, Liverpool and Edinburgh but each has

been a disappointment to greater or lesser degrees.[1] At the peak of their popularity one would have thought that speciality centres in places like York, Bath and Edinburgh itself would have been obvious candidates. It does, however, appear that for a variety of reasons here is another road down which we are not destined slavishly to follow the Americans. Time, of course, will tell but few of the speciality centres currently being hawked in Britain will see the light of day.

Even in the USA the pattern is uneven. In Minneapolis, two centres, St Anthony on Main and Riverwalk, seem to have the necessary water ambience with the Mississippi flowing nearby but they are clearly struggling and are candidates for remarketing or even closure. Although in the same city and in the shadow of a successful regional centre, a new delightfully detailed speciality centre called Bonaventure is trading well.

So the road to success is not even and in addition to the pitfalls there are other unique problems. Because the traders are not multiples they are likely to be inexperienced and will need careful nurturing. Because each trader is unique to the centre it is very unlikely that units will pre-let before construction is complete. Funding is therefore difficult. Many traders will be new to shopping centre trading and they may not have access to shop front designers, or the capital to provide shop fronts and fittings. The developer will have to fund this. At Waverley for instance we designed a 'kit of parts' from which traders could build a variety of shop front configurations. They worked excellently and the result won a national prize but they cost the developer half-a-million pounds he could ill-afford.

Nevertheless, from a townscape point of view these speciality centres are a godsend. When they work well the bonus to the environment is priceless. Faneuil Hall, Riverwalk and South Street, Seaport have revitalised whole areas of derelict waterfront and Trolley Square in Salt Lake City has galvanised a characterless wilderness of suburbia. The Tabor Centre in Denver is a vital ingredient in the return to downtown as part of the famous 17th Street regeneration. Difficulties abound but success is sweet.

Food courts
Like speciality centres, food courts are an American idea and a stroll through any leisure orientated facility in the United States will tell you why. Americans love to nibble and munch away at anything that takes their fancy regardless of the hour or normal meal times. Nobody would dream of opening a public building of any kind without food as an adjunct. Dedicate a special area of a shopping centre of any kind to food kiosks and, given certain criteria, it will attract custom. To watch Americans grazing their way through the food lined central building at Faneuil Hall in Boston is an awe-inspiring sight.

The fad for food courts has now taken firm route in Britain and, unlike speciality centres, they are much less speculative. There is probably not a single substantial shopping centre on the drawing boards anywhere in the UK which does not sport one. And therein lies a danger because merely proposing a food court does not guarantee success.

The basic ground rules are that a food court should offer a wide choice of food and to provide this means substantial size. The total facility consists of a number of units all selling different dishes – Greek, Italian,

American burgers, salad bars, deli's, ices, yoghurts and so on. The units are quite small, 250 to 400 square feet (23 to 37 sq metres), and completely self-contained with their own cooking and washing facilities. Some centre managements offer a central pool of disposable crockery and cutlery but that is only to offer the tenants the price benefit of bulk purchasing.[2]

The tenants dispense the food over the counter and that is the limit of their responsibility. The customer takes the food to a table of their choice and the centre or food court management clear it away and make sure the 'front of house' operation is clean.

So much for the facts. The success of the basic idea has led to much analysis of why they work and how to get the best results. Size has already been referred to and it is fairly clear that a scheme with less than seven or eight units cannot offer a wide enough choice of food and this must limit its effectiveness. It is also a matter of fact that a shopping centre must be a certain minimum size if it is going to sustain ten or more units. The food court must live off the shopping centre it is in. It is not a 'magnet' in the sense that people will go to the centre because a food court is there. They go to centres because there are 'magnets' like John Lewis or Debenhams and will visit the food court as part of the trip. That, however, is a most important function because, once replenished, the shopper is very likely to stay in the centre to do more shopping. That makes food courts, in shopping parlance, an 'anchor' within the centre itself and it is generally considered that 250,000 sq ft (23,000 sq metres) of retail space is needed to give sustenance to the food court.

A centre which could be described as a magnet in that people will go to it as a unique experience is the dramatic food court at Atrium Court, Fashion Island, Newport Beach south of Los Angeles. There is a magnificent central space with fashion shops on two levels overlooking a food court which is excellently laid out and food is purchased from stalls at the perimeter. It is a destination in its own right.

Another matter for debate is location. British commentators often assume that a food court should be located close to a good pedestrian flow. Such is not the case in most recent American centres. American shoppers now expect there to be a food court in a centre of any substance and they will go out and find it. Frequently they are placed in remote places and therefore act as an anchor or even a magnet.

Two 'state of the art' centres at present are the St Louis Centre and Westside Pavilion in Los Angeles. Both have food courts in excess of 600 seats and both are located on the third level of trading to one side of the mall. They cannot be seen from the ground floor and both are the least satisfactory part of the centre from a design standpoint. Specifically, they both are too noisy and much too dark, neither has top light. Both are extremely successful trading entities, they frequently overflow and neither have any significant benefit from adjacent pedestrian flow.

In more detail, and as a design guide, between 40 and 50 seats are required per unit and a multiplication of between 25 and 30 sq ft (2.3 and 2.8 sq metres) per seat gives about 8000 sq ft (750 sq metres) for a 250 seat operation. This figure is gross and includes the food outlets themselves. For that reason the lower end of the square foot rate per seat is more applicable to bigger courts and 12,000 to 13,000 sq ft (1,100 to 1,200 sq metres) is likely to be ample for a 600 seat food court.

South Bay Galleria, Redondo Beach, Los Angeles

Many layouts are possible but a continuous display of the various units is often preferred. From the moment a shopper or a family enters the food court they should be able to survey the options for food and get easily to the unit of their choice. This means at least 10 feet (3 metres) in front of the counters to allow circulation and some queueing. It is also good to be able to see easily what is going on in adjacent units and this argues for cutaway walls of the stable-like partitions that are used at South Bay Galleria in Redondo Beach, California.

The seating area should be interesting and varied in layout. People like to go to a unique area and feel rather special. Changes in level are quite acceptable and the old reluctance on the grounds that people will trip with loaded trays is largely unfounded. The visual advantages far outweigh the practical disadvantages and a classic example to remaining doubters is the multi-level food court at first floor level at The Esplanade in New Orleans. It is quite delightful.

Management is absolutely critical. A dirty, ill-kempt public side will kill the operation. British shoppers make things more difficult because many will not take their trays and trash to the waste bins before leaving. Americans do this automatically so the food court is in no danger of looking like a works canteen when the tables are empty. Constant attention is therefore doubly critical in Britain, but there is no doubt that properly designed and managed food courts will now be a permanent adjunct to all future major centres in Britain.

Design for fire
(in association with Stuart Boott)
Among the many factors which make shopping centre design one of the most challenging obstacle courses for

Trump Tower, New York
Open multi-level shopping atrium par excellence.

the architect is the problem of fire hazard. There is now a fair amount of technical literature covering this aspect of an architect's work and in the realm of central area design the subject merits a specialised book. Here the intent is to outline the problems that are likely to be encountered. Many of them must be addressed at the outset because some aspects of design for fire have far reaching consequences on the eventual configuration of the shopping centre. The primary aim should be to create a 'Fire Strategy' document as a first stage in 'firming up' the fire design requirements of any shopping project. This document should be agreed between the design team and the external professionals, the fire officer, the building inspector, and it should incorporate the advice of external bodies such as the Fire Research Station and specialist fire engineers. The sooner this is done and agreed the less likely are costly design changes, creating client frustration and consequent acrimony.

In the early days of enclosed shopping mall design, inexperience on the part of both architects and statutory authorities led to misunderstanding. Architects tended to take a cavalier stance, the authorities a hesitant caution based on inadequate support from guidelines which had not been framed to cope with the conditions under review. The result frequently led to a compromise which was far from satisfactory. The consequence is that in the refurbishment of many shopping centres built in the 60's they are now seen to be firetraps fraught with potential disaster. During the 70's a number of fires of fatal proportions were experienced and a period of extreme caution was experienced with a good deal of 'shroud waving'. More recently the lessons of those early fires have been assimilated and careful work done by Morgan, Hinkley and Marshall and the Fire Research Station has resulted in a balanced body of information for use by designers.

Although no two shopping centres are alike and each presents a different problem, the past ten years has seen the widespread dispersal of hundreds of shopping centres throughout Britain. This has meant a growth in the body of knowledge available to many authorities and a uniformity of approach in resolving fire design problems. Chiefly this means that since the conventional rules governing fire strategy in 'ordinary' building types need re-examination, a solution must be reached based on principles and probabilities. It results in a fine balancing act between the demands of compartmentation, means of escape, fire resistance of the structure and smoke control and detection.

So far as fire is concerned the problems created by covered centres are caused by ideal shopping requirements being inimical to good theoretical fire safety and fire fighting techniques. Modern retailers look for large open spaces (atria), ease of movement with no physical barriers, multi-use with differing fire-ratings and lightweight, look-through materials which entice shoppers to move from one area to another with no break between one retail activity and another. Each of these criteria strikes at the heart of the fire officer's golden rule: compartmentation. Practically every other building type can be 'layered' or compartmented floor by floor, whereas the ideal shopping experience is enhanced by volumes and mixed uses which produce spaces far in excess of the theoretical limits of building legislation.

Much of the negotiation with fire authorities hinges therefore on the balance of 'trade-offs': larger compartmentation against improved precautions and control. In practice this means that if the rules governing maximum volumes are to be breached, the most hazardous zones must be isolated. It is not difficult to separate storage areas, plant rooms and car parks. Access can be protected by fire doors and lobbies with smoke detectors or alarms and detection of fire can be improved. The problem is most acute in public areas where different user classes need separation: where a cinema or a library, for instance, shares a common mall area with shopping. Visual continuity is then difficult to achieve with safety, but recent developments in fire resistant glass and framing certainly make things easier – albeit at extra cost.

Fire is a frightening phenomenon but, as every fire officer knows, the great enemy is smoke. Smoke is the barrier to public escape and to fire fighting access. Heated smoke travels and expands with amazing rapidity and its containment is the prime purpose of compartmentation. The spread of fire itself is a secondary worry. All architects should master the basic principles and AP Morgan's work, BRE 34 'Smoke control methods in enclosed shopping complexes of one or more storeys: A design summary',[3] required reading for any architect working in this field and most fire officers carry a copy.

The basic approach to smoke extraction is simple: contain and remove it. Application in practice is a good deal more complicated.

In the early 'open' centres the problem was solved because a fire in a shop could be naturally vented out under a canopy and from there to the atmosphere. Even when the single level mall was enclosed smoke reservoirs could be formed in ceilings which could be vented by 'chimneys' using a 'stack effect'.

The rules were set out in the Orange Book 'Fire Precautions in Town Centre Developments'.[4] The book was a favourite in the fire officers' library and although slightly out of date it is still frequently quoted.

The dawn of the huge retail development, often in excess of 500,000 sq ft (46,000 sq metres) with multi-levels and mixed uses, brought a new and vastly more complex set of parameters to be considered. The natural extraction of smoke in lofty, multi-level atria is no longer acceptable. Smoke cools and expands as it rises and at about 60 feet (18 metres) it stops rising and builds downwards to cause smoke logging in the areas below. The horizontal spread of smoke has long been counteracted by downstand smoke curtains and exhausting from the compartments created, but in these relatively new lofty halls automatically activated mechanical means must be used to clear the danger. Though adding to the expense of development, the new requirements are in fact welcome because the mechanical systems have much greater control and can overcome the negative effect of some wind conditions which can make natural smoke extraction impossible.

With the advent of multi-level trading there is also a need to exhaust the smoke from the level in which it originates, and so avoid it rising to cause danger to higher trading levels. This is usually accomplished by downstand screens; either permanent features or activated and dropped by smoke sensors, so that the smoke can be extracted before it spills into the main void. As smoke is removed, however, care must be taken that replacement air is introduced in such a way as to avoid turbulence and premature cooling of the smoke. Additional mechanical means may need to be provided to introduce the replacement air.

Controlling smoke is just one aspect of the problem of fire in buildings. Providing ample and clear means of escape is another. It is axiomatic that in an emergency people will tend to try to get out the way they got in – and that means the main entrance doors and the main atrium space, feeling that there will be more space and less claustrophobic conditions there. Actually the large space is potentially the most dangerous for the reasons we have seen; cool, expanding smoke could actually descend on them.

Ealing Broadway Centre, London
Library and shopping share the same mall area. The two different uses are compartmented by 2-hour shutters across the library windows and entrance doors.

**Les Terrasses,
Montreal**
*Downstand smoke
curtains in glass
protect the perimeter
of an opening – a
permanent feature.*

**The Pavilions,
Birmingham**
*Automatic smoke
curtains within the
ceiling zone, activated
by the fire alarm system.*

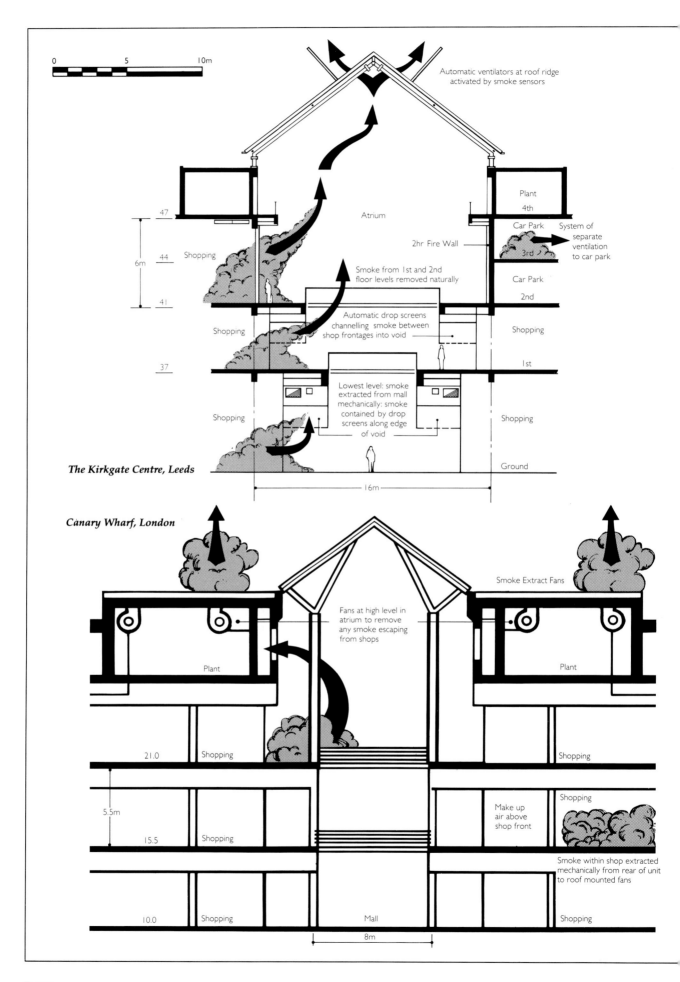

0   5   10m

Automatic ventilators at roof ridge
activated by smoke sensors

Atrium

Plant
4th

Car Park
3rd

System of
separate
ventilation
to car park

2hr Fire Wall

47

Shopping

Smoke from 1st and 2nd
floor levels removed naturally

Car Park
2nd

6m

44

Automatic drop screens
channelling smoke between
shop frontages into void

Shopping

Shopping

41

Lowest level: smoke
extracted from mall
mechanically: smoke
contained by drop
screens along edge
of void

1st

37

Shopping

Shopping

Ground

The Kirkgate Centre, Leeds

16m

Canary Wharf, London

Smoke Extract Fans

Fans at high level in
atrium to remove
any smoke escaping
from shops

Plant

Plant

21.0   Shopping

Shopping

5.5m

Make up
air above
shop front

Shopping

15.5   Shopping

Smoke within shop extracted
mechanically from rear of unit
to roof mounted fans

10.0   Shopping

Mall

Shopping

8m

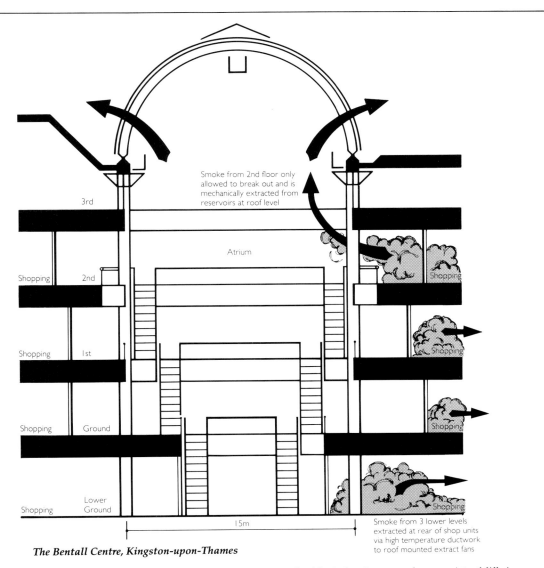

The Bentall Centre, Kingston-upon-Thames

These cross sections through a number of shopping developments completed in the last few years, show a variety of differing approaches to the problems of smoke extract. Natural and mechanical ventilation are illustrated as well as principles of extracting from within the retail area as distinct from allowing smoke to escape into the mall to be extracted.

The proposed solution should be resolved at as early an date a possible since a late change of mind could be costly.

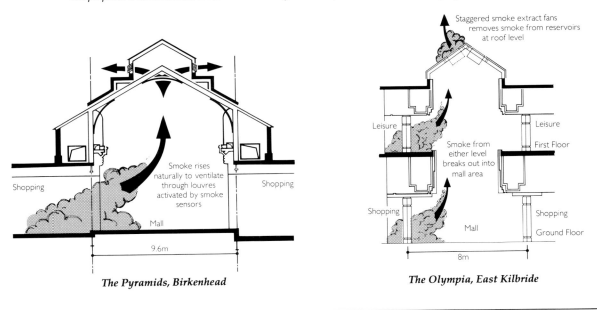

The Pyramids, Birkenhead

The Olympia, East Kilbride

In a place of work like an office building or a factory people can be trained to use unfamiliar routes in an emergency and they can be taught the geography of their building. In a shopping centre all but the traders know only the malls and the retail areas of the shops. The back-stage rooms, corridors and service ways are a private world of which they know nothing. It is therefore a difficult matter to sign and make obvious a safe exit route which is a novel and untapped experience to someone in a panic. Some centres have provided vast lineal footage of mall length to allow batteries of doors into enormous corridors. It is open to question how many people make for them in an emergency, especially when the doors are painted to look like shop fronts, decked out in colourful graphics or clad with mirrors – anything to pretend they are not doors and do not form a break in the continuity of the shopping frontage. A further ingredient to confusion is that all mechanical means of movement like lifts, escalators and travelators stop in an emergency, and these are the means whereby many people will have entered the precinct.

If accent is to be placed on either fire limitation or means of escape the former should be stressed. Fire limitation and access for professional fire fighters can be measured with a good deal of certainty. Whilst in no way suggesting that means of escape should be skimped, the behaviour of large numbers of people in a panic is not easily predicted especially when there is a wide range of possibilities causing the panic in the first place.

A good knowledge of BS 5588 [5] is essential to shopping centre designers and an early discussion of its implementation with the fire officer is desirable. In fact the extensive area requirements of means of escape can be second in importance only to ordinary customer flow through the building. The architect is likely to be the only team member who has knowledge of the fire fighting implications and much responsibility devolves upon him or her to make allowances for escape as early as possible – certainly before the letting agent gets his or her hands on the plan and starts quantifying the rents on an area basis. Agents are prone to moan like banshees at any subsequent reduction in area,

particularly when they share everyone's hope that emergencies will be so rare that the only people ever to use the escape corridors will be the cleaning staff.

All calculations start from an assessment of building occupancy and Table 2 of BS 5588 Part 2 states the area occupied per person for different uses. This causes immediate difficulties because no one knows the precise nature of occupancy at this stage of the design. Overkill and overprovision will solve nothing because it will simply ensure a non-viable scheme. Judgement is needed. Strangely BS 5588 is silent on figures for mall occupancy but the fire officer will have his own estimate which can be as high as one person for 8 sq ft (0.75 sq metres) – a rate often quoted for Christmas Eve. In road width calculation one can safely ignore such extreme congestion because it would result in a sea of asphalt and no buildings. The percentage rate of inconvenience on an annual basis is minimal. Fire, however, is lethal: one must demonstrate how it can be made safe in conditions of maximum occupancy when the risk is greatest.

The provision of escape revolves around the number of people who can pass through a given width of exit and people must be no further than 145ft (45m) from a place of safety – the door to that exit. The complex must be capable of evacuation in two and a half minutes (in theory) and the calculations to achieve this can result in some alarming widths of doors and corridors. Such widths often cut drastically into mall frontages and one can see the result at Gateshead's Metrocentre where football stadium sized vomitories have been required to cope with the calculated occupancy.

Conventionally a place of safety has meant fresh air but in today's complex and enormous buildings we look for staged escapes leading people by horizontal and downward movement (upward movement 'feels' wrong) into parts of a building unaffected by fire. A fire protected corridor is such a place because it is unlikely to be made untenable by smoke or fire before the building is evacuated. All such corridors must terminate in an ultimate place of safety, which means not only fresh air but a space large enough for the dispersal of escapees.

St Annes Centre, Harrow 'Mirrored' fire exit.

After smoke and occupant evacuation come fire fighting systems: smoke detection at the early stages of a fire is critical. Fires can remain undetected for long periods and frequently start in the unlikeliest of places, away from supervision and usually out of trading hours. Smoke rather than heat detection is the best form of defence since smoke is the primary product of most fires and will be released well before detectable heat is produced. Smoke detectors can unfortunately be over-sensitive and can be activated by vehicle exhausts, and even dust. This can be overcome by reducing sensitivity settings or double circuiting so that two signals have to be confirmed prior to triggering off the alarms. The purpose of smoke detection is to initiate alarms, inform the central management control centre and confirm the location of a fire, possibly at the same time alerting the fire service direct and switching the fire ventilation system to emergency mode.

Fire alarms are eventually 'zoned' so that the sounder bells in each 'zone' give a different message dependant on the zone's nearness to the fire. This in theory allows a phased evacuation and the public address system can save much confusion in an emergency.

Fire fighting provisions are still in the main waterbased. For the vast majority of internal spaces a sprinkler system is now mandatory since they are most effective in containing the size of fires until the arrival of the fire brigade. Linked to the fire alarm system they also alert centre management and their provision has the additional bonus of reducing insurance premiums.

The design and provision of these systems is not with-out problems. Many authorities now require a tank supply to sprinkler systems, particularly in areas of low water pressure and this can be the size of a modest swimming pool in a large centre. Its location should be resolved at an early stage. The location of sprinkler heads, particularly in lofty 'atrium' type malls should be considered. Sprinklers are normally activated by heat unless it is a 'dry' system. The further away from a heat source the sprinklers are located the longer the delay in activation. The result is that by then the fire has become so intense that the sprinkler's spray will evaporate before reaching the seat of the blaze. Furthermore the

spray will cool the smoke, slowing the rate of rise, speeding up the smoke logging of the centre and impeding escape and fire fighting. Sprinkler heads therefore have to be placed where they are likely to be most effective, near to the fire hazard, and side walls. Voids may have to be protected by sprinklers – especially above suspended ceilings.

At an early stage in the design the team will have to consider fire fighting access to the building from the surrounding streets. The fire officer will ensure that his or her appliances can get to as many points around the building as practicable and that stairs and lifts, the latter under the fire officer's control, are strategically placed. The provision of dry or wet risers in a centre is a matter for negotiation dependant upon how vandal proof the area is deemed to be. The provision of access for tenders can have an impact on external circulation and landscaping with provision being required for 'hard standing' for emergency vehicles immediately adjacent to dry risers and the building.

As in any building, whether public or private, good housekeeping is essential if everything is to work properly. Management strategy should therefore be considered. Until recently management has not been too concerned about visibility and offices have been tucked away in any odd corner which was not of immediate benefit to the letting agents. This attitude is changing. Some developers now take the view that a high management profile is a good investment and a deterrent to the vandal. Since management centres are also security centres the location of them is of great interest to the fire officer who never liked them tucked away in the bowels of the basement and certainly did not want to take fire appliances down there and risk losing them.

Monitors for security alarms, closed circuit TV, electrical and air-conditioning systems will all converge on the management office and in an emergency it will become an operations centre for police, fire and ambulance services. This argues for ease of access as well as visibility and it also presumes that the control centre will itself be a place of safety, unaffected by fire and smoke.

Metrocentre, Gateshead
'Disguised' fire escapes as part of the shopping frontage decorated to the point of invisibility.

So far as fire is concerned, management means more than keeping things clean for the benefit of the image of the centre. It means a constant care to keep litter off the malls and any sort of waste or impediment (flammable or not) clear from all escape routes. Constant supervision is needed to keep rubbish, tenants redundant materials and assorted trolleys out of these areas. A fire with fatalities usually uncovers a cupboard full of skeletons: of blocked corridors and chained doors. To minimize risk of rubbish accumulation the architect must provide ample and convenient bin storage or compactors. Shopping activity is a prodigious waste generator so there must be no excuse for piles of paper waiting like a tinder box for a stray spark or cigarette stub. Because fires can smoulder unseen for many hours before breaking into open conflagration, many fires 'occur' in the small hours of the morning. Early detection is essential if damage is to be limitated. Ruinous though these fires may be to the fabric of the building, the silver lining to this cloud is that the malls are usually empty of shoppers.

These are the principles behind the precautions that must be taken in a heavily used public building. There is no gainsaying the right of the fire authorities to impose high standards though, as in most things, a good and final balance is best achieved by people who respect each other and get on well together. The fire officer has all the powers he needs to ensure compliance with his wishes, though it is open to any designer who feels aggrieved to call for a second opinion from Marsham Street. There complete professionalism prevails and the presumption is always that the developer is entitled to want to build a profitable building. From this, creative discussion flows.

Cost and the quantity surveyor
(in association with Roy Taylor)

When the developers say, as they do at regular intervals, 'if this scheme doesn't tick, there is no job' they mean just that. Profit and promise of enhanced value are the developer's prime motivation. Self or other people's aggrandisment are of minimum account: the benefit to the quality of the townscape is not the developer's concern. The job of making sure there is a viable development from the building side of the equation falls squarely on the shoulders of the quantity surveyor whose influence will be of great importance from the earliest days of the job. His or her appointment is of second priority to the selection of an architect only because the architect has to draw something before there is anything for the quantity surveyor to price.

The difference between the retail scheme and general practice

There is a very important difference in the cost reporting climate between a quantity surveyor working on a commercial development and the same profession working in almost any other field of building. In the public sector for instance there is a painstaking structure of cost limits – cost per bed space in hospitals, cost per student in schools and so on. In the private world the client usually has a clear idea how much he or she has to spend on a house, a factory, a bank or a block of offices. In all these cases there is a budget to aim at and the clients want value for money. In the public sector especially there is no point in trying to save on the target: the money will simply be lost to the project. The jam must be spread as far as it will go. The quantity surveyor in these circumstances should become part of the design team. From the earliest days

he or she needs to be at the designer's elbow, advising on value for money and pointing out ways to optimise the concept. As soon as possible the first estimate of cost needs breaking down into the main cost elements of a building – about 32 of them – and from then until contractors tenders are received this cost plan must be regularly honed and revised until it becomes a very accurate prediction of the winning tender.

Ideally such a process should also apply to speculative development work, but the reality is very different. As we have seen throughout this book, the developer's relationship with the architect is ambivalent at best. They need each other: the developer values the gifts and the experience that a good architect can bring, but the architect is the money-spender. In spite of endless warnings and repeated lecturing, the architect will spend money like water if he is not watched. So a watchdog is needed and a good quantity surveyor fills the bill admirably.

The quantity surveyor as watchdog

It is no use asking the developer for a cost target for the same reason that it is fruitless asking for a planning brief. These matters are beyond him. All the developer knows is that a plot of land presents a development opportunity and that planning permission is either granted or is in reasonable prospect. What he needs to know is what kind of building will yield optimum profit when let at market rents.

In these circumstances the developers are usually at pains to dig a ditch between themselves and their designers, and to keep the quantity surveyor on their own side of the ditch. The game then develops as follows. The architect is called upon for outline ideas: the outline cost is then compared with an expected rental income which the developer provides either from in-house knowledge or with help from a letting agent. From a simple set of equations the developer can then tell whether the scheme is worth pursuing.

Keeping architects in the dark

From this point onwards the designers are urged to maximise the scheme's potential to produce profit from the rental income. Since there is no budget in the usual sense of the word (only a cost at which the scheme becomes non-viable), it is impossible for the designer to know whether his or her proposals are value for money and there is a depressing tendency for the developer and the quantity surveyor to greet every proposal as 'too expensive' and every saving with 'why didn't you think of that in the first place?' Getting a detailed cost plan out of a quantity surveyor in the development world is a near impossibility and many designers get right through to tender stage without knowing the cost of the job. Indeed on one current project the only way we acquired the knowledge was because we needed to know the figure for fee calculation and stage payments.[6]

The lesson is clear. On the one hand the developer must be able to rely on the complete impartiality and even, on occasions, the confidential nature of cost information. It is felt that there are financial calculations and predictions which must be kept away from designers in order for them in turn to give impartial advice to the client on desirable standards, unencumbered by impact on development profit.

Ensuring value for money

On the other hand value for money can only be ensured when the designer – quantity surveyor relationship is interwoven. Otherwise designers are reduced to working to ever lower standards (and the results are plain to see on developments throughout the 60's and 70's) or keeping things from the quantity surveyor in the hope that the detail will not be spotted until the contract is under way and cannot be stopped. The quantity surveyor quickly realises what is going on and 'loads' those parts of the job the architect is disinterested in – like work below ground level – so that he or she is not eventually accused by the client of underestimating the project. All a very silly and time-consuming charade [7].

Extraneous areas covered by the estimate

Now to the nuts and bolts. At the first cost conference the quantity surveyor and developer must agree the area of cost reporting which falls to the consultant's responsibility. The building cost can be taken for granted but other items like site clearance, diversion of services, accommodation works for affected peripheral owners, purchase of additional properties, purchase of rights of light or other covenants, contribution to archaeological excavations, physical and geological surveys, professional fees and so on may or may not form the basis for separate contracts. Together they constitute a very significant percentage of the overall development cost so they should be itemised and considered carefully.

Peripheral accommodation

Peripheral accommodation works are worth a special mention. In the present climate of concern for the existing fabric of towns, developments must nestle unobtrusively into the surrounding buildings instead of demolishing everything in sight within a given block of streets. The Hounds Hill Centre at Blackpool for example was particularly difficult where we had to rearrange rear service access, loading bays and storage

areas to shops on the site boundary. They all had to be lifted from ground to first floor to suit the new service deck. Other shops were provided with new stairs and access lifts and a connection was made to an existing multi-storey car park to double its size. At Carlisle we found ourselves trying to underpin a wall to a row of shops that turned out to have no integrity with any return wall. The quantity surveyor will be called upon to put a figure to what work can be anticipated (and to have an educated guess at what cannot).

On site hazards

On the site itself the very fact that almost all British centres are in towns will ensure that a host of problems arise from the activities of past generations. By reason of the project's centrality, electric cables, telephone wires, switchgear, substations, sewers, water and gas pipes will all be at their largest and therefore most difficult to move or bend – let alone cut off. Old basements abound, earlier settlements need recording, roads need closing and the quantity surveyor must be alert to the cost repercussions. He or she will advise when specialists should be consulted so that the cost estimate will be more accurate. Again at Blackpool we found it more economical to construct an underground walkway tunnel around a large diameter water pipe for constant access rather than pay for diverting the service to a position where 24 hour access could be guaranteed.

During this period the quantity surveyor must advise on the range of possible external contributors to development costs. Local Authorities may have budgets to assist: Enterprise Zones, Urban Development Corporations, EEC funds and development grants of various sorts may be available and the best surveyors take pains to keep up to date and make themselves invaluable to developers.

Hounds Hill Centre, Blackpool
Ground floor plan – works required to peripheral accommodation.

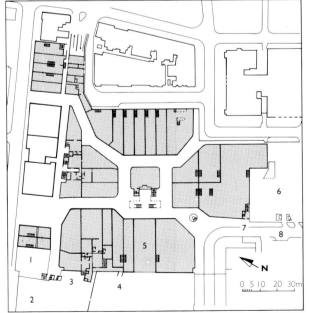

Hounds Hill Centre, Blackpool
First floor plan.

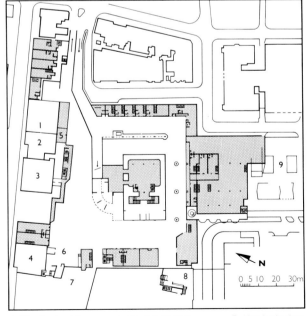

1 New basement storage areas formed : new service stairs and goods lift

2 Existing Boots store

3 Existing ground floor loading bay removed and shop area extended

4 Existing Binns department store

5 Existing ground floor loading bay removed and shop area extended

6 Existing multi-storey car park

7 Replacement stairs and lift access

8 New exit facilities

1 New Service stairs and goods lift

2 New Service entrance at first floor level

3 New Service entrance at first floor level

4 New Service stairs and goods lift

5 Three new service access bridges

6 New first floor beer store and fire escape

7 New loading bay at first floor level

8 New loading bay at first floor level

9 New internal circulation ramps

Demolition and archaeological excavation

Estimating the cost of demolition prior to new construction is another difficult area. The surveyor needs to balance three factors. First, the difficulty of the demolition process itself, constrained as it often is by city centre access problems, second the value in the second hand market of materials which can be salvaged (and the extra cost of salvaging them intact rather than driving a bulldozer through them), third the distance and therefore the transport costs to the nearest tip and the tipping costs themselves. Much of this work lies in the realm of judgement and experience: very little of it can be learnt from pricing guides and cost indices. Yet wide margins or error on so substantial an element can wreck viability. To omit them from consideration could be disastrous.

Nor is it easy to estimate the cost of archaeological exploration and recording. The days are thankfully gone when contractors could blast through a site destroying evidence of past societies in the rush to build anew. Statutory provisions give archaeologists the right to examine a site which has become available for redevelopment prior to building work starting. The historians themselves have very limited funds to finance a 'dig' and although they may be full of curiosity to know exactly what is below ground, they usually know from records what they would expect to find if they had the funds to examine it. For the most part, therefore, they have to be content with knowing something of interest exists until a proposal to build comes along. The cost of archaeological excavation usually becomes part of the price of building and thus the surveyor's task to estimate its impact.

Archaeologists will usually give a fair estimate of the time and money they need but pressure is usually needed to speed this up for, whilst time is often of scant interest to historians, it is crucial to developers. Inflation is public enemy number one as far as they are concerned. Surveyors must not only build the archaeological cost factor into their calculations but must also take a view about the probability of uncovering unsuspected remains. Their exploration and recording will add further cost and allowance needs to be made in the level of contingencies.

Areas of shared costs

Turning to the new building work itself, the quantity surveyor must ascertain as quickly as possible which elements are going to be shared with others or paid for completely by the Local Authority. Multi-storey car parks, public toilets, new road works and other public amenities can all come into this category and the method of dealing with shared costs like foundations, structure and preliminaries must be established. The larger space users may prefer to pay the entire capital cost of their unit, especially if they had previously an interest in the site as a landowner.

In the standard units too the level of provision must be established. Fire and smoke control can make very onerous demands with sprinklers, fire curtains, smoke reservoirs, incombustible materials – all carrying cost implications which may or may not be shared. Sometimes staff toilets are provided and fitted out. In other developments the area is merely designated and services are capped off ready for tenant connection. Heating, cooling and ventilation have similar variants.

The aim is to eventually reduce the estimating process to areas that are without doubt the developer's sole risk and responsibility. At that stage the quantity surveyor and client need to define the parts that appear to be well established as distinct from sections of the scheme that are known to exist but not yet located and therefore not shown on drawings. Plant rooms are a classic example. All such cases are best allowed for on a 'worst case' basis and by taking a view on the probability of the need arising.

Experience of the design factor

Here again experience is more reliable than academic theory. It is no use assuming that Sod's Law will ensure that everything that can go wrong will. Such an approach will simply price the project out of viability. The right approach is to allow a design factor to cover areas not yet identified or resolved on drawings and reduce this progressively as greater certainty is evidenced. Such design factors can be as high as 10% of the project value in the early stages but the aim should be to get that down to about 2.5% at tender stage. These percentages are quite separate from and additional to the contingency sum that is incorporated into every normal building contract. This latter percentage is to give moneys to deal with problems that arise during construction and the client must recognise this. Such sums are not to be used to finance changes to the brief. Changes of that nature (of which there will be legion) must be accommodated by revising the cost brief figure both before and even during the building contract.

These many and diverse points have been raised to emphasise that in the entrepreneural field all costs to the developer are real and must be met with real money. There can be no excuses for omissions or 'getting it wrong'. The client knows he is in the risk business and does not want to contemplate the possibility that consultants have forgotten something. Equally the quantity surveyor will get no thanks for overloading the cost: a realistic estimate for viability testing is the requirement. In the 70's this was a particularly tricky high wire act because, in addition to all the factual costs that can be listed, quantity surveyors had to crystal ball gaze in a period of rampant inflation and try to predict out-turn costs on completion. At one stage contractors' tender levels were increasing at 1.5% a month – far above the inflation level of rents. It is to the credit of some developers that, when the tide turned in the early 80's and tenders became absurdly keen, they ploughed back some of the windfall savings they had reaped into higher quality finishes to enhance their investment. It would be sad if the present forecasts of sharply rising costs were to persuade developers to fall back from the excellent standards of finishes and materials that the best of them have achieved.

Image, location and design variables

The question of standards raises the issue of appropriateness of image for the location and the degree to which the developer wants to 'lift' an area or simply to merge discreetly into the ambience of the town or city. There is, for instance, a significant difference between building a shopping complex in Oxford Street, London and one in Hull. In the former, the Zone A rentals will be pushing £200 per square foot (£2,150 per sq metre); in the latter £35 (£375 per sq metre). Even in the less esoteric world of Corporation Street, Birmingham or Ealing Broadway, the rents will be well over £100 a square foot per annum. Such huge variations make developers take quite different views of the money they are prepared to risk.

The Lanes, Carlisle
Elevations with lower Zone A rental levels.

Ealing Broadway Centre, London
Elevations with high Zone A rental levels.

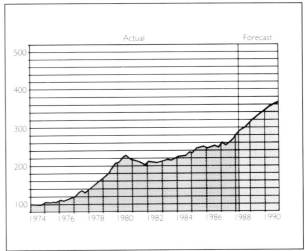

Graph showing increases in tender levels.

To take another aspect; if the proposed development is in the centre of Norwich or Worcester, it will be sufficient to get the pedestrian flows working properly. The location should be assured. From a design standpoint one need not strive to impress. Indeed the priority will be to respect the urban fabric. If the site is just 'off pitch' however and on the edge of the commercial centre, an architectural statement of some substance is necessary because the development team's job is to create a pitch which will attract good covenants, assure the funding and lure custom.[8]

All these matters must be understood by the surveyor whilst the plan is still an architect's felt pen doodle. There are, in fact, three prime considerations which a good quantity surveyor must bear in mind when pricing in this critical early stage. The first two have already been mentioned; rent levels and location. Both will tell the quantity surveyor something about the appropriate level of pricing. The third is the design reputation of the architect. This is not to say that good design is necessarily expensive but high quality building does not come cheap. Some architects have a reputation for making working drawings of the first idea that comes into their heads. Their standards are low so the contractor can respond accordingly. Other architects agonise after perfection and their attitude repercusses directly on the cost of the job. These well meaning people get a reputation in the industry and are awarded a 'beggaration factor' that a quantity surveyor will anticipate.

The point is being made that, with projects for schools, hospitals, prisons, factories and a host of other building types, there is a well established set of standards which vary little from job to job. With shopping centres a whole set of variables must be overlaid on the basic idea of a retail mall which makes the job of the quantity surveyor very much more exciting and creative than is normally the case. It reinforces also the benefit of a design team working and staying together over a number of projects. And, at risk of repetition, it underlines the importance of the quantity surveyor being considered part of the design team rather than a drag anchor of a policeman on their activities – without taking away from the quantity surveyor's duty to report independently and, if need be, critically to the client.

Sharing experiences of other centres
There is no better way of welding a team together in pursuit of a common standard than to undertake a joint tour of 'state of the art' centres. Some – happily an increasing number – are in Great Britain, but many are overseas. Arcades in Germany, speciality centres in Paris, regional malls and theme centres in the USA are all required viewing and no designer can claim to be fully up to date unless they have been studied. It is like claiming to be an expert on Michaelangelo before one has been to Florence: photographs are not enough. The quantity surveyor is an essential member of these tours (and this is an architect saying it) because he or she needs to listen to what excites the designers and clients. He or she can then allow for the appropriate level of quality when looking at a line or a space on a drawing.

Balancing design flair with practical reality
A first class commercial quantity surveyor is in fact an economic consultant rather than the stereotype of a column of figures in a Bill of Quantities. Whilst the architects are fanning their egos with vast public areas and high domes reminiscent of Brunelleschi, it is the quantity surveyor's job to remind them that the ratio of public to lettable area is the most crucial equation in the project. The former costs three or four times more than the latter (merely a shell) yet the income to make the scheme happen will come from the cheapest area to build. Hence the high cost areas must be designed for maximum impact yet with optimum efficiency. Similarly basements: every cubic metre saved in excavation reaps a handsome reward in viability as long as the planning remains efficient. Basements are without doubt the most satisfactory means of servicing but every square metre must be made to work. The land fall across a site sometimes makes it possible to get natural ventilation on the lower side, as at Carlisle but it is easier to achieve with basement car parking than with servicing because there are no storage areas to block the flow of air. Natural ventilation reduces the extent of sophisticated mechanical provision.

Cost of 'open' versus congested sites
One area of planning which normally has a marked influence on cost is the proportion of external wall to floor area. One would suppose that an island site with finished materials on all sides would cost more than the external wall element of an infill site but the reverse is often true. The quality of materials may be less for elements that are not seen on an infill site, but two factors act against economy. One is the high cost of accommodation works to peripheral properties. The other is the irregular perimeter which causes non-standard situations to arise with every design discipline. Architectural, structural and mechanical variants arise every few metres and the effect is not confined to the outside walls. Roofs, especially pitched roofs, become non-standard and the proliferation of design details has a direct effect on the construction cost.

Infill sites are also, by definition, locked into the existing fabric of the town. This has a number of other implications apart from the building side. Firstly, when the site is in a town centre, there is usually a need to keep public access open across the area during construction. This leads to complex programming schedules because the hoarded passageways sometimes have to be moved three or four times to keep the contracting process going whilst ensuring public access and safety.

Secondly, the infill site is usually a congested site. Tower cranes may have to be moved and cabins and other accommodation shifted several times. If the infill site is also a refurbishment project, the additional costs accumulate even further. The centre must be kept trading so there will be a great deal of out of sequence working imposed on the contractor. All these vagaries add cost to the job and are not easily quantified. They are therefore covered in what are called preliminaries to the building contract. Whilst preliminaries can be in single figures for simple repetitive work they can easily rise to 20% on the cost of the measured building work for complex sites.

The first cost estimate
Almost certainly the first cost estimate must be computed on the basis of a set of single line 1:500 scale plans. They will usually be drawn freehand and if they are lucky the quantity surveyors will get a section indicating the number of levels and floor heights. If given an outline specification of building materials they will think it is Christmas.

Years of experience and judgement of the many factors discussed in this chapter will now be brought to bear

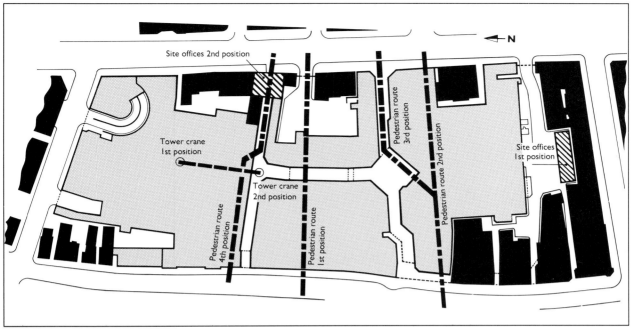

The Lanes, Carlisle
Temporary works required on the infill site.

on this first cost assessment. Any journeyman surveyor can plod methodically through the measurement of a good set of working drawings but here is another level of skill. On the basis of this estimate the developers will call for an estimate of rental income from their agents and then take a view about the viability of the scheme. The document is perhaps the most important contribution the surveyor will make to the project.

There is no point in the quantity surveyor calling for more detail or pleading that it is too early to provide estimates. The developers may have spent years assembling the site and expended huge sums in the process. They now want to know whether their investment is capable of yielding profits through development or whether to cut their losses, sell and get out. As we have seen in the chapter on fees, the developers want to spend the absolute minimum on professional fees at this stage so the surveyors are called upon to use their best judgement on the many factors involved. They should also be aware that the first figure they come up with will be remembered throughout the project and may return to haunt them.
It is a very serious – even litigious business.

The first cost estimate can only be produced on a square metre basis and, because so much is left to judgement, the quantity surveyor will be anxious to begin eliminating areas of uncertainty as quickly as possible. As further information becomes available the next step is to break the cost down into elemental form so that variations can be pinpointed more easily.

The elemental cost plan
While the estimate based on rates per square metre does reflect the cost of the overall planning efficiency, the production of the elemental cost plan gives a check on the more particular features of the project being considered. It indicates whether the rates initially used adequately reflect some of the vagaries although there may not yet be any drawings showing the proposed elevations or the structural profiles. However, there must be plans at all levels and cross sections, together

with a brief outline specification for the building. This should cover the structure and services content in order for a full measure to be undertaken and realistic rates assessed. The cost plan will have a significant level of 'design reserve' and areas of uncertainty identified. It forms the first stage in the long process of refinement that eventually becomes part of the contract documentation, and reaches a conclusion in the final account.

From now on there should be maximum communication between the quantity surveyor and the design team, and the surveyor and the client. The design team should be made aware of the consequences of the decisions they are taking and the surveyor should advise on economic forms of construction and possible savings to be made through shorter construction periods. The client should be given the implications of different levels of specification: durability and maintenance costs being crucial. There is also no financial return in specifying expensive finishes to concrete and brickwork that will subsequently be covered up. The finished quality of the structure in the building shell can be made lower than, say, the exposed structure of an multi-storey car park whose final coat of paint will highlight every blemish.

Contract procurement methods
As the design process proceeds another aspect assumes great importance. The most appropriate contract procurement method can have profound cost implications. Speed is often assumed to be the overriding criterion and it is true that cutting the contract time reduces not only contract costs but the cost of borrowed money. It ensures that income begins to flow earlier and these factors are a bonus. Nevertheless there are significant benefits to be obtained through detailed preparation and keen tendering – especially in competitive tendering climates such as we have experienced in the 80's. It is well to remember that unwanted speed encourages over-design so that errors and omissions can be minimised. Such elements of over-design have cost penalties. Whatever

method is chosen, the team must make sure
that adequate financial control of the contract
can be maintained once building has commenced.
Significant changes can and do take place in the course
of every development as the client responds to better
opportunities. Each amendment must be effectively
cost controlled.

The best way to do this is to price and agree all
variations with the contractor quickly so that the
change can be fed into the agreed cost plan. Tenant
variations also crop up with great frequency and
the client will want an agreed price so that he or she
can finalise the letting. If the change shows a greater
profit or an added value, it will be approved: if not, it
is likely to be shelved. Either way the work on site must
not be delayed so decisions should be decisive – and
irrevocable.

These factors all point to a traditional contract with a
full Bill of Quantities which itemises every aspect of the
construction so that the competing contractors can price
it and comparisons can be made. In an ideal world such
a process is commendable but commercial development
is far from that. Indeed for some years no retail
project in BDP has had the luxury of such a timescale.
Americans cannot either comprehend or begin to
agree with the notion of a Bill of Quantities; in fact they
dispensed with the whole quantity surveyor profession
at the turn of the century. It was much too cumbersome.[9]

Programme, cash flow and delays
This makes programmes and the ability to monitor
them against site performance a prime requirement.
Quantity surveyors have an important role because
they advise on an appropriate cash flow throughout
the contract. When the cash flow falls behind target the
quantity surveyor should sound warning bells because
the client must not be allowed to sign deals with tenants
on an assumed occupancy timescale if it is becoming
increasingly clear that the job will not be finished in
time.

Contractors have a proclivity to optimism which can be
misleading but they cannot avoid the clear cut
implications that their rate of spend indicates significant
delays.

When the prospect of delays can no longer be avoided,
the quantity surveyor has another important role.
Delays can be caused by either contractor ineptness, the
team's failure to provide information to the contractor's
programme, inclement weather or one of the many
other events covered by the building contract. There is
always an Ascertained or Liquidated Damages clause
in a contract between a builder and a client which is
intended to give the client financial redress if the
builder fails to deliver on time. The penalty is many
thousands of pounds a week and it hurts so much
that the moment delays are in prospect the builder
starts preparing his case for claims to mitigate the
penalty.

Acceleration Payements
It is strange how a contractor will swear that he is
irrevocably delayed due to some misdemeanor or act
of God, yet the moment extra cash is dangled before
him astonishing savings in time become possible. The
developer will want to take a view on the prospect of
paying extra money to accelerate the building process
and the quantity surveyor is central to these
negotiations.

These acceleration payments are a minefield for the
professional team. The client may be minded to pay
them to assure completion on time. An opening for
trade in October for the Christmas bonanza is crucial to
the retailers. Most of them will say that, if they cannot
be trading before Christmas, then they will not open
until Easter: a loss to the developer of six months
rent. If one capitalises that rent the resultant figure
is usually several hundred thousand pounds. Two
issues immediately arise. Do the contractors pay all or a
portion of it; do the consultants pay some of it; or do the
clients fund the lot out of their funding contingency for
such matters? Degrees of fault must be established and
quantified. Then, if acceleration costs are agreed and the
clients pay, they are certain to look askance at the extra
fees such sums attract.

Fees are, or should be, based on a percentage of the
final account for the contract and it is not easy for the
clients to understand why they should pay fees on extra
money to speed the contract. They have to be taken
carefully through the hours, even weeks, of negotiation
that are entailed in settling such matters. In the end it
comes down to the consultant's perceived reputation
for impartiality. He or she regularly spends hours
negotiating down a contractor's price or claim for
additional moneys in the full knowledge that it is
actually lowering the fee remuneration. The same
degree of professionalism must be assumed when
the cost is going the other way. Although under the
contract, architects are the official arbitrators in these
matters, it is in fact to the quantity surveyor that they
turn for advice under its provisions.

Finally, it is to everyone's benefit that the final
account is closed quickly with the contractor.
Protracted wrangles over the contract sum mean that
the developer does not know exactly how much the
investment has cost. This in turn can delay the final
gearing of the income between the developer and the
fund. Whereas in other forms of building the various
parties seem to spend years settling the final account,
one great benefit of working in the retail world is
that usually, once the building is handed over and the
traders are in place, a deal is done. Volumes of claim
and counter-claim documentation (which would
keep claims clerks in the public sector employed
until their retirement) are swept aside in bargaining
that would do credit to an Arabian casbah. Everyone
in this entrepreneural club is much more interested
in breathing life into a new scheme than combing
through the entrails of one that is finished. At these
times good quantity surveyors are not just essential;
they are worth their weight in gold.

**Landscape in shopping centres
(in association with Janet Jack)**
Interior landscape includes a number of elements in
addition to plant material. Water, sculpture, paving,
changes of level, seating, glazing, lighting, heating,
drainage, irrigation, water-proofing and the spatial
concept of the design all have a part to play. It is
clearly a multi-profession concern.

Success is dependent on the quality of the concept, the
development of the design by the multi-professional
team, the implementation by the contractors and
the commitment of the client to the maintenance
and management programme. Interior landscape
relies on an artificially created environment, but it can
increase our appreciation of nature, and enhance our

Grand Avenue, Milwaukee
The combination of steps, water, paving, tree grids, seats and sunshine create a welcoming urban atmosphere.

experience of spaces within the building. The scale, volume, form, and function of the space and the availability of light are primary design considerations. Access for maintenance, the quality of the environment and the quality of materials which can be afforded are also fundamental.

Examples from North America and the United Kingdom show that good interior landscape can improve the environment within buildings, make better use of lettable space and enhance rental values. Where developers and funding institutions are aware of these advantages and have invested in a well considered scheme, the results are most rewarding.

In the design of a successful interior landscape there are certain principles to be remembered. The design team must work together from the beginning and the landscape architect must persuade the architect that a number of aspects must be borne in mind to avoid plants being added merely as decoration to an unsuitable environment.

It is equally important that the landscape architect understands the architectural concept and can see where planting can enhance or modify it. The client, too, must be committed to the maintenance implications. In the most successful schemes these aspects have been addressed at the outset. In a speculative development the future can never be predicted, but when the landlord has the responsibility for running the building and where the planting concept is a part of the corporate image, the landlord's concern for the planting has a good chance of maintaining the investment value.

Other chapters have touched upon the issue of an ongoing commitment to standards but in the present context of landscape it is especially relevant to say that continued ownership by the original developer is by far the best way of assuring quality in the long term. Local authorities and their professional advisors would do

well to look askance at any development team who announced at their interview that their policy was to 'sell on' and create cash for the next venture. Yet many do just that.

It is difficult enough to get the new owner to agree to the management regimen that the inert materials of the floor and wall finishes demand. It is almost asking too much to expect that the purchaser will share the originator's sensitivity to organic, living plant material.

A major design factor is the relationship between the scale of the space and the scale of the planting. It influences both the selection of the individual species and the way plants are combined within the overall design. Landscape designs are seen in many different ways: from above, at a steep angle, at close range, at a distance or with light shining from behind. Colour, texture, plant and leaf form and translucency are therefore important.

The landscape architect has to be alive to the space which is being created. It is the product of two things. Firstly the physical boundaries and secondly the light, both natural and artificial, and how they are handled. The quality of the space is defined by form, materials, colours and lighting.

In addition to spatial and three dimensional criteria, access and maintenance requirements, the quality and the quantity of light, heat, water and nutrients have to be established. To appreciate how these factors shape a design it is useful to analyse some outstanding examples of interior landscape.

The Ford Foundation building, New York
The atrium of the Ford Foundation building is one of the finest examples of interior landscape design. Twenty years ago the North American climate, with its extremes in summer and winter, had been mastered by developments in heating, ventilation and air-conditioning systems. The scene had been

set for the creation of large interior public spaces with a comfortable environment far more welcoming than the external climate.

Roche and Dinkeloo, the architects, asked Dan Kiley the landscape architect, to work with them on a great space created by completing the square of a 14 storey L-shaped office block. Sheer glass walls on the outer sides enclosed a garden that overlooked 43rd Street. After 20 years it is still an influential and inspirational example of the concept of gardens in buildings. It was a seminal building and an initiator from which has developed a new approach to the design of buildings with internal public spaces. Its understated elegance and quality are unsurpassed. The designers and the client had high ideals, wishing to create a serene park-like environment for the staff and public that would enhance and enrich their lives and the work of the Ford Foundation. It is now commonplace to see developments in the corporate and commercial sectors which use atria as marketing attractions.

More recently the extension to the John Deere Administration building at Moline in Wisconsin has been similiarly influential. The same architects, working this time with Gerry Leider of Tropical Plant Rentals, Illinois, USA, created a much lower, more extensive garden fully environmentally controlled below a fully glazed roof. The two level offices look out directly into the central space, unencumbered with glass enclosures. Thus the gardens appear to penetrate the workspaces themselves.

As control of interior environments developed, increasing discomfort externally was experienced by the pedestrian caused by increased car ownership. City centres became increasingly congested, residential areas more widely dispersed and shopping in high streets became more unpleasant and inconvenient. The Eaton Centre in the centre of Toronto solves these problems with the advantages of year-round temperature control, easy parking, connection into public transport, a dozen or so cinemas, numerous restaurants, and an Oxford Street range of shopping facilities. All this combined with down-town visual excitement and an interior landscape similar to that of small urban parks.

Paramas Park, New Jersey

Constructed out of town in the 70's, Paramas Park shopping centre was in the first generation of shopping centres to use substantial planting combined with water and seating. Despite its modest cost it has continuing popular appeal and was a seminal piece of work. Its upper level is reached by escalators and stairs rising through large scale stepped rock gardens, dense with the canopies of ficus trees and the ornament of foliage and flowers. The food court surrounding the escalator garden has a pleasant view into the tree canopy with the unexpected bonus of small birds which have colonised the interior adding to the bustling activity of the scene with their flight and song. Planting and water in innovative three dimensional interior landscape designs was used to ease and enhance the movement of people from one level to another.

Water Tower Place, Chicago

Planting was clearly part of the architectural concept of Water Tower Place. The architects, Loebl, Schlossman, Bennet & Dart, had the problem of enticing people off Michigan Avenue and up two floors to an internal shopping centre which itself was to trade on seven floors. They audaciously created cascading gardens with monumental street scale travertine features, through which shoppers ascend by escalator and stair. They are bathed in brilliant artificial sunshine and surrounded by superbly detailed waterfalls and vibrant planting. The trompe l'oeil effect of escalators and the massive detailing, the scale of which increases towards the top, make the two storey journey appear shorter. Fourteen ficus trees in rusticated travertine containers form a canopy in the three dimensional design. Low growing trailing foliage and seasonal plants provide additional colour and detailed interest to the remaining stone planters.

Mayfair in the Grove, Miami

More recently again this remarkable two level scheme near the ocean side in Miami has central spaces that are open to the sky (in an ideal climate) and, more remarkably, open to the public 24 hours a day. So exotic is the planting and so extensive and intriguing the water, fountains and special lighting effects that it is sometimes difficult to see the shops themselves. The effect of the design by night is quite magical.

In the USA the first generation of out of town shopping centres is now more than 20 years old, and as these have succeeded, the downtown areas of many cities have declined. The old run-down centre at Grand Avenue, Milwaukee, was one such area but, by the enlightened collaboration of developers and the local authority, it has been regenerated. Traffic was diverted onto streets round three city blocks and then linked by creating three storey pedestrian malls, where the streets had been. The buildings were cleaned up and some historically interesting buildings carefully restored.

An atrium was formed at the intersection of the main streets, with an interesting off-set, which adds to the vitality of the space. Some delightful details using steps, water and large scale tree planting, have helped to enliven a dead central city area. There is scope for this sort of development in many cities.

Some innovative buildings have paved the way for a new generation of shopping centres in Great Britain. They vary in concept from the idea of a simple roofed street to a very sophisticated, environment controlled atrium: four BDP schemes exemplify the diversity.

The Lanes, Carlisle

The character of The Lanes in Carlisle was designed to be redolent of the old cross-town alleys that had characterised the city. They are therefore narrow and certainly of insufficient width to permit planting at street level. The landscape of the malls is therefore 'hard' with granite setts, sandstone and brick, developing patterns that lead one through the shopping centre. Soft landscaping is restricted to hanging baskets whose effect must be seen from below. Variegated colours brighten, soften or enhance the surrounding · architecture as the season demands. The Lanes are covered but open at the sides and the entrances, so external temperatures must be expected, modified only by the solar effect of the glass roof and heat spill from the shops below.

The Broadway Centre, Ealing

A large 150,000 sq ft office complex rises above the shopping and one of the car decks. The photographs show how Water Tower Place influenced the scheme to provide an attractive route up through two levels to the reception desk. There the comparison ends because one is carried up into a large glazed foyer to the offices.

Though the space is heated, no cooling is provided other than natural ventilation from glass louvres and some very localised cooling at either end of the topmost galleries to the lift foyers. Travertine paving, water, large scale tree planting and artificial light were all integral design features of the interior.

The client agreed to cover the car deck in two large courts on either side of the atrium and this gave opportunity for planting and paving. One walks out into these courts from galleries in the atrium so the relationship of the landscape ideas is perceived. Moulded land forms for both pavings and soft materials gave opportunity for water features with the former and a variety of plant material from grass, through shrubs to trees for the latter.

The Waverley Market, Edinburgh
At present the west court of Waverley Market is probably the most luxuriantly planted shopping centre in Britain. The top lit space is, like the whole scheme, air conditioned, and ideal conditions for plant growth are maintained. A large escalator takes one down three storeys into an underground plaza and the planting is therefore first appreciated from above. As one descends through the tree canopy a world of smaller plants, pools, waterfalls and rock gardens is revealed and the sound of running water is important. From very extensive planting boxes trailing plants grow densely and fall over the deep fascias in garlands of green. Artificial lighting is crucial to the night time effect. The photograph illustrates the result.

The Arndale Centre, Manchester
This is an example of a refurbished shopping centre. It was completed as one of the largest indoor shopping complexes in Europe only six years ago. Building Design Partnership was recently asked to refurbish a section of it. The original design had been based on the now out-dated concept of no internal daylit spaces; on the theory that natural light might direct attention away from the shop fronts.

The design for improvements suggested opening parts of the roof to create a lively, wholesome environment into which planting could be introduced. New interior lighting, signs, plant containers and seats create a welcoming place for people to meet and enjoy the shopping experience.

The benefits of interior landscape
Planting has a therapeutic effect, relating us to our origins on the land, far from cities. Shopping is often a very tense experience and successful large scale planting can be calming. Water is similarly therapeutic. People gravitate to relax and watch moving water whether it be a tiny rivulet in a Japanese garden or Niagara Falls. By combining water and plants in an interior landscape some shopping stress can be smoothed away.

Dining outdoors in sunshine and amongst planting under a pergola, is a most pleasurable experience. Many Californian food courts are outside but in Britain it is possible with the techniques of environmental control and lighting now available to us, to simulate sundrenched gardens with year round greenery. This theme of creating a summer outdoor atmosphere within buildings has been most successful. It creates incident and interest and combines the two natural functions of dining and enjoying plant material on every scale from large trees to flowers on the table.

Well nurtured plant material lends unique qualities to interiors. Firstly it conveys a feeling of care for living things: shoppers therefore feel they are being looked after carefully. Secondly fresh green foliage with glistening new growth and seasonal plants give colour throughout the year and even in inhospitable weather makes people feel welcome. Thirdly the colours, forms and textures of the plants themselves add interest to the interior. By contrast there is nothing worse than artificial plants gathering dust and conveying a cheap, neglected appearance. Some developers mistakenly feel that manufactured plants are cheap and require no care. In fact they are more expensive in first cost and must be washed regularly if they are to look 'real' and add quality to the area.

Some particular areas of importance

Entrances
The entrances to the shopping centre must make it evident that the centre is going to be lively, interesting, well cared for and efficient. The quality and character will be apparent here as an immediate impact. The entrance is the transitional zone between outside and inside. The urban and civic function of the centre can be enhanced by using good quality, well finished materials such as granite, marble and stainless steel which when combined with water, seats and planters of the right scale introduce a sense of nature indoors and reinforce the significance of a modern shopping centre.

When eating is associated with entrance areas there is an opportunity to create interest and liveliness by the suggestion of a street cafe under a canopy of foliage with the additional sparkle of water.

The mall
The mall replaces the traditional shopping street and for that reason it can with some justification take advantage of street scale trees, There are on the market trees of great quality and character with substantial trunks denoting age and conveying a sense of establishment and maturity. Tree grids and 'street furniture' help to create the image of the interior street.

The atrium
The atrium is frequently used as a focal point linking malls, entrances, and the heart of the shopping centre. It is usually an impressive volume with large scale trees of 30 to 33ft high (9 to 10 metres) as in many of the North American shopping centres. Huge atria house cafes and restaurants. Large ficus trees and other species provide canopies for sitting under, as in an outdoor grove, and upper level terraces look directly in to the foliage.

Trees must be carefully specified if they are to have a chance of success in the artificial environment of shopping malls. Their natural habitat is in the rain, sun and wind. Few species find the transition to an internal life congenial. At the Royal Bank in Toronto the central space was planted with tall Norfolk Island pines (Araucaria excelsa) which looked wonderfully elegant for a few months. But they missed the conditions of their native habitat and expired. A sad and costly mistake. Trees which are appropriate to large scale spaces are ficus, shefflera and palms. Ficus are obtainable in many heights but can be bought as high as 36ft (12m). Shefflera are obtainable up to 30ft (10m) in height but are difficult to transport and settle in. Palms are available in sizes up to 20ft (6m). In addition bamboo is available in large sizes up to 40ft (14m).

Interior gardens with seats and water features can be incorporated into this type of space. Vine covered pergolas are a device whereby space can be partially enclosed and a sense of seclusion created within a large volume

Vertical movement
Vertical movement is an essential part of the transition from one level to another and the landscape design can enliven the journey. Reference has already been made to schemes which contribute in this way so a summary of methods will suffice.

Firstly the restrained classicism of Water Tower Place in Chicago. Escalators rise between massive rusticated stone planters filled with luxuriant herbage. Canopies of ficus trees, the brilliant colour of seasonal planting, the calm of green foliage plants, water pouring elegantly down a rivulet of refined knife edged stone weirs all contribute to the sense of vertical movement. The artificially sun drenched scene captivates the interest of shoppers as they are transported up two levels.

Secondly the exciting escalator ride at Paramas Park, New Jersey, through the vertical rough concrete rock garden under a canopy of ficus trees. Shoppers are surrounded by planters with foliage, plants, steps and seats all under a daylit heaven. Again there is an intriguing sense of adventure as one is carried up from mall to food court.

Thirdly the exciting descending (only) escalator in Edinburgh's Waverley Market from Princes Street down two floors into the unexpected subterranean world of tree canopies, water, foliage plants and rockery as an introduction to the shopping experience.

These three examples show the following design elements:

1 the drama of movement;

2 they keep the shoppers' interest;

3 they use planting, water and large scale elements.

Balcony planting
There are many examples of balcony planting and two methods are used frequently:

1 linear containers set behind solid balustrades;

2 smaller 'flower-pot' containers supported on a metal framework outside balcony railings.

The plants most frequently used for these purposes are;

Grape Ivy (Rhoicissus), Chinese Evergreen (Aglaonema), Peace Lily (Spathiphyllum 'Mauna Loa'), Sweetheart Plant (Philodendron scandens), Devil's Ivy (Scindapsus aureus).

Window planting and other details
An effective way to obtain maximum light, which is an essential ingredient in successful plant growth, is to design a glazed shop front to support plant containers. It is a sensible use of daylight and easy to achieve by using a framework on which pots sit. Flowering perlargonium and small leafed ivies are suitable plants. They flourish in the daylight available in the window and create an intimate character inside the room by filtering and softening the light. The plants are seen against the light giving their translucent green leaves a lively appearance.

Eaton Centre, Toronto
The raised and balcony planting add colour and life without using valuable space at ground level.

The Ford Foundation atrium, New York
One of the finest and earliest examples of interior landscape design.

Paramas Park, New Jersey
Shoppers rising up the escalators to the food court are surrounded by foliage.

Water Tower Place, Chicago
Cascading gardens with monumental street scale travertine features entice the shopper to the upper levels.

The Broadway Centre, Ealing
The attractive route passes between planting through two levels to the fully glazed office foyer above.

Mayfair in the Grove, Miami

The Lanes, Carlisle
*The hanging baskets make good use of space and add colour to the
architecture.*

The Waverley Market, Edinburgh
An escalator descends three storeys through a tree canopy and luxuriantly planted garden with the sound of running water in the pools.

The Arndale Centre, Manchester
Daylight and interior lighting have been introduced to a formerly dark internal space permitting planting to be added.

Madrid Dos, Madrid
Landscaped canopy masking the external walls.

The Gallery, Baltimore
An avenue of ficus trees, a pool with a geometric arrangement of foaming jets, seats and bright street scale lights form the focal point of the atrium.

The Broadway Centre, Ealing
Travertine, stainless steel and large ficus trees are the classical materials used in the fully glazed foyer.

209

A variation is the use of a simple bookshelf framework with plant pots inserted as a partial screen between the restaurant and public areas of a shopping mall. The plants are easily accessible for maintenance and replacement.

A cutlery and tray collection point in a food court can be made into an attractive feature by forming a dais for plant material. Trees or shrubs can also be incorporated into a practical layout without using valuable space. These devices can be seen at both The Woodbine Centre and The Eaton Centre in Toronto.

Screens
A screen of planting can be used to divide one area from another or to indicate a difference in use, as in a bustling mall adjacent to a quieter cafe. This can be done in many ways. A few options include:

1 a vertical semi-transparent screen of bamboo or a planted trellis;

2 linear raised planters create a physical barrier;

3 definition of the space by the edge of a pergola with supporting structure adorned by trailing and climbing plants;

4 a canopy of small trees which reduce the scale from large to intimate, defining the space and indicating a change in function.

Plants can also be used to screen unsightly mechanical apparatus and service areas, provided that the foliage is protected from damage by the increased speed of either hot or cold air passing close to the plants. The architect should not rely on plants to solve difficult design problems as it will be obvious that it is an expedient and not part of an overall concept. There is a temptation to resort to artificial plants in this kind of situation.

Living plant material cannot stand on its head and perform unnatural antics. Where plants cannot thrive naturally they should be omitted altogether and another art form employed.

A range of plant materials
There is a range of about 100 reliable foliage plants suitable and relatively tolerant of interior conditions. They range in size from a few inches to 40ft (12 metres) in height and from under £1 to £10,000 in price.

Recommended lighting requirements range from 700 lux to over 10,000 lux. The scale of foliage varies from leaves measuring a few inches to leaves of 3ft or 6ft (1 or 2 metres) in length.

There are many growing habits from small carpeting ground cover plants through climbers which cling to or twine round their support to large scale trees with substantial single or multi-stemmed trunk structures: some are symmetrically formal, others more natural and romantic.

Some strike a classical note and others are exuberant and sometimes even vulgar. There are varieties which have been manipulated and deformed by growers in the search for something new, like poodle clipped topiary shapes or distorted plaited trunks.

Most plants used in interior landscape projects have evergreen foliage and are capable of living for quite a few years. If seasonal colour is needed this is supplied by flowering bedding plants massed together to make a striking display. These last only a few weeks and need regular replacement: as much as 18 times per year to maintain a good show.

Interior landscape design and horticulture are highly specialised skills and should be left to professionals but it is useful for the whole project team to have an appreciation of the varieties, the environmental requirements and the availability of plant material.

A short descriptive list will give an idea of the species available. Very good illustrations have been shown in Richard L Gaines' book 'Interior Plantscaping' published by Architectural Record Books, New York.

Trees	Height	Scale of Foliage
Ficus benjamina Weeping fig	5ft - 40ft (1.5m - 12m)	Medium/fine
Ficus nitida Java fig	5ft - 33ft (1.5m - 10m)	Medium/fine
Ficus nuda	5ft - 33 ft (1.5m - 10m)	Medium/fine
Ficus retusa Indian laurel	5ft - 33ft (1.5m - 10m)	Medium/fine
Ptychosperma elegans Alexander palm	Up to 20ft (Up to 6m)	Medium/large
Caryota mitis Fishtail palm	Up to 20ft (Up to 6m)	Medium/large
Washingtonia filfera Washingtonia palm	Up to 13ft (Up to 4m)	Medium/large
Livingstonia chinensis Livingstonia palm	Up to 15ft (Up to 4.5m)	Medium/large
Chrysalidocarpus Lutescens Areca palm	Up to 13ft (Up to 4m)	Medium/large
Schefflera actinophylla Umbrella tree	5ft - 33ft (1.5m to 10m)	Large
Magnolia grandifolia Southern magnolia	Up to 20ft (Up to 6m)	Large
Bambusa Bamboo	Up to 33ft (Up to 10m)	Fine
Bucida buceros Black olive	Up to 16ft (Up to 6m)	Fine

Environmental requirements
Interior plant material although tolerant and selected to grow in an artificial situation has basic requirements without which it would not survive. The correct lighting, temperature, water supply, growing medium, drainage and maintenance are all essential and the correct balance must be achieved.

Lighting
Lighting should be part of the planting concept. To compensate for the absence of natural light artificial daylight must be introduced and the prime

requirements are intensity, quality and duration. Light is the major stimulant to the life cycle of plants, triggering the process of photosynthesis, or the manufacture of food. Sunlight is the best light source but inside buildings it is not always possible or desirable to provide adequate sunlight.

There are some points about light which are worth remembering:

1   plants survive only by virtue of light;

2   on a clear sunlit day outside one might expect 100,000 to 120,000 lux;

3   on a winter day it might be 30,000 to 70,000 lux;

4   in areas in the tropics where the plants we use for interiors grow, the light intensity reaches 140,000 lux and higher;

5   typical offices have a light level of between 200-1000 lux;

6   the recommended light intensity requirements for typical plants used in interior landscape ranges from 750 lux to over 5000 lux. Plants will survive with less light, but probably in a stressed condition and not put on healthy growth which is one of their most attractive qualities.

Quality
There is not a great deal of difference in growth rates between blue-light energy and red-light energy except in the appearance; blue giving short, stocky growth and deep colour; red giving leggy, straggly elongated foliage, light in colour.

There are basically three types of lamp which are suitable for interiors and none is best for all situations:

1   filament lamps;

2   fluorescent lamps;

3   high intensity discharge, mercury and metal halide lamps.

The considerations regarding their use are:

1   the scale and function of the space;

2   the height of the ceiling and the position of light fittings;

3   the colour rendering for people as well as plants;

4   lighting for plant growth or for seeing the plants;

5   efficiency. Incandescent lamps produce heat and are expensive; the more efficient lamps produce less heat;

6   cost. The high intensity discharge lamps are more expensive to install but cheaper to run;

7   is the status quo expected in plants or are they expected to grow? If the latter use blue and red light sources;

8   consider maintenance and the ease of replacing bulbs.

There are advantages and disadvantages in all types of lighting but in the main blue light energy emitting sources are recommended. These are fluorescent, high intensity discharge, mercury and metal halide because they produce wave lengths that are perfect for healthy growth.

Duration
The daily duration of lighting of the recommended level should be 12-14 hours throughout the year including public holidays. If lower than recommended lighting levels are required, 18 or even 20 hours per day should be considered. If low lighting levels are essential during trading hours (to avoid contrasts for example) then lighting purely for plant growth should be in operation outside those hours.

Temperature
Most interior plants thrive in the human comfort range of $21°C - 24°C$ ($70°F - 75°F$) during daytime and prefer a cooler night of $10°C$ minimum. Hot stagnant air can 'burn' foliage and rapid temperature changes will damage plants.

Temperatures for the range of plant material most commonly used should not go below $10°C$. Avoid placing plants in the direct path of airstream from hot or cold supply grilles.

Good natural ventilation however is needed to replenish the carbon dioxide used in photosynthesis and to prevent heat build-up round foliage in high light.

Irrigation
The preference in the USA is to irrigate manually. There they expect intensive maintenance care to a high standard. We should follow this example more often in Britain because in the act of manual watering plant health can be observed and monitored.

Various irrigation techniques are used in the UK such as hydroculture (leca and water), half hydroculture (compost, leca and water) or subterranean reservoirs for background irrigation.

To avoid trailing hoses, irrigation can be achieved by a mobile watertank with a small hand-held spray nozzle. This is a versatile and practical piece of equipment. More sophisticated methods using automated valves are appropriate where long stretches of perimeter trailing plants are used.

Relative humidity
Although interior foliage plants are grown in conditions of 60% to 90% relative humidity (RH), they can tolerate conditions in which humans thrive, i.e. 30%-50% RH. They will dehydrate below this. Some plants will suffer below 40% RH and the RH in the vicinity of the plants should be maintained by soil moisture or aerated fountains.

Installation
Planting should be the last operation in the completion of a new building or refurbishment.

Foliage is delicate, living material which should be treated with great care. It can be damaged seriously by deposits of dust, by deprivation of light and moisture, or by careless handling and incorrect temperatures. Specialists should always be used to avoid expensive disasters.

IBM Plaza, Fifth Avenue, New York
Bamboos, 40-feet high, placed on a grid in a granite floor, give a civic scale to this interior urban space which is open to the public.

As an example:

In January 1985 the planting of eight large ficus trees was carried out in the Ealing Atrium during the coldest weather for 30 years. There was a determined attempt to keep the temperature above 10°C (50°F), but the building was not finally completed and there had been some difficulties with the heating installation. With a concerted effort using emergency heaters the correct temperatures were just maintained and a very costly failure was averted. A fall below the critical temperature would certainly have killed the trees. It is essential to recognise the risks of installing planting in buildings which are not fully commissioned and to avoid it if at all possible.

Maintenance

Maintenance is an essential part of the interior landscape and without a commitment to long term care interior landscape cannot succeed. Shopping centre owners and management must understand this.

Accessibility is important for ease of maintenance. Plants have to be cleaned and dead leaves removed on a regular basis which, dependent on the species, can be as frequent as once a week. (There is no wind and rain in a mall to do the job naturally.) Large fig trees such as Ficus benjamina, nitida and retusa whose copious foliage can be out of reach, benefit from hand spraying with soft water to keep their leaves glistening and healthy, therefore thought should be given to the floor finish to avoid the possibility of damage.

The intention of the landscape architect regarding the long term development of the planting and the form and growth to be expected over the years should be understood. A management regimen working towards this goal should be instigated so that clear maintenance instructions can be given.

Regular checks on lighting and temperature levels, the condition of the growing medium, nutrient levels and watering requirements should be made. Maintenance should be carried out by specialist contractors to achieve good results, and they should be made fully responsible.

Conclusions

There is a wide range of experience in interior planting for shopping centres on both sides of the Atlantic and it is clear that a well designed scheme makes a significant contribution to the comfort and enjoyment of shoppers. To achieve the best results the design should reflect close collaboration between developer, architect, landscape architect, environmental consultants and the contractors.

The primary requirement is light and it should be sufficient to promote attractive new growth. Temperature, humidity, irrigation and long term maintenance are additional vital considerations. If adequate thought is given to these factors at the right time the interior environment can be significantly enhanced and a worthwhile contribution be made to the success of the enterprise.

There is a growing awareness among architects, landscape architects and other members of the team, of the design factors which have to be considered in creating good interior landscape where it is fully integrated with the architecture. There are many good schemes to be seen, where the elements of planting, seating, changes of level and water have been successfully implemented and many new ideas to explore and perfect. There is now no excuse for failure.

---

1. *The one I understandably know best at Waverley in Edinburgh would have been a runaway success in the USA. In Princes Street with millions of tourists a year, only the food court was immediately successful (it is still reputedly the best trading court in Britain) but the speciality shops themselves took several years to let fully.*

2. *The Pavilion opened in Birmingham in 1987 and the food court was the first to go up market with crockery. This is very nice but centre management must provide both a wash-up and a full disposable back-up in case the wash-up fails.*

3. *HP Morgan-smoke control methods in enclosed shopping complexes of one or more storeys. A design summary. London HMSO 1979.*

4. *Fire precautions in town centre redevelopment. London: HMSO, 1972. (Fire prevention guide 1)*

5. *Fire precautions in the design and construction of buildings: Part 2. Code of practice for shops. London: British Standards Institution, 1985 (BS5588: Part 2)*

6. *On another job the developer and his quantity surveyor released to us a figure of £50m and the cash flow against the percentage fee was based on that sum. BDP's own quantity surveyor priced the job at £68m and of course that would have produced a far better cash flow on the same percentage fee. Some two years later with the design at a more advanced stage the cost is acknowledged to be 'between £60 and £70m'. There is no doubt it will be nearer the latter. We will get fees on the final cost all right, but it is frustrating to know that payments in the design stage could (and should) have been much higher.*

7. *It will occasion no surprise that I advocate a complete all-in service for optimum value for money because this is the philosophic bedrock on which BDP is founded. To those who doubt quantity surveyor confidentiality, I reply that the clients who have worked with us in this way are still our valued clients. I also believe that it is not wholly coincidental that at Blackburn, Blackpool and Carlisle where our quantity surveyors were retained, all three were recognised in the Civic Trust Award Scheme, and Carlisle received both an RIBA Award and the BCSC Award for the best shopping centre opened in 1985.*

8. *A good example of this is at Kirkgate Market, Leeds. There a £100m development is on the 'wrong' side of Vicar Lane which bounds the shopping district. The highest quality design is not only the local authority's hope, it is the developer's necessity. Shoppers must be attracted.*

9. *As my boss in Boston used to say 'we couldn't have got America built in time if we had kept your system'. He was right: indeed some form of management contracting, parallel working, negotiated tendering or a device to shorten the timescale is common in Britain today.*

FURTHER READING

Arcades: The History of a Building Type Geist, J.F. Cambridge (Mass): MIT, 1983

The Architect as a Developer Portman, J. and Barnett, J. New York: McGraw Hill, 1976

Atrium Buildings Saxon R. 2nd ed. London: Architecural Press, 1986

The Book on Value Retailing St Petersburg, Florida: Value Retail News, annual

Canadian Directory of Shopping Centers Toronto: Monday Report on Retailers, annual

Design and Planning of Retail Systems Gosling, D and Maitland, B. London: Architectural Press, 1976

Design for Shopping Centres Beddington, N. London: Butterworth, 1982

Directory of Department Stores New York: Business Guides Inc, annual

Directory of Leading Chain Stores in the US New York: Business Guides Inc, annual

Directory of Major Malls Spring Valley: MJJTM Publications Corp, annual

Dollars and Cents of Shopping Centers Washington DC: Urban Land Institute, 1987

The Effect of a Sprinkler on the Stability of a Smoke Layer beneath a Ceiling Bullen, M.L. Borehamwood: Fire Research Station, 1974. (Fire Research Note 1016)

Enclosed Shopping Centres Darlow, C. London: Architectural Press, 1972

Fairchild's Financial Manual of Retail Stores New York: Fairchild Publications, annual

Fire Precautions in the Design and Construction of Buildings: Part 2 Code of Practice for Shops London: British Standards Institution 1985 (BS 5588: Part 2)

Fire Precautions in Town Centre Redevelopment London: HMSO, 1972 (Fire prevention guide No 1)

The Fire Problems of Pedestrian Precincts: Part 5. A Review of Fires in Enclosed Shopping Complexes Wright, H.G.H. Borehamwood: Fire Research Station, 1974. (Fire Research Note No 1012)

Fires in Shopping Malls Hinckley, P.L. et al. Bracknell: Heating and Ventilating Research Association, 1974

The Future of the City Centre Davies, R.L. & Champion A.G. (eds). London: Academic Press, 1983

Gestalt Magnetism or what is Special about Speciality Shopping Centres N. Gruen. Urban Land. January 1978. pp 3-9

Guidelines for Shopping London: British Multiple Retailers Association, 1980

The History and Conservation of Shopping Arcades MacKeith, M. London: Mansell, 1986

Interior Plantscaping Gaines, R.L. New York: Architectural Record Books, 1977

Investigations into the Flow of Hot Gases in Roof Venting Thomas, H. et al. London: HMSO, 1963. (Fire research technical paper No 7.)

Men of Property: The Canadian Developers who are buying America Goldenberg, S. Toronto: Personal Library, 1981

The Minneapolis Skyway System: what it is and why it works Irvin, L.M. and Groy, J.B. Minneapolis: City Planning Department, 1982

New Dimensions in Shopping Centres and Stores Redstone, L.G. New York: McGraw Hill, 1973

Parking Requirements for Shopping Centers Washington DC: Urban Land Institute, 1982

The Planning of Shopping Centres London: Multiple Shops Federation, 1963

Property Development Library Jolly, B. (ed). A series of handbooks on different aspects of property investment and development in the UK, Australia and North America – see entry under Shopping Centres (I. Northen and M. Haskoll)

Retail Tenant Directory National Mall Monitor's Trade Dimensions, annual

Retailing and Retail Planning Kirby, D.A. Stamford: Capital Planning Information, 1986

Shop Fronts and Facades Pegler, M.M. New York: Retail Reporting Corporation, 1986

Shop Spec Skyne, R. Tonbridge Wells: Pennington Press, annual

Shopping in the Eighties Kirby, D.A. London: British Library Science, Technology and Industry, 1988

Shopping Arcades: A Gazetteer of Extant British Arcades MacKeith, M. London: Mansell, 1985

Shopping Center Development Handbook Washington DC: Urban Land Institute, 1985

Shopping Center Directory Chicago: National Research Bureau, annual

Shopping Centers and Malls Rathbun, R.D. New York: Retail Reporting Corporation, 1986

Shopping Centers: Planning, Development and Administration Lion E. New York: Wiley, 1976

Shopping Centre Development Dawson, J.A. and Lord, D.J. London: Croom Helm, 1985

Shopping Centres: A Developer's Guide to Planning and Design Northen, I. and Haskoll, M. Reading: Centre for Advanced Land Use Studies, 1984. (Property development library.)

Shopping Centres: From High Street to Hypermarket Peek, E. Fire. December 1979. pp367-368

Shopping Centre Progress 1988 British Council of Shopping Centres, and Estates Gazette, 1988

Shopping Towns USA: The Planning of Shopping Centres Gruen and Smith. New York: Reinhold, 1960

Shops: A Manual of Planning and Design Mun, D. London: Architectural Press, 1981

Smoke Control Measures in a Covered Two-Storey Shopping Mall having Balconies as Pedestrian Walkways Morgan, H.P. and Mashall, N.R. Garston: Building Research Establishment, 1979. (BRE Current Paper 11/79.)

Smoke Control in Large Stores connected to Extensive Covered Shopping Malls: Design of 'Slit-Extraction' Systems for Openings on to the Mall Borehamwood: Fire Research Station, 1978. Provisional

Smoke Control Methods in Enclosed Shopping Complexes of One or More Storeys: A Design Summary Morgan, H.P. London: HMSO, 1979

Smoke Hazards in Covered, Multi-Level Shopping Malls: A Method of Extracting Smoke from Each Level Separately Morgan, H.P. and Marshall, N.R. Garston: Building Research Establishment, 1978. (BRE Current Paper 19/78)

Speciality Shopping Centres Jones Lang Wootton and DI Design & Development Consultants. London, 1986

Standards for Service Areas in Shopping Centres London: British Multiple Retailers Association, 1968

GROUP PUBLICATIONS:

College of Estate Management, Reading

A Nation of Shopkeepers?: A User's Guide to the 1971 Census of Retail Distribution and Other Services 1976

Service Charges in Property: Report No 3: Shopping Centres 1986

Shops for Shopkeepers: Tenants' Requirements in Modern Shopping Developments 1977

Hillier Parker Publications, London

British Shopping Developments 1965-1986 1987

Central London Shops Survey 1987

The Effects of Tourism on Central London Shop Rents 1985

The Effect of Town Centre Size on Shop Rental Growth 1979

A Forecast of Shop Rents 1987

Multiple Shop Branches 1981

Proposed Out-of-Town Regional Shopping Centres 1988. Map

The Relationship between Shop Rents and Town Centre Size 1979

Shopping Centre Refurbishment 1986

Shopping Centres in Scotland 1986

Shopping Centres in the Pipeline Quarterly

International Council of Shopping Centres, New York

Architectural and Construction Contracts King, H M. 1980

Developing for the Future 1979

Food Courts: How to Develop a Food Court in Your Shopping Center 1987

Market Research for Shopping Centers Roca, R A (ed). 1980

Planning and Developing Mixed Use Projects Childress, J D. 1983

Public Access: The Rights of Shopping Centers to Restrict the Use of Malls for Political and Other Non Commercial Activities 1987

Renovating a Small Center Castro, D M and Trott, R W. 1977

The Scope of the Shopping Center Industry in the US Annual

Shopping Center Operating Cost Analyses Report 1989 1988

Shopping Centers and the Accessibility Codes Fishman, D. 1979

Unit for Retail Planning Information, Reading

British Town Centre Shopping Schemes: A Statistical Digest 1979. (U11)

Car Parking and Retailing 1979. (U13)

GB Businesses Based Retail Expenditure Estimates and Price Indices 1987. (Information brief 87/3)

The GB Top 100 Shopping Centres (Information brief 86/8)

Key Demographics for the Top 100 Shopping Centres in GB 1987. (Information brief 87/2)

M25: An Opportunity for Retail Development? 1985. (U27)

Managed Shopping Schemes: General 1988. (Information source sheet 28)

Managed Shopping Schemes: Impact Assessment 1987. (Information source sheet 26)

Pedestrian Flows at Selected Retail and Service Businesses (Information brief 86/8)

Planning for Department Stores 1979. (U10)

Planning for Fast Foods 1980. (U20)

Publications in Print

Register of Managed Shopping Schemes 2nd ed. 1987

Restricting Retail Deliveries 1980. (U19)

Retail Planning in the 1980's 1982. (U24)

Retail Warehouses Supplement 2 1988. (Information source sheet 27)

Retailing in the Inner Cities 1980. (U19)

Tomorrow's Shopping Environment 1983. (U26)

Trading Features of Hypermarkets and Superstores 1978. (U7)

Trends in Furniture, Electrical and DIY Goods Expenditure (Information brief 87/6)

UK Goods Based Retail Expenditure Estimates and Price Indices (Information brief 88/1)

1987 List of UK Hypermarkets and Superstores 2nd ed. 1987. (P1)

PERIODICALS:

Buildings (USA publication)

Carlson Report for Shopping Center Managers

Chain Store Age Executive

International Journal of Retailing

Jones Report for Shopping Center Marketing

National Mall Monitor

National Real Estate Investor

Shopping Center Digest

Shopping Center Newsletter

Shopping Center World

Shopping Centers Today